SELF-KNOWLEDGE AND THE SELF

SELF-KNOWLEDGE AND THE SELF

David A. Jopling

ROUTLEDGE
New York London

Published in 2000 by
Routledge
29 West 35th Street
New York, NY 10001

Published in Great Britain by
Routledge
11 New Fetter Lane
London EC4P 4EE

Routledge is an imprint of the Taylor & Francis Group.

Copyright © 2000 by Routledge

Printed in the United States of America on acid-free paper.
Design and typography: Cynthia Dunne

Library of Congress Cataloging-in-Publication Data
Jopling, David A.
Self-knowledge and the self / David A. Jopling.
p. cm
Includes bibliographical references and index.
ISBN 0-415-92689-0 (hardcover) – ISBN 0-415-92690-4 (pbk.)
1. Self. 2. Self-perception. 3. Self-knowledge, Theory of. I Title.

BF697.5.S43 J66 2000
155.2—dc21   99-462009

For my parents,
Alan and Rhoda Jopling

CONTENTS

ACKNOWLEDGMENTS

Over the years I have benefited enormously from discussions about the issues addressed in this book with the following philosophers and psychologists: David Carr, Steven Czar, Theo de Boer, Greg Dubord, Christina Howells, Tom Flynn, Barbara Held, Cary Isley, Ran Lahav, John Macquarrie, Mary Warnock, and Eugene Winograd. I owe special thanks to Ulric Neisser and Henry Pietersma for years of vigorous and insightful philosophical discussion about these and related issues. I owe a special debt of gratitude to Owen Flanagan, Hazel Barnes, and Mike Martin for their careful reading of an earlier draft of this book; and to my editor at Routledge, Gayatri Patnaik. Above all, I would like to thank my wife, Rebecca Wells Jopling. This book is dedicated with love and gratitude to my parents, Alan and Rhoda Jopling.

Thanks also are owed to the Emory Cognition Project at Emory University's Department of Psychology, where I was Mellon Postdoctoral Fellow; and the Humanities Research Centre at the Australian National University, where I was a visiting research fellow.

Some portions of this book began as journal articles or book chapters and have been modified along the way. I am grateful for permission to use them. Parts of Chapter 2 began as an extract from my chapter "'A Self of Selves?'" in *The Conceptual Self in Context: Culture, Experience, Self-Understanding* (New York: Cambridge University Press, 1997), edited by Ulric Neisser and David A. Jopling. Chapter 4 began as an extract from my chapter "Sartre's Moral Psychology" in the *Cambridge Companion to Sartre* (New York: Cambridge University Press, 1992), edited by Christina Howells. Parts of Chapter 6 began as extracts from my article "'Take Away the Life-Lie . . .': Positive Illusions and Creative Self-Deception" in *Philosophical Psychology*, volume 9, number 4 (1996); and from my chapter "Cognitive Science, Other Minds, and the Philosophy of Dialogue" in *The Perceived Self* (New York: Cambridge University Press, 1995), edited by Ulric Neisser.

SELF-KNOWLEDGE
AND THE SELF

I

◀

INTRODUCTION

▶

When does the butterfly in flight read what's written on its wings?

— Neruda, *Book of Questions*

By setting off you would never find out the ends of the soul,
though you should tread along every path: so deep a
measure [logos] *does it have.*

— Heraclitus

THREE TRADITIONS

The inscription above the gates of the ancient temple of the oracle at Delphi served as an injunction to all those who passed below it: *Gnothi seauton*, "Know thyself!" This injunction, which became a popular theme in ancient philosophy and drama, and which served as a terse and easily memorizable maxim for moral conduct in everyday life, continues to exert its hold over the popular imagination. In commonsense psychology, clinical psychology and psychotherapy, religion, and philosophy, among other domains of life, we are enjoined to know ourselves better than we currently do; to clarify our lives and our life histories, and the values that inform them; and to live with a greater awareness of how we are perceived by others and how our characters and decisions affect others. The injunction appears to be universally applicable: that is, it appears to be compatible with almost any morally and psychologically complex situation involving the self in its relations with others. But this does not mean that it is vacuous, or that it is merely a convenient rhetorical device with little moral import. The assumption behind the injunction is both plausible and reasonable: there are many situations in which it is easy *not* to know oneself, to be deceived about oneself, or to be misinformed. Self-knowledge, in other words, is not only something that one ought to work at; it is something that can *only* be had by working at it. It is an achievement and not a given. It is not something that I merely happen to have, like eye color or temperament. Nor is it something that I obviously or unproblematically have. My simply *claiming* to know who I am, for instance, is not enough to establish that I *in fact* know who I am. To begin with, I must call into question the veracity and plausibility of my conventional self-understanding, which supplies me with a reassuring and ready-to-hand account of who I am; and then I must move on to the more difficult task of raising the question "Who am I?" in a more fundamental manner.

The self-knowledge that results from the process of reflective self-inquiry and reflective self-evaluation is ascribed to those who know with some acuity the shape and development of their moral personality, the direction their lives are taking, and the values that matter most to them; who have achieved a level of personal integrity through the adoption of a stance of self-criticism toward their immediate desires, beliefs, and volitions; and who have not accepted uncritically any conventional and ready-to-hand forms of self-understanding as descriptive of the true nature of the self, but who have, by reasoning, choice, dialogue, or moral reflection, arrived at their own ways of making sense of themselves and their life histories. Not everyone actually attains this level of moral, psychological, and existential self-awareness, but it is held as an ideal to which all persons should aspire. Those who display a degree of self-knowledge in their conduct are typically praised; and barring certain exempting conditions such as childhood or mental illness, those who display self-ignorance, self-deception, or self-misunderstanding in their conduct are typically subject to moral criticism.

This is a broad *description* of what self-knowledge—the kind of knowledge that answers to the Delphic maxim—is like. But how is self-knowledge to be *explained?* How is it possible? Are there limits to what I can know of myself? And what is the self that is the object of self-knowledge?

Across the history of Western philosophy, at least three broad traditions in moral philosophy and philosophical psychology have emerged to address these questions. In one tradition, self-knowledge has been regarded as a virtue that is expressed in prudential action, and that is essential for leading a good life. In another, self-knowledge has been regarded as a morally valuable but largely unrealizable goal, because of the elusiveness of the self that is its putative object. In another, self-knowledge has been regarded as a form of reflexive critique, because of its destructive impact on conventional ways of understanding the self, and because of its potential for moral and psychological destabilization. While at the borders of these traditions there is some overlap, each one pulls in a different direction, and each undermines central commitments of the others.

Consider the first tradition. In ancient Greek and Roman moral philosophy, the kind of moral self-knowledge that is commanded by the Delphic maxim is considered to be one of the highest goods of human life. There are two ways this claim about the value of self-knowledge can be interpreted. First, self-knowledge can be considered as intrinsically valuable: that is, its possession is good in itself, independent of any consequences it may have in action, character formation, or the relative well-being of the agent. The assumption here is that knowledge is always a good, and ought always to be maximized. Second, self-knowledge can be considered as instrumentally valuable: that is, it can serve as a means to ethical action, and as the basis upon which other virtues, especially prudence and self-control, can be cultivated. But it is not good in itself. This is because it is not impossible to be both self-knowledgeable and immoral, or self-knowledgeable and unhappy. It is possible, for example, to cultivate an exceptionally deep and clear understanding of one's antisocial character and cruel impulses, which one then uses to good effect in furthering one's socially destructive ends. Under both interpretations, those who are self-knowledgeable will know such things as the limits of what they can do; their place in the world; the limits of their understanding; and the extent and nature of their faults.[1]

The Aristotelian ideal of magnanimity, for example, illustrates one interpretation of the ideal of self-knowledge as a virtue.[2] Magnanimity is an ideal mean between what Aristotle calls petty-mindedness and conceitedness, both of which states arise from the moral agent's state of self-ignorance or self-deception. Those who are magnanimous have a true and action-guiding estimate of their character, an awareness of their flaws, and an understanding of their limits as finite human beings. It is because of their balanced self-knowledge that they are worthy of great things: they aim neither too high nor too low in their projects and plans. Those who are petty-minded, by contrast, have the potential of greatness, but it remains unrealized because they systematically underestimate the true worth of their own talents and traits, which flourish only with proper cultivation and rational direction: they do not, in other words, know their own measure. Conceited persons are just as self-ignorant as the petty-minded, but their self-ignorance takes a different form: they are convinced of their superiority, counterevidence notwithstanding, but their talents and traits fail to live up to their inflated self-assessments. Because they systematically overestimate themselves, their actions consistently fall short of, and often far afield of, their most carefully considered intentions and plans.

Socrates' interpretation of self-knowledge also has a strong moral and practical bearing, but it places more emphasis on knowing one's soul than on the Aristotelian goal of knowing one's character. The central concern of Socratic ethical intellectualism—the view that knowledge and virtue are one—is care for the soul. But to care for the soul adequately presupposes knowledge of what, in general, the soul is; and this entails knowing what the soul needs, how it flourishes, and what is detrimental to it. Socrates thus distinguishes self-knowledge as an understanding of the nature of the soul in relation to virtue and vice from self-knowledge as knowledge of particulars, such as empirically discernible character traits, talents, and motives. While self-knowledge is embodied, as it is in the Aristotelian view, and must determine the particular kind of character that one becomes, it also transcends the knowledge of mere particulars. Because the true object of knowledge is the universal, in terms of which particulars are understood, those who are self-knowledgeable frame their personal knowledge in terms of a robustly philosophical understanding of the nature of the soul. In Socratic thought the universal and the particular are dialectically intertwined, with self-knowledge coming to be suffused with Eros, desire, and existential commitment.

Despite the differences between the Aristotelian and Socratic views, there is still broad agreement that self-knowledge is an essential component in the formation of good character, and in care for self; and that it is a necessary condition for living a good life and being a responsible citizen. Those who are self-knowledgeable are better equipped for the practical and political duties of life than those who suffer from self-deception, or from the kind of self-ignorance or self-misunderstanding that comes from obsession with material things, social status, or sensual pleasure. Concern with these transient goods undermines the development of self-knowledge, and therefore the development of related virtues such as integrity, political and moral responsibility, and self-direction.

But the idea that self-knowledge is a virtue, and that it is a necessary condition for leading a good life, rests on a crucial assumption: viz., that the self is something that is knowable in the first place. If this assumption is false, then the role of self-knowledge in the acquisition of virtue is rendered highly problematic. Exploring this assumption generates a number of questions about the conditions and limits of self-knowledge, and the very possibility of knowing the self. If character or soul are not knowable as such, if they are only knowable indirectly, or if they are known only as appearances rather than as they are in themselves, then the ideal of self-knowledge as a virtue may be unattainable.

The tradition that begins with Heraclitus and continues through Nietzsche and Freud defends precisely this view: self-knowledge is not a fully realizable ideal, because the self is elusive and cannot be adequately identified and conceptualized as it is in itself. Human beings are cognitively and phenomenologically constituted in such a way that they are strangers to themselves, and their efforts to improve their lives through reflective self-inquiry are destined to failure or incompletion. There are two ways these claims can be construed. The weak construal holds that the self is such a complexly configured and multilayered reality that many aspects of it simply cannot come into full view for the person whose self it is: that is, there is always more about the self that can be identified and represented at any one time. This is an important construal, and one that serves as a useful constraint on any theory of self-knowledge. But it is a construal that is trivially true: it is a version of the claim that reality is always richer and more complex than our knowledge of it. The strong construal is more philosophically interesting: the cognitive powers—and especially the reflexive powers—of human beings are structured in such a way that there is a blind spot to the self and its existence. The self is not merely something that is difficult to know because of its complexity; it is something that systematically eludes knowledge—despite first-person claims to the contrary.

Both interpretations of the nature of the elusive self are compatible with at least two different explanations. According to one, the self cannot be known as it is in itself because it is too familiar and too pervasive to be noticed; it is like a horizon that frames objects within it, but it is not itself framed by anything else because it is not itself an *object*. This is a familiar theme of existential and phenomenological theories of the self. According to another explanation, the self cannot be adequately known because the only available access to it is distorted by inadequate descriptive language, or by conceptual schema that are poorly fitted to the contours of experience. Nietzsche defends a version of this idea. Whichever explanation is the most plausible, it is clear that the claim that the self is elusive introduces into the relation between the self and itself a disjunction between reality and appearance: who I am is not who I think I am. My access to the self that I am is necessarily underprivileged, even if that self belongs to me, and *is* me, in a way that no one else can possibly replicate, and even if my attempts to explore my self and describe it are constitutive of what it is. It is more than a mere logical possibility that my most carefully considered self-descriptions and self-evaluations, those that form my best self-understanding, are widely off the mark; it is an empirical fact.

Suppose that there is a clear disjunction between reality and appearance in matters pertaining to self-knowledge. It does not follow from this that the self is unknowable. The claim that the self is unknowable is to be distinguished from the claim that the self eludes knowledge. The former is a principled claim: it establishes a dichotomy between reality and appearance, and restricts all legitimate knowledge claims (and the epistemic practices that lead to them) to the dimension of appearances. The latter claim, by contrast, establishes a disjunction between reality and appearance, and gives support to the idea that self-knowledge is difficult to acquire and difficult to maintain over time. If the principled claim is true, it makes the self a mystery, and self-knowledge regarding anything beyond the dimension of appearances an unattainable ideal. If the weaker claim is true, considerable pressure is placed on the approach that holds that self-knowledge is a virtue, and is to be pursued either for its own sake or for its extrinsic value.

Nietzsche is one of the philosophers in this tradition who forcefully expresses the disjunction between the self as it appears, and the self as it is:

> We are unknown to ourselves, we men of knowledge—and with good reason. We have never sought ourselves—how could it happen that we should ever find ourselves? . . . Present experience has . . . always found us "absent-minded": we cannot give our hearts to it—not even our ears! Rather, as one divinely preoccupied and immersed in himself into whose ear the bell has just boomed with all its strength the twelve beats of noon suddenly starts up and asks himself: "what really was that which just struck?" so we sometimes rub our ears afterward and ask,

utterly surprised and disconcerted, "what really was that which we have just experienced?" and moreover "who are we really?" and, afterward as foresaid, count the twelve trembling bell-strokes of our experience, our life, our being—and alas miscount them. —So we are necessarily strangers to ourselves, we do not comprehend ourselves, we have to mis-understand ourselves, for us the law "Each is furthest from himself" applies to all eternity—we are not "men of knowledge" with respect to ourselves.[3]

Nietzsche locates the roots of self-estrangement in the logical principles of discrimination and identification that are embedded in the psychological vocabulary of everyday discourse. According to Nietzsche, the language of psychological self-reference is inherently imprecise, with first-person descriptions of the passing moods, feelings, and traits of which selves are constituted being pitched at levels that systematically misrepresent the actual phenomena. Nietzsche's claim that referential imprecision is the norm is plausible, but only if it is restricted to a description of a narrow range of uses of ordinary language: for instance, casual self-reports and habitual self-descriptions. Owing to the constraints of context, linguistic parsimony, and functionality, these forms of self-reference are often highly simplified. But it would be false to say that all the uses to which the ordinary psychological language of self-reference is put are inherently imprecise. It is the goal of novelists and autobiographers, for instance, to describe the pas-sage of lives, and the changing states of mind and traits of character of their subjects, with exacting detail. But to do this successfully, they must draw from the same fund of psychological and phenomenological descriptive terms as that deployed in nonliterary contexts. The difference is that they use these terms more carefully and precisely, and without regard to the demands of communicative economy that structure non-literary descrip-tions. Nietzsche, however, writes:

Language and the prejudices upon which language is based are a mani-fold hindrance to us when we want to explain inner processes and dri-ves: because of the fact, for example, that words really exist only for *superlative* degrees of these processes and drives; and where words are lacking, we are accustomed to abandon exact observation because exact thinking there becomes painful. . . . Anger, hatred, love, pity, desire, knowledge, joy, pain—all are names for *extreme* states: the milder, mid-dle degrees, not to speak of the lower degrees which are continually in play, elude us, and yet it is they which weave the web of our character and our destiny. . . . *We are none of us* that which we appear to be in accordance with the states for which alone we have consciousness and words, and consequently praise and blame; those cruder outbursts of which alone we are aware make us *misunderstand* ourselves, we draw a conclusion on the basis of data in which exceptions outweigh the rule, we misread ourselves in this apparently most intelligible handwriting on the nature of our self.[4]

Nietzsche appears here to be committed to calling for a global overhaul of the language of moral and psychological self-reference, on the grounds that our current language is systematically distorting and misleading. This is an implausible requirement. First, it is doubtful that it is linguistically and psychologically possible to revise the psychological vocabulary of everyday discourse *as a whole*. But even if such a revision were possible, it would result in an overmagnified psychological vocabulary that would function successfully in referential and communicative contexts only if a number of extralinguistic conditions of human life were also to be overhauled. But there is no need for this. The language of psychological self-reference has evolved in such a way that it is scaled to size, and fitted to the action demands of the contexts in which it is relevant. Across this evolutionary history, some degree of referential imprecision and semantic vagueness has proven adaptive, and has served the needs of cognitive and linguistic economy.

The philosophical tradition that views the self as elusive, and self-knowledge as an unattainable ideal, is complicated by yet another philosophical, religious, and dramatic tradition, exemplified in the writings of Ecclesiastes and Sophocles and continuing through the philosophies of Spinoza, Nietzsche, Heidegger, and Sartre: the pursuit of self-knowledge is unavoidably destructive of conventional forms of understanding the self, and therefore has the potential to be morally and psychologically destabilizing.

According to this third tradition, there is more to self-knowledge than the simple knowledge of immediate de facto desires, beliefs, and emotions; and there is more to it than the "thicker" knowledge of character traits, life history, and moral personality. Focusing only on these targets yields an incomplete view of the self. It is possible to know certain truths about the desires or character traits that constitute the self, and yet to remain ignorant of more fundamental dimensions of the self: for example, the normative issues of whether one *should* have these desires and traits, and whether one *really* wants to have them; and the ontological issue of the *being* of the self that has such and such desires and traits. If de facto knowledge is all that self-knowledge amounts to, then it has relatively little practical and moral bearing; it is not sufficient to change the self, or to situate it in moral or existential space. Self-knowledge therefore involves normatively structured reflective critique: that is, self-criticism, self-evaluation, and self-inquiry. To acquire a lucid and morally relevant self-awareness is to call into question the framework in terms of which one conventionally or habitually thinks about one's self. This is not an easy task to carry forward. It is deep in a way that renders appeal to previous precedent-setting achievements in self-inquiry irrelevant or incomplete; and it is comprehensive in a way that undermines the plausibility of the investigative and evidentiary norms deployed in previous self-inquiries, because those norms too are subject to inquiry and reevaluation. Critique thus calls for deep interpretation and deep self-evaluation. This does not leave the self unchanged: given the close proximity between the knower and the known in self-inquiry, changes in the way the self is interpreted and evaluated bring changes in the self.

But self-knowledge as reflective critique is disruptive, because it calls into question the validity of the psychological, metaphysical, moral, and religious concepts that inform the conventional modes of self-understanding: concepts, for instance, about the soul, personal immortality, evil and sin, and human nature, as well as the conceptual distinctions that are operative in the commonsense vocabulary of sentiment and desire. So basic are these core categories and concepts that they are not normally considered as falling within the range of potentially investigable, and therefore potentially revisable, subjects of inquiry. Because they are presupposed by those beliefs that are considered to be normal subjects of inquiry, they are less amenable to empirically or conceptually driven revision.

If core concepts such as these have served an adaptive capacity, then the result of sustained reflective inquiry into their cogency and plausibility may be disenchantment with the self, and the self-understanding with which it is associated. A critique that is informed by the Heideggerian hermeneutics of suspicion, for instance, discloses the groundlessness of one's being in the world. In doing this, the inadequacy of one's "ontic," or entity-oriented, ways of self-understanding that constitute one's "average everyday" behaviors is revealed. This is a kind of self-knowledge, situated within an ontological rather than moral or psychological context of inquiry; but it is disruptive, and its reintegration into prereflective life is problematic. As carried out by

Sartrean existential phenomenology, for instance, reflective critique reveals the radical contingency of one's self, and one's abandonment in a world devoid of intrinsic meaning. With this comes the disturbing realization of the explanatory and hermeneutic inadequacy of "serious" forms of self-understanding, infected as they are by layers of motivated concealment and bad faith. In both cases, self-knowledge as critique involves the self in a kind of "dark enlightenment."[5]

The destructive element of critique is not, however, an end in itself. There would be little point in raising the question "Who am I?" with a view only to eradicating false beliefs about the self, and the misguided knowing practices leading to them. If critique served no other purpose than the removal of unsupported beliefs, it would amount to nihilistic ground clearing. To avoid this, critical self-knowledge must be placed ultimately in the service of a higher end: namely, liberation, enlightenment, or authenticity.

FOUR PHILOSOPHICAL PSYCHOLOGIES

The goal of this work is to examine some of the epistemological, phenomenological, and moral dimensions of self-knowledge. These can be grouped into three sets of questions:

i. What is the question "Who am I?" a question about? Is the self targeted by the question an independently existing reality that makes the descriptions about it true or false? Is it discovered, or is there a nontrivial sense in which it is constituted by the very descriptions and evaluations under which it is identified?

ii. Is it possible to know the self as it really is? Are there in self-knowledge determinate matters of fact, in virtue of which it would be possible (at least in principle) to terminate reflective self-inquiry—or is it, by contrast, interpretation "all the way down"? Is reflective self-inquiry limited to the resources of the first-person point of view, or is there a role for the second-person and third-person points of view?

iii. What role in moral conduct and moral improvement does self-knowledge play? Is self-knowledge a necessary condition for human flourishing, one of the beneficial consequences of flourishing, or a cognitive competence that is not significantly related to flourishing? Is it possible, for instance, that certain kinds of self-deception, self-ignorance, or self-misunderstanding are more psychologically adaptive, and more conducive to well-being, than self-knowledge?

To explore these questions, attention will be focused upon four contemporary philosophical psychologies, each of which falls into one or more of the three broad traditions of interpreting self-knowledge, and each of which has corresponding offshoots in contemporary clinical and psychotherapeutic practice: the neo-Spinozist philosophical psychology of Stuart Hampshire, the existentialist philosophical psychology of Jean-Paul Sartre, the neo-pragmatist philosophical psychology of Richard Rorty, and dialogic philosophical psychology.

There is broad agreement among these four philosophical psychologies on the following substantive issues:

i.   Self-knowledge is an important (though neither a necessary nor sufficient) condition of responsibility for self.

ii. Self-knowledge is an important (though neither a necessary nor sufficient) condition of rational agency.

iii. Self-knowledge is action-guiding.

iv. The target of self-knowledge is the self qua embodied agent, in contrast to the self qua thinking subject, or substantial ego, or immediate self-consciousness.

v.   The self qua embodied agent is constituted by character traits, an ongoing life history, and central values, as well as by core beliefs, desires, dispositions, and emotions.

vi. A philosophical account of self-knowledge is essential for making sense of the concept of insight in psychodynamic psychotherapy.

These six commonalities form the basis for a comparison of what would otherwise appear to be four unrelated philosophical psychologies, each situated within divergent philosophical traditions, and each deploying divergent explanatory principles and technical terminologies. Obviously, these differences should not be minimized. A closer analysis of each of the four will reveal a number of salient differences on the following issues, which are independent of differences in philosophical terminology and method:

i.   the role of objectivity in the acquisition of self-knowledge;

ii. the relevance of the first, second, and third-person points of view in the acquisition of self-knowledge;

iii. the specific nature of the self qua embodied agent (e.g., the self as a fundamental project, as a complex configuration of traits, as a self-weaving text, or as a dialogically constituted interlocutor); and

iv. the transformative potential of self-knowledge.

Hampshire considers self-knowledge as one of the goods of human life, and as a necessary condition for freedom of mind. His philosophical psychology is traceable to the work of Spinoza and Freud, and it serves as a broad (and multiply interpretable) philosophical framework in contemporary psychodynamic and psychoanalytic psychotherapies. Hampshire interprets self-knowledge in largely naturalist terms, as the acquisition of knowledge of the causal factors that determine the traits, dispositions, and mental states that constitute the self: for example, unconscious desires and motives, childhood conditioning, and unacknowledged passions. Working out the question "Who am I?" adequately requires a process of rational reflective detachment from the agent's first-person point of view: that is, "stepping back" from the self to a more independent standpoint, with a view to observing those aspects of the self, and those causal mechanisms of behavior and motivation, that are typically obscured by conventional self-understandings.

Hampshire's emphasis on rational detachment from self derives from Spinoza's idea that the improvement of life, and the eventual attainment of liberating insight, requires that the understanding of self be placed in the largest and most objective context of explanation possible: the understanding of the self, in other words, is ultimately to be integrated into an understanding of all things *sub specie aeternitatis*. The search for self-knowledge is therefore necessarily incomplete, because the self is a part of nature, which is infinitely extensive. Still, this thoroughly naturalized account of self-knowledge preserves for the self a kind of freedom of mind. As a part of nature, the self is to be explained in terms of a natural history of causes and effects that extends endlessly back in time. The acquisition of self-knowledge involves learning to identify the causes that make the self what it is, and learning to see the self, and the reflexive powers of the mind that permit this learning, as themselves causal determinants in the formation of the self. Self-reflection has the peculiar power of modifying the very states of mind (and traits of character) that are the object of reflection, and making them different from what they would otherwise have been had they not been targeted for reflective self-inquiry. The more that I learn of the causal mechanisms that explain my mental states, dispositions, and traits of character, the more I am in a position to anticipate them, and to either modify them or reinforce them in ways that more adequately conform to my rationally governed ideals and plans. Thus with increases in self-knowledge come increases in the range of self-determination.

Sartre's philosophical psychology, by contrast, is dinstinctly antideterminist and antinaturalist. It is traceable to the work of Kierkegaard and Heidegger, and is instantiated in contemporary existential psychotherapy and psychiatry. Sartre's view of self-knowledge falls within both the second and third traditions: self-knowledge is not a fully realizable ideal, because the self—or more precisely, the self qua fundamental project—is systematically elusive with respect to my cognitive grasp. Whatever limited self-knowledge I manage to achieve in spite of this barrier tends to undermine my conventional forms of self-understanding, which are vulnerable to a variety of forms of reification and self-deception; and it has the potential to be morally and psychologically destabilizing, and to generate anxiety, even as it brings me closer to the goal of existential authenticity.

Sartre emphasizes the importance of the relation between temporality and existing as central in the acquisition of self-knowledge. If, as existential ontology suggests, *being* ought to be understood as a transitive verb rather than as a noun, then the ultimate goal of raising the question "Who am I?" is not psychological insight but ontological lucidity: that is, lucidity about the relation I have to being, and to the fundamental life possibilities (or possibilities of being) that I must at all times confront simply by virtue of having to be. Sartre argues that the relation to being that is constitutive of the self takes the form of a dynamic and open-ended fundamental project: that is, a project to be. Character and the psychophysical ego are secondary structures in relation to this fundamental project, and are therefore to be explained in terms of it. But this reconceptualizing of the object of self-knowledge comes with a high price: the understanding of the self qua fundamental project is necessarily incomplete, because the project resists description and conceptualization as it is in itself. It is lived but not known: it is a "mystery in broad daylight."

Sartre is also critical of the centrality of place given in contemporary moral theory to rationality; hence the demotion in his philosophical psychology, and in his existential ethics, of such concepts as deliberation, rational volition, and rational self-criticism. This does not mean that he favors irrationalism. With Heidegger, however, he argues that the fundamental questions of existence, including the questions "Who am I?" and "How do I want to be?" must be worked out by actually existing. This process does not involve rational detachment from the self, as Hampshire argues: there is no stepping back from the fundamental project, because it is inseparable from the very movement of existing. My attempts to regard myself from a detached point of view are themselves an expression of my fundamental project, rather than a bona fide independent point of view that allows me to observe myself impartially. Nor is the answer to the question "Who am I?" framed in terms of knowledge about the causal mechanisms that have shaped my fundamental project; this is because causal determinants are intelligible only in terms of the meaning they have within the fundamental project.

Sartre's emphasis on the finite and contingent first-person standpoint clearly derives from Kierkegaard's suspicion of the use of objective methods of investigation in matters subjective: life is understood backward, but can only be lived forward. But Sartre's claim that "one can't take a point of view on one's life while one's living it" seems to block the very possibility of knowing oneself. This is problematic, because the ethical demands of his theory for a plausible form of escape from the self-opacity of bad faith and existential inauthenticity necessitate self-knowledge.

Richard Rorty's philosophical psychology appears to be closely related to Sartre's, given its emphasis on the radically contingent nature of the self, the centrality of self-determination, and the role of interpretation and the hermeneutic circle in self-inquiry. But there are also significant differences between the two, the most salient of which is Rorty's rejection of the existential ideal of authenticity. Rorty's philosophical psychology is traceable to the existential hermeneutics of Heidegger, and to the pragmatism of Donald Davidson, John Dewey, and W. V. O. Quine; and it serves as a broad (and multiply interpretable) philosophical background to contemporary narrativist and postmodern psychotherapies. Rorty defends an antifoundationalist and anti-epistemological interpretation of self-knowledge. The self that is the object of self-knowledge is more like a text requiring a creative, ironic, and open reading than a determinate substance or thing to which subjects enjoy privileged access, and in which they can expect their self-inquiries to be successfully terminated. The question "Who am I?" can only be worked out holistically and contextually, and with a critical eye to the deeply contingent and friable nature of the self that is its object; it is thus an inquiry marked by incompleteness, and by the ambiguities of hermeneutic circularity.

Rorty is as skeptical of the idea that there is one particular way that the self "really" is, to be captured by one finalized form of self-knowledge, as he is skeptical of the idea that there is one way the world "really" is. Once objectivity as correspondence to "the facts" about the self is relinquished, and with it the notion that self-knowing delivers privileged truths that all responsible knowers would ultimately converge upon, there remains only a proliferation of free-floating and ultimately contingent discourses about the self. It does not follow from this, however, that anything goes in matters pertaining to self-inquiry: its results are shaped as much by pragmatic, artistic, and social constraints as by historical circumstance. But none of the discourses about the self that serve as answers to the question "Who am I?" enjoy privileged epistemic status. Thus no final limits can be set in advance to the number of interpretive innovations I may generate in making sense of the question, and to the number of criteriological innovations I may generate in attempting to evaluate the changing answers I give to the question. It is simply a matter of finding newer —but not thereby more objective, or better justified, or more existentially authentic—ways of describing the self to cope with the vicissitudes of life. The metaphoric language of "depth," to which philosophical discussions of self-knowledge are so closely attached, and which plays a key role in Hampshire and Sartre's philosophical psychologies, drops out as an idle cog.

The differences between Hampshire's, Sartre's, and Rorty's interpretations of self-knowledge can be summarized roughly as follows: in Hampshire's philosophical psychology, self-knowledge is interpreted in naturalist terms as constituted by relations between the self and the natural world, of which the self is a finite and initially self-opaque part. In Sartre's philosophical psychology, self-knowledge is interpreted in existential-phenomenological terms as constituted by relations between the self and its existence, or its being in the world, much of which is overlooked because of the mind's tendency in matters ontological to focus on things or entities instead of the *being* of things. In Rorty's philosophical psychology, self-knowledge is interpreted in textualist terms as constituted by relations between the self and the contingent public vocabularies used to describe selves.

In addition to the six shared themes (i–vi), there is the following shared theme:

vii. The acquisition of self-knowledge is to a significant extent an action *of* the self, *for* the self, and *by* the self.

Hampshire, Sartre, and Rorty regard self-knowledge as ultimately an individual achievement, for which one and only one person can take full responsibility: viz., the person whose self it is. In reflective self-inquiry and reflective self-evaluation, the self is thrown upon its own resources: it must confront itself by itself, and it must make its discoveries by itself. The assumption that makes such a view intelligible is that the question "Who am I?" that motivates the inquiry rigidly designates one and only one respondent, and one and only one author. The question "belongs" to the self that raises the question: no one else can take it over—with a view (for example) to relieving the inquirer of his or her burden—without the inquiry risking epistemic and interpretive contamination.

The idea that one ultimately has only oneself to answer to in reflective self-inquiry is closely tied to the concept of responsibility for self. Both kinds of self-relation are characterized by a special sense of ownership or "belongingness." Just as it is only I who can take up the task of knowing who and what I am, so it is only I who can ultimately take responsibility for what I am and what I make of myself. In neither case can someone else take up this stance, or serve as a substitute.

The individualistic construal of self-knowledge is most clearly developed in existential philosophy, where the self (or *Dasein*, or the for-itself) that is pursuing reflective self-inquiry is depicted as thrown entirely upon its own resources, and as confronting itself qua existent in isolation from the alienating influences of others (for example, *das Man*, or the look of the Other). In existential ethics and psychology, self-knowledge is regarded as constituted by a unique and irreducible relation of the self to itself that finds its purest expression in existential authenticity. Only the self can authentically take a stand with respect to the fundamental questions of existence forced upon it by the simple fact of existing. No one else can serve as a substitute for the question; and the very attempt to assign the question to others is a manifestation of a uniquely personal though evasive stand on the question. In existential terms, the existence that is targeted by the question "Who am I?" is characterized by "mineness."[6]

The individualism that informs these three philosophical psychologies is problematic, because it is purchased at the cost of an implausible account of the social and interpersonal dimensions of self-knowledge. The purpose of the chapter on the dialogic nature of self-knowing is to suggest ways in which a philosophical account of self-knowledge might be reshaped to accommodate the dimension of interpersonal interaction, social influence, and the moral encounter with the other person. The view that will be developed is that self-knowledge is essentially a kind of dialogue-based social and interpersonal knowledge; that is, it is a dialogic competence that is constituted by the confrontation of the self with the other, rather than a monologic state that is constituted by the confrontation of the self with itself. To be self-knowledgeable is to know oneself insofar as one is known by and responsible to others.

The dialogic view is to be distinguished from George Herbert Mead's behaviorist view that self-knowledge is constituted by knowing oneself *as* others know one. This is incomplete. Self-knowledge involves more than the introjection of the views that others happen to hold about one's personality and behaviors. It also involves knowing what effects one's desires, actions, and character traits have upon others, and what effects others have upon one's desires, actions, and traits. Knowing these things makes it possible to respond appropriately to the morally reactive feelings and morally reactive attitudes of others: that is, to respond to feelings and attitudes such as love, resentment, guilt, shame, approbation, respect, blame, gratitude, forgiveness, and condemnation. Self-knowledge such as this is a kind of social and interpersonal articulacy.

By contrast, one of the distinctive characteristics of self-opacity is interpersonal inarticulacy. Those who are self-deceived or self-ignorant characteristically fail to respond appropriately to the feelings, actions, and attitudes of others. Literature abounds with characters who misread and mistreat others because their own self-understandings have been stunted by self-deception or self-ignorance. The psychological novels of Stendhal and James, and the plays of Ibsen and O'Neill, are populated with characters whose self-understandings are not adequately responsive to the dynamics of their immediate social worlds: characters, for instance, who think of themselves as kind and caring, but whose neurotically selfish actions leave in their wake a trail of hurt feelings that are rarely recognized for what they are; characters who are deeply egocentric, but who persist in believing, to the detriment of others, and despite massive counterevidence from the responses of others, that they are altruistic and generous. The theme uniting these different character portraits is that the self's failure to respond appropriately to others is a function of its failure of moral self-perception, which is too underdiscriminating and stereotype-driven to do justice to the complex reality of the needs, rights, and experiences of other persons; a failure, in other words, to appreciate the alterity of others.

If the essential character of self-knowledge is to serve the ends of interpersonal responsiveness and moral responsibility, it does not follow that it is always socially and interpersonally oriented. Self-knowledge can be put to work in an exclusively individualistic and monologic context, and it can be framed in nonmoral terms as purely factual knowledge. But this is a derivation from its original state.

The idea that self-knowledge is socially and dialogically constituted is clearly a broad idea, and can be interpreted in several ways. It might, for example, be construed as meaning that the encounter between the self and the other serves as the primary means of access to moral and psychological truths about the self. On this construal, social and dialogic relations perform an instrumental function, as a kind of via media. This is a weak construal of the idea. If it is true, then such relations are a means of accessing truths about the self that could be accessed by nonsocial and nondialogic means as well, if such means were available. It is a contingent fact that these relations lead to self-knowledge, and that other means do not.

This is not the only interpretation available. It can also be argued that the act of engaging the other in a dialogue directed to working out the question "Who am I?" is itself a way of knowing. Dialogue is not merely a means of accessing truths that could be accessed by nondialogic means: the dialogic encounter of self with other is *constitutive* of self-knowledge. This too is a broad idea, and supports several interpretations: for example, (1) self-knowledge involves agreement between the self and like-minded persons within a coherent community on substantive issues about the good, and the good life, as well as on procedural issues involved in the practical reasoning supporting these substantive issues; (2) self-knowledge presupposes consensus between rational interlocutors who have some degree of expertise in matters pertaining to reflective self-inquiry; and (3) self-knowledge is constituted by a response to the call from the other, and takes the form of interlocutive injunction and attestation. Each of these interpretations will be explored.

What is the point of analyzing these contemporary philosophical psychologies, rather than, say, the philosophical psychologies of Rousseau, Augustine, or Kierkegaard, each of whom also addressed the problem of self-knowledge? First, each one is distinguished by a certain philosophical depth and systematicity that is not readily found elsewhere in contemporary philosophical psychology. Each one, for instance, focuses on the phenomena of self, self-understanding, agency, and emotions, not just as isolated phenomena but as essentially interrelated components of more generalized philosophical anthropologies, which themselves are representative of widely shared but implicit conceptions of human being found in contemporary Anglo-American and European philosophy.

Second, each philosophical psychology has clear-cut applications in contemporary psychotherapy and clinical psychology, where bringing clarity to questions of self, agency, and self-knowing is more than a matter of theoretical interest. This is particularly obvious in the case of the psychodynamic psychotherapies, the goal of which is to help clients attain a level of veridical insight into the structures of their personalities and behaviors, and the causes of their psychological problems, which prior to therapeutic intervention was not available to them. It is a widely held assumption in the psychodynamic tradition that the client's psychic suffering is alleviated by *insight*. The particular content of insight varies from one type of psychotherapy to another. In some therapeutic traditions, insight involves acquiring knowledge of the previously concealed causal determinants of the presenting psychological disturbance: e.g., childhood traumas or unresolved complexes. In other traditions, it involves developing a degree of existential lucidity about the nature of one's being in the world. In other traditions, it involves reweaving the past and present into an internally coherent and personally satisfying narrative. In each of these cases, insight is considered to be a necessary condition for therapeutic change; without it, change is short-lived, and the client's presenting problems would be liable to recur later in only slightly altered form. The insight-oriented psychotherapies provide an environment that affords clients opportunities for reflective self-inquiry, through experimentation with new forms of self-understanding and interpersonal relating, and the acquisition of new problem-solving skills.[7]

But while the concept of insight in the clinical practice of the psychodynamic psychotherapies is intuitively plausible, its epistemic and hermeneutic conditions have remained to a large extent unclarified at the level of the *theory* of psychotherapy. It is often assumed without argument that insight just is veridical self-knowledge; that when insight is followed by therapeutic change, it must be a true insight; and that the specific contents of the client's insight make a significant and specific difference to the therapeutic outcome.[8] Each of these assumptions is problematic, and conceals a number of important epistemological and phenomenological complexities. The mere occurrence of insight in psychotherapy is no guarantee of its veridicality and accuracy. Some insights that are therapeutically beneficial and subjectively reassuring, for example, also happen to be false, or driven by therapeutically induced self-deception; their effectiveness can be explained adequately in terms of placebo effects, therapeutic suggestion, and the client's doctrinal compliance, and not as a function of the acquisition of veridical self-knowledge. Moreover, the mere fact that therapeutic change follows (in some cases) upon the acquisition of insight is not a guarantee that the insight represents veridical self-knowledge. To assume otherwise is to commit the fallacy of *post hoc ergo propter hoc.*

The third reason why these four particular philosophical psychologies will be explored is that each casts light, from one narrow angle, upon a series of important tensions in contemporary moral philosophy and philosophical psychology on the nature of rationality, truth, and realism. These tensions are sharply articulated in the postmodernist critique of the essentialist, substantialist, and transcendentalist models of the self in modern and contemporary philosophy. The postmodernist critiques do not hold that the self is elusive, or that self-knowledge is potentially dangerous—both of which views assume the reality of the self; they hold that the self that is the putative object of self-knowledge is a construct or an artifact whose ontological status is deeply problematic. The self in postmodernist thought has been characterized variously as a fictional center of narrative gravity, as an infinitely polyvalent text, and as a fragmented and non-self-identical flux. If these depictions of the self are valid, then there are grounds for thinking that the reflective self-inquiry that is motivated by the question "Who am I?" is not, and cannot be, about antecedently existing matters of fact. What reflective self-inquiry "uncovers" is layers of interpretive, narrative, or linguistic artifact, laid down one upon the other with each successive attempt to address the question "Who am I?" Reflective self-inquiry penetrates into an ultimately groundless, and ultimately disunified, layering of artifacts, while at the same time contributing to it yet another artifactual layer.

The postmodernist models of the self, however, bear little resemblance to actual human psychology, and to the phenomenology of actual moral experience. They are at once oversimplified and overidealized. One way their poor fit with experience becomes manifest is in the clinic. Victims of dissociative personality disorder or schizophrenia, for instance, suffer from a fractured self that closely matches postmodernist descriptions of the decentered self. But their experience is a source of suffering and maladaptivity, not of insight, irony, or liberation from the insidious normalization of power/knowledge technologies. If realized in clinical settings, the postmodern idealization of the fragmented self would have negative iatrogenic consequences, the result of confusing the theorized properties of texts with the psychology and the experiences of embodied human beings.[9]

SELF-KNOWLEDGE IN LITERATURE AND DRAMA

Literature, drama, and case histories from the insight-oriented psychotherapies supply a fertile field of robust examples of many of the varieties of self-knowledge, self-deception, self-ignorance, and self-misunderstanding. One of the litmus tests of the empirical plausibility of the four philosophical psychologies that will be discussed in later chapters is their capacity to accommodate and explain examples from these domains. Literature and drama will provide the central examples, because in them are found repositories of the exploration of self-interpretations and models of moral personality that have developed across many centuries. Thus Sartre's autobiography *The Words* will serve to illustrate his own existential-phenomenological account of self-knowledge, Robert Musil's novel *The Man without Qualities* will illustrate Rorty's account, and Margaret Laurence's novel *The Stone Angel* will illustrate the dialogic account. Several examples from psychoanalytic psychotherapy will be used to illustrate Hampshire's philosophical psychology.

Despite the variety and robustness of depictions of morally self-reflective characters in literature and drama, the goals of psychological and phenomenological realism do not always receive the attention they deserve. Literary depictions are often driven more by dramatic, stylistic, and characterological conventions than by concern for psychological verisimilitude and phenomenological precision. A clear example of this is found in the account of self-knowledge in Sophoclean drama, with its convention of the "single hidden truth" driving the dramatic machinery: hidden from the view of the protagonist, but indirectly manifest in all of his or her behavior, is a single overwhelmingly significant moral truth about his or her identity. The protagonist's actions slowly converge upon the discovery of this truth, each action supplying a piece of a puzzle that unfolds with the inevitability of a natural disaster; and each action remains relatively insignificant until the truth is finally uncovered in one cathartic moment. The acquisition of self-knowledge in Sophoclean drama is at once tragic and liberating, effecting a global reevaluation of self and occasioning an untraversable divide in the protagonist's life history. The clearest example of this is the tragedy of Oedipus.

The aesthetic demands of dramatic tension, however, are not always consistent with the demands of psychological and phenomenological realism.

The acquisition of self-knowledge is not always a case of uncovering a "single hidden truth" about the self. Nor is it always a matter of all-or-none insight: ambiguity, uncertainty, and incompleteness inevitably interfere with the acquisition of self-knowledge, rendering it less final, and less finalizable, than that portrayed in drama. Sophocles' play, however, would lose its dramatic power if Oedipus suffered only from nagging doubts about his identity, after having acquired merely a fragmentary and poorly evidenced understanding of his past.

Another convention affecting the way the acquisition of self-knowledge is portrayed in literature and drama is the convention of the "extreme situation." This is especially common in existentially oriented literature, with its emphasis on the disruptive and disenchanting potential of self-knowledge: literature such as Tolstoy's autobiographical *Confession* and his novella *The Death of Ivan Ilyich*, Kierkegaard's philosophical parables and stories, and Sartre's novels. The starting point of existential self-reflection is often depicted as occurring during extreme situations in which the central character faces a critical turning point in his or her life: in situations of extreme danger, in dark nights of the soul, during fatal illnesses, or confronting dilemmatic decisions about life possibilities. One of the clearest variations of this dramatic convention links up a character's impending death with his or her felt need to bear witness to life in terms that are finally stripped of protective illusions or self-deceptions. The authentic realization of mortality is often depicted in literature as somehow forcing a "squaring off" of accounts, an "owning up," or what W. Somerset Maugham called "the summing up":

> We know that all men are mortal (Socrates was a man; therefore— and so forth), but it remains for us little more than a logical premiss till we are forced to recognize that in the ordinary course of things our end can no longer be remote. An occasional glance at the obituary column of *The Times* has suggested to me that the sixties are very unhealthy; I have long thought that it would exasperate me to die before I had written this book, and so it seemed to me that I had better set about it at once. When I have finished it I can face the future with serenity, for I shall have rounded off my life's work. I can no longer persuade myself that I am not ready to write it, since if I have not by now made up my mind about the things that seem of importance to me there is small likelihood that I shall ever do so. I am glad at last to collect all these thoughts that for so long have floated at haphazard on the various levels of my con-

sciousness. . . . When I have finished this book I shall know where I stand. I can afford then to do what I choose with the years that remain to me.[10]

One of the literature's most well known cases of "owning up" in an extreme situation is to be found in *The Death of Ivan Ilyich*. Tolstoy's description of the last-minute reflections of the dying Ivan Ilyich is guided by a thinly disguised Christian interpretation of the lost soul's struggle toward redemption and salvation. Ilyich's journey toward a final clarity about his life illustrates the Augustinian theme that one must first die to one's alienated self before one can find one's true self. Tolstoy's description captures some of the main themes of the existentialist concept of inauthenticity. Ilyich is "a capable, cheerful, good-natured and sociable fellow, though strict in the performance of what he considered as his duty; and he considered as his duty whatever was so considered by those in authority over him."[11] Ilyich is a self-centered conformist who has spent his life "smoothly, pleasantly and correctly," never stopping to examine his life in anything other than the conventional terms supplied by his social milieu, and never subjecting his moral and religious beliefs to rational scrutiny. He is unaware of how his life displays a consistent pattern of denying or evading serious self-reflection. But at the low point of an incurable illness, when his defenses are most vulnerable, he finds himself forced to confront a series of troubling questions about what he has done with his life:

> Ivan Ilyich saw that he was dying, and he was in continual despair. In the depth of his heart he knew he was dying but, so far from growing used to the idea, he simply did not and could not grasp it.
>
> The example of a syllogism which he had learned in Kiezewetter's *Logic*: "Caius is a man, men are mortal, therefore Caius is mortal," had seemed to him all his life to be true as applied to Caius but certainly not as regards himself. . . . That Caius—man in the abstract—was mortal, was perfectly correct; but he was not Caius, nor man in the abstract: he had always been a creature quite, quite different from all others . . . with all the joys and griefs and ecstasies of childhood, boyhood and youth. . . .
>
> And Caius was certainly mortal, and it was right for him to die; but for me, little Vanya, Ivan Ilyich, with all my thoughts and emotions—it's a different matter altogether. It cannot be that I ought to die. That would be too terrible.[12]

Ilyich is unable to integrate the knowledge that he is mortal in such a way that it becomes *self*-knowledge: it remains an abstract truth that can be understood without making any practical difference to his moral self-perception, and to his conduct of life.[13] His feeling that his case was incomparably different from Caius's is only one instance of a lifelong pattern of denying potentially disruptive facts about himself. The dawning of insight is painful: "It can't—it can't be, and yet it is!"

> Then he was still and not only ceased weeping but even held his breath and became all attention: he listened, as it were, not to an audible voice but to the voice of his soul, to the tide of his thoughts that rose up in him.

> "What is it you want?" was the first clear conception capable of expression in words that he heard. "What is it you want? What is it you want?" he repeated to himself.

> "What do I want? Not to suffer. To live," he answered.

> And again he listened with such concentrated attention that even his pain did not distract him.

> "To live. Live how?" asked his inner voice.

> "Why, to live as I used to—well and pleasantly."

> "As you used to live—well and pleasantly?" queried the voice. And he began going over in his imagination the best moments of his pleasant life. But oddly enough none of those best moments of his pleasant life now seemed at all what they had seemed at the time.[14]

The train of Ilyich's deathbed questioning progresses relentlessly, terminating at the disturbing thought that he may not have lived his life as he should have lived it. His first reaction of denial is consistent with his inauthentic stance to life: he has lived a proper and dutiful life "just like the others." But this evasion fails to silence his doubts. The thought returns to haunt him, each time acquiring larger implications, and each time forcing him to review his life in deeper and less familiar terms. Eventually he finds himself confronted with a horrifying question: "What if in reality my whole life has been wrong?" The sense of the question is not that *some* of the ideals, actions, and decisions in terms of which he defined his life were of morally questionable value; it is, rather, that the framework in terms of which these values make sense is morally questionable *as a whole.*

During the course of the night, as the struggle between his conventional self-understanding and the horrifying question put to him by his conscience plays itself out, he comes to see himself in a profoundly different light.

> He lay flat on his back and began going over his life entirely anew. In the morning when he first saw the footman, then his wife, then his daughter, then the doctor, every movement they made, every word they uttered, confirmed for him the awful truth that had been revealed to him during the night. In them he saw himself—all that he had lived for—and saw plainly that it was all wrong, a horrible, monstrous lie concealing both life and death.[15]

This is not the end of Ilyich's crisis. With the collapse of his conventional self-understanding, and the system of intellectual and emotional defenses that protects it, he is finally capable of experiencing a redeeming self-transformation through which he can justify his life. Moments before he dies he undergoes a kind of epiphany: he discovers the truth—the essentially spiritual truth—that it is others for whom he must live. The implication is that this insight has the potential to exert a profound retroactive effect on Ilyich's life: the *meaning* of his past life (e.g., his lifelong coldness and selfishness), if not the facts of his life, changes with the newly won change in his self-understanding. This may be the most psychologically implausible part of the story. Tolstoy does not address the issue of whether the transformation effected by Ilyich's insight is authentic, or a selfish last-ditch act of self-deception driven by the fear of oblivion. Nor does he ask whether it has genuine interpersonal consequences. How, for instance, does Ilyich's essentially solitary transformation affect others? Would his wife have been disposed to engage in a fundamental re-evaluation of the past decades of marital unhappiness simply as a result of witnessing firsthand her husband's revelation?

Literary accounts of extreme situations give the impression that the realization of impending death inevitably forces an honest confrontation of the self with itself that could otherwise be postponed indefinitely. This is false. Nothing about an impending death prevents those who are creatively and positively self-deceived from continuing to deceive themselves. Ilyich's illusions may have been so resilient and entrenched that even the fear of death could have been temporarily neutralized by a harmless pseudo-insight.

Literary accounts also give the impression that the confrontation with death is sufficient to certify the authenticity of the insights that ensue. This too is false. The intensity or timing of an insight is no guarantee that it is veridical. Ilyich's deathbed insights may be systematically off track—complex artifacts of the self-deceptive and self-evasive strategies that characterized his entire stance to his life—and yet bear the outward marks of authenticity.

Whatever the dramatic demands, however, the literary conventions that tie together self-knowledge and death still capture some important components of self-knowledge: for instance, the relation between self-knowledge and the felt need to bear witness to one's life; the relevance of self-knowledge to moral and existential integrity; and the potential of an impending death to dispel the veils of self-deception or self-ignorance.

Bearing in mind the constraints placed by literary conventions on psychological verisimilitude and phenomenological precision, examples such as these will serve to orient the discussion of self-knowledge in the following chapters. Without this attention to literary examples, the discussion would risk floating free of the very experience whose epistemological and phenomenological conditions it seeks to make intelligible. A descriptive phenomenology of the experience of self-knowing is propaedeutic to the analysis of the epistemic and hermeneutic conditions of self-knowledge.

ZASETSKY

To forestall the impression that self-knowledge is exclusively a matter of acquiring deep and complex insights of the sort portrayed in the literature of depth psychology—as if being self-knowledgeable is a matter of being "finely aware and richly responsible"[16]—it is appropriate to turn to the case histories of neurology and cognitive neuropsychology. Here the pursuit of self-knowledge is pitched at a less refined but no less morally and existentially significant level.

Consider the Russian soldier Zasetsky, a man who was injured on the Russian front during World War II, and who was treated by the neuropsychologist Alexander Luria.[17] Zasetsky suffered massive damage to the temporo-parieto-occipital area of his cerebral cortex, the area of higher cortical functions that controls the analysis, synthesis, and organization of complex associations of information into a coherent framework. Left aphasic, perceptually and proprioceptively disoriented, and densely amnesic (with retrograde and anterograde amnesia), he struggled to piece together the fragments of a once robust identity and self-understanding with only the slimmest of resources available to him. He had to relearn how to read and write, how to perform basic movements, and how to name objects. So impaired were his visual capacities that the right-hand side of objects within his visual field—including the right-hand side of his own body—was nonexistent (hemianopia, with corresponding topographic field defects). Objects no longer appeared to him as complete and continuous entities, but flickered erratically like shadows. Accompanying his fragmented external world was a severe impairment of kinesthesis, proprioception, and body image: "Sometimes when I'm sitting down I suddenly feel as though my head is the size of a table—every bit as big—while my hands, feet and torso become very small. . . . When I close my eyes, I'm not even sure where my right leg is; for some reason I used to think (even sensed) it was somewhere above my shoulder."[18] Zasetsky had difficulty locating parts of his body, and could not remember how they functioned. Simple gesturing was incomprehensible to him. He also found that he had an impoverished sense of the affordances of objects. Wielding an ax or hammering a nail quickly deteriorated into meaningless sequences.

The most important goal of Zasetsky's rehabilitation was not physical in nature: it was to recover his sense of self. Because he had lost large portions of his memory, his ability to form a coherent account of his past, and to plan for the future, was almost nonexistent. He had no clear idea of his preferences, beliefs, values, and goals. "My head was a complete blank. I just slept, woke, but simply couldn't think, concentrate, or remember a thing. My memory—like my life—hardly seemed to exist. . . . At first I couldn't even recognize myself, or what had happened to me."[19] Zasetsky resolved with Luria's help to dedicate his energies to the project of reclaiming his self, and to recovering a "subjective sense of an invigorating sameness and continuity."[20] His efforts at self-recovery were no less significant than those of more psychologically sophisticated self-knowers. While equipped with fewer cognitive resources than most, Zasetsky endeavored to raise the question "Who am I?" in a manner that was, at least for him, fundamental.

Zasetsky's memories after the injury consisted only of random fragments that would come to mind involuntarily, and which were difficult to piece together into coherent wholes. But as his long-term memory had not been destroyed (it was only the access to the stored memories that had been damaged), a great deal of information about his past was preserved, although it was not available by the ordinary means of simply summoning up memories at will. It was with Luria's help that Zasetsky found a key to unlock the store-house of his long-term memory. The brain damage had left him illiterate and aphasic, but it had not affected certain lower-level kinetic-motor functions, including the hand and digital movements deployed in writing. Zasetsky discovered that he could write if he allowed his hand to flow automatically across the page, without consciously guiding it, or visualizing the words he had to spell.

The discovery of automatic writing was the turning point in a life that would otherwise have been imprisoned in the present moment. Zasetsky committed himself to writing a journal, with the goal of reclaiming his former self, and leaving behind a first-person account of the conquest of amnesia. Although writing was an exhausting task, he produced over the span of twenty-five years a three-thousand-page journal that he entitled *I'll Fight On!* "Writing about and studying myself is my way of thinking, keeping busy, working at something. . . . If I shut these notebooks, give it up, I'll be right back in the desert, in that 'know nothing' world of emptiness and amnesia."[21]

Why did he embark on such a monumental and painful task of self-recovery? Luria writes:

> What was the point? He asked himself this question many times. Why bother with this difficult, exhausting work? Was it necessary? In the end he decided it was. . . . [He] could try gradually to assemble the bits and pieces of his past, compose and arrange them into episodes, create a coherent view of what his experience and desires were. . . . It was essential in that it was his only link with life, his one hope of recovering and becoming the man he had been. Perhaps if he developed his ability to think, he could still be useful, make something of his life. Reviving the past was thus a way of trying to ensure a future.[22]

The singular tragedy of Zasetsky's case is that while he gained access to information about his past, he was unable to transform it into anything that resembled the rich sense of self, and the robust form of self-understanding, that he had enjoyed prior to the injury. His rehabilitation remained incomplete: he could write automatically, and thereby access parts of his past, but the impairment to his other memory systems prevented him from keeping in mind for more than a few moments the few recognizably true passages that he did manage to read successfully. He did not have the mnemonic resources that would enable him to identify with the autobiographical passages that flowed from his pen. While he externalized himself on the page, he was unable to internalize and integrate what he had written in such a way that he could feel that he had a reasonable and more or less truth-tracking grasp on the question of his identity.[23]

But Zasetsky is relatively lucky among those who have suffered severe neurological damage. He at least had some access to autobiographical memory, and some use of the tools needed to create an account of who he was. Others lack even this degree of leverage, having suffered damage to both the access and the storage systems of autobiographical memory. Without some vestige of long-term memory, it is not possible to form the complex plans, reflexive attitudes, and forms of self-understanding that are essential for a robust sense of self. This does not mean that for such people there is "nobody home." Those who are densely amnesic still have a subjective point of view that is tied perceptually, somatically, and proprioceptively to a certain way of being in the world, and to a certain way of experiencing the passage of time. One of the baseline conditions for this is the preservation of short-term memory. But this is insufficient to generate a robust self-understanding.

The Zasetsky case illustrates even more poignantly than many literary cases a number of salient features about what is involved in coming to know oneself: the fragility of self-knowledge, the complex multidimensional nature of the self, the importance of proprioception and kinesthesis for higher-order cognitive tasks, and the interpersonal conditions of self-inquiry. It also illustrates how with certain kinds of neurological trauma, selfhood is subject to fading, leaving in its place an identityless mind, or in the most extreme cases an identityless organism subsisting at rudimentary physiological levels. The case suggests that selfhood can be thought of as ranged along a continuum, at one end of which is a relatively well-integrated self, and at the other end of which is a variety of forms of relative disintegration. Self-knowledge is an equally fragile achievement. Certain kinds of trauma can lead to its erosion, leaving in their place a variety of forms of self-opacity or self-misunderstanding. It too can be ranged along a continuum, ranging from robust, plausible, and integrated to shallow, misinformed, or fragmentary. Zasetsky's experience showed that the kind of knowledge called for by the Delphic command "know thyself" is not the exclusive preserve of those who are "finely aware and richly responsible."

2

◄

APPROACHES TO
THE SELF

►

Self-knowledge has been characterized as an achievement and not as a given. This is because it involves subjecting the various parts of the self—especially those desires, beliefs, traits, and emotions that are central to the self's configuration—to the difficult work of reflective self-inquiry and reflective self-evaluation; and because it involves subjecting conventional self-understandings, which are not themselves normally scrutinized, to self-criticism. But these are not the only ways the self can be accessed; nor are they, developmentally, the first. The self is also something that can be imagined, narrated, remembered, conceptualized, and perceived. Each of these ways of approaching the self may serve as a source for self-knowledge—but they are not to be confused with self-knowledge proper. This is because it is possible to be self-knowledgeable without being proficient in any one of these alternative approaches to the self; and it is possible to be proficient in any one of these alternative approaches without being self-knowledgeable. I may for example simply have a knack for formulating outwardly plausible self-concepts that appear to capture essential features of (for example) my character traits, without having an adequate grasp of the actual psychological salience, historical development, and causal role of those character traits.

Self-knowledge thus needs to be distinguished from a number of alternative ways of approaching the self. In psychology and philosophy these alternative approaches, including self-concepts, self-narratives, and the psychosomatic sense of self, are sometimes confused with self-knowledge. The work of distinguishing self-knowledge from these superficially similar approaches to the self is thus largely ground-clearing work. Once completed, it will be possible to turn to the analysis of the four philosophical psychologies that address self-knowledge proper.

JUDGMENT DAY

Since we are considering the variety of ways by which the self can be approached, let us take the strongest case first, and work backward to weaker cases. Consider the approach to the self that can be had from an ideally objective point of view—say from a God's-eye point of view, or from the point of view of a completed science of mind, behavior, and personality. Would this approach serve the ends of self-knowledge—the sort of knowledge that answers to the question "Who am I?" Could I ground my claims to self-knowledge on the basis of what I know about my self from an ideally objective point of view?

Owen Flanagan addresses this question by developing a thought experiment that rests on the distinction between "actual full identity" and "self-represented identity."[1] This corresponds to the distinction between who I *actually* am, as revealed from an objective point of view, and who I *think* I am, as revealed from a personal point of view. The objective point of view is not the view occupied by disinterested observers of the self: it is an *ideally* objective point of view. It thus has none of the marks of incompleteness and uncertainty that characterize the viewpoints of others who are in a position to comment objectively upon the self. One of the goals of the thought experiment is to highlight the differences between these two ways of approaching the self. Another more prominent goal is to show that self-represented identity necessarily falls short, and in some cases far afield, of actual full identity. The thought experiment thereby serves to push to the limit our naive intuitions about the mutual relevance of the first-person and third-person perspectives.

What is actual full identity, and how do I relate to it? Flanagan characterizes actual full identity as the identity "which is normally to some significant degree unknown to us but which, according to a useful fiction, we come to see with clarity on Judgment Day, when all memories are restored and all distortions are removed." Superficially, this may look like a version of the concept of the noumenal self that is hidden behind a veil of appearances. But actual full identity is not something that is beyond all possible experience, as a condition of possibility of experience of the apparent self. It is no more and no less mysterious than complex natural phenomena that have yet to be fully identified and explained. Actual full identity is a dynamic configuration of many parts and layers, the sheer complexity of which means that very little of its true nature will ever be known to the person whose identity it is. It is constituted by "the dynamic integrated system of past and present identifications, desires, commitments, aspirations, beliefs, dispositions, temperaments, roles, acts, and actional patterns, as well as by whatever self-understandings (even incorrect ones) each person brings to his or her life."[2]

The point of introducing this idealized epistemic condition is to show that knowledge of actual full identity cannot be reliably obtained from the first-person point of view by pursuing the question "Who am I?" in the mode of reflective self-inquiry. This is because reflective self-inquiry is too subjective and too interest-relative to yield anything other than narrow and relatively impoverished results. One reason this is the case is that reflective self-inquiry can result only in *representations* of the self; it does not give direct access to the self. Representations approximate actual full identity with varying degrees of success. Some are more accurate than others, but none, ex hypothesi, are complete in the sense in which the Judgment Day account of the self is complete.

What then are the differences between a self-representation that happens to have a high degree of accuracy, and the Judgment Day account of that same self? Is it simply a matter of degree of completeness? One of the distinguishing marks of self-representations is that they are necessarily *simplified* with respect to the actual full identity they represent. This might appear to be a trivial claim: it is simply the nature of the case that representations are simplified with respect to the objects they putatively represent. If actual full identity is in fact an enormously complex natural phenomenon, then it is reasonable to expect that any attempted representation of it will be simplified. But it is the nature and degree of simplification that is significant here. Flanagan's claim is that the first-person representation of the self is necessarily *over*simplified, in the same way that a theoretical fiction (rather than a bona fide theoretical explanation) is oversimplified. Just as the concept of a center of gravity is a useful theoretical fiction for understanding some of the highly complex properties of physical objects, so the first-person representation of the self is a

useful fiction for understanding and unifying the highly complex properties of
the psychology of human organisms. But just as the concept of a center of
gravity is too simplified to serve an adequate explanatory role in physical science, so the first-person representation of the self is too simplified to count as
a serious candidate for an adequate explanation of actual full identity: it is,
Flanagan claims, "emblematic" of what the self is, but its fit with the facts is
severely restricted.

But the analogy between first-person representations of identity and theoretical fictions is strained, because it assumes that all forms of self-representation
are fictional. This is simply not the case. Some self-representations are fictional,
if their unification of the properties of the self floats free of the real configuration of those properties. They may, for example, be fictional in the way that a
deliberately nonrepresentational (e.g., expressionist) portrait is fictional. But
self-representations may be simplified *and* nonfictional, if they accurately and
economically depict the salient properties of the self while unifying those properties in ways that remain relevant for explanatory purposes. Conversely, self-
representations may be fictional and highly complex, as in an imaginative
autobiography that blends fiction with fact. What determines the fictionality of
a self-representation is something other than its degree of simplification.

Flanagan's point, however, can be made independently of the adequacy of
the analogy. Actual full identity can only be known from the ideally objective
perspective; and it can only be adequately explained in terms that have been
purified of the distortions and simplifications of the first-person point of
view. The ideally objective perspective, Flanagan claims, is the perspective
constituted by the collection of the best theoretical perspectives that would
be converged upon by an ideally realized scientific inquiry: "Actual full identity is the self as described by the most enlightened version of the story of the
self that emerges as science advances and first-person opacities and distortions are removed. It is described in abstract terms."[3]

It should be clear from this that Flanagan is concerned with the nature of
actual full identity as it is *in itself*, independent of the issue of *whose* identity
it is, and how it *matters* to that person. Facts of a subjective nature such as
these are accounted for by the explanation of actual full identity, but they do
not themselves have explanatory value. The particular affective and volitional
dimensions of the self-relation, including reflexive feelings of self-concern,
moral emotions of self-regard, and acts of avowal and self-identification, do
not have any explanatory privilege in the final account of actual full identity:
their significance is phenomenal rather than explanatory.

But is this plausible? What sorts of considerations would block assigning an explanatory role to reflexive feelings of self-concern and moral emotions of self-regard? One consideration is that the phenomenon of identity mattering to the person whose identity it is, is constituted by that person's relations to a notional or self-represented identity, and not to his or her actual full identity itself. That is, the concern that I feel about my self, and my acts of identification or disavowals, are actually directed to what I *consider* to be my self: but this is not the same as being directed to my actual self—my actual full identity as it is in itself. This is because it is only possible to feel concern for (and a sense of ownership of) those aspects of the self to which there is access. But it is no more possible for me to identify with and feel concern for a self of which a large portion is hidden from my view, and which will remain hidden until Judgment Day, than it is possible to feel concern for the self of a stranger.

This strategy is problematic. One of the difficulties in trying to give an impersonal analysis of actual full identity is that it underestimates the importance of a range of phenomena that play a constitutive role in the identity of persons: viz., the phenomena associated with *being* a self. To see this, consider how the relation that I have to my self is different from the relation that another person has to it. Someone else can relate to who and what I am in a theoretical, aesthetic, or representational manner. But the one relation that I cannot avoid, and that other persons necessarily cannot have, is relating to my self in the concrete manner of having my self *to be*. This can be called the existential self-relation: I am the one who must continue *being* me; and I am the one who must assume such and such an identity, and continue to do so. But the taking up of this relation is not the assumption of a theoretical, aesthetic, or representational stance toward my self, based on certain beliefs I have about what my self is in an absolute or "actual full" sense: it is a practical relation. I do not, in other words, *have* a self in a straightforwardly factual sense, as objects can be said to have determinate properties in virtue of which their identities are "actual" and "full"; rather, I *am* a self in such a way that I must take up a practical and existential stance toward my self. But if this is the case, then the self cannot be analyzed independently of the existential issue of whose self it is, how it matters to me, and how I identify with it. The objective information about my self that is disclosed to me on Judgment Day does not help alleviate the task of having my self to be.

There is a way to preserve the impersonal analysis of actual full identity in the face of this criticism, but it comes at a high price. This is to argue that the existential self-relation is *itself* a fictional representation. My relating to my self in the concrete manner of having my self to be is constituted by fictional representations of the self I have to be. These representations at best approximate how I actually stand in relation to my actual full identity. Only an impersonal analysis can accurately identify actual full identity, and the actual full nature of the existential relations that I have to it.

This argument reduces the existential self-relation to a fictional representation. But this is problematic, because it leads to skepticism about the very possibility of self-knowledge. If first-person self-representations are fictional, then it is logically possible that the truths revealed on Judgment Day in response to the question "What sort of person is it that I am?" bear no significant resemblance to the putative truths revealed by first-person self-inquiry in response to the question "Who am I?" What Flanagan calls the "most enlightened version of the story of the self that emerges as science advances and first-person opacities and distortions are removed" may preserve little of those first-person self-understandings.

Two consequences follow from this. First, it is logically possible that the fictional representations of the self that are supplied by first-person inquiry are *radically* mistaken in what they purport to represent. My self-representations could be coherent and consistent, and display a high level of functionality, without corresponding in any significant sense to my actual full identity. They could float free of the facts of my self and my life history that will be revealed to me on Judgment Day. This systematic failure to represent the self might be the case, despite my subjective certainty about the validity of the representations, the presence of intersubjective consensus, and the functionality of the representations. Similarly, it is logically possible that the entire range of acts of identification and disavowal that I have made under the assumption that such acts play a central role in determining what is constitutive of my identity have in actuality missed their mark; and, similarly, that the entire range of feelings of self-concern and self-regard that I have experienced have in actuality been feelings about something other than the self that I actually and fully am: viz., feelings about what is in fact a fiction.

Second, the truth of the Judgment Day account cannot, ex hypothesi, be challenged; it is a final and authoritative account of who and what I am. But the putative truth claims of the first-person account can be challenged: they are revisable claims, subject to both empirical and conceptual revision. This means that the Judgment Day account would have the authority to correct, revise, or even eliminate the truth claims of my first-person account. On

Judgment Day it is logically possible that I could wake up and realize that I have never before known who and what I am. The full range of a lifetime's worth of attempts to deal with the question "Who am I?" have floated free of, or far afield from, their target, subjective certainty and intersubjective consensus notwithstanding.

These are unwanted consequences. The problem with skepticism about the very possibility of self-knowledge is that it commits the fallacy of changing the subject. It is one thing for the ideally objective account of the self to go beyond the experientially based claims of the first-person perspective, with a view to providing a rigorous explanation of the nature of the self. This is a reasonable claim that is in keeping with the aims of science to explain the lawlike patterns of phenomena. But it is another thing to claim that this dimension of experience fails to provide the proper subject matter that is to be inquired into, or that it requires radical redescription because of its fictional status. This violates the principle of saving the phenomena. To deny the relevance of the first-person perspective (including the experience of being a self, and the existential self-relation) is to deprive the explanation of the self of its very subject matter: viz., the self. This perpetuates a variation of what has been called the "retrospective fallacy": namely, replacing the accurate description of experience (which is the object of explanation) with the theory-driven conception of how that experience must be.

PERSONALITY PROFILES

In trying to distinguish self-knowledge from a variety of superficially similar approaches to the self, we have begun with the strongest possible case: viz., the self as it is seen from a God's-eye point of view, or from the point of view of a completed science of mind and personality. The question this raised was whether it is logically and phenomenologically possible to ground a claim to a personal and practically relevant form of self-knowledge on the basis of an ideally objective knowledge about the self. The Judgment Day thought experiment served to challenge our naive intuitions about the relevance of an ideally objective point of view for reflective self-inquiry. Several difficulties were encountered along the way, although none were fatal.

The thought-experiment strategy, however, is not the most felicitous way to resolve the issue. One of the problems with thought experiments as a general strategy for illuminating philosophical problems and suggesting tentative solutions is that they get off the ground only by remaining silent about a number of obvious questions about boundary conditions. For example, is the account of my self that I receive on Judgment Day a description, an explanation, or an evaluation? Is it framed in terms that are intelligible to human beings? Is it of any *use* to me? What would it be *like* for me to understand it, and to form identifications with it? Could I reject portions of it? Questions such as these could be addressed with the addition of further variables and stabilizing background conditions. But this is a potentially endless process; and simply adding more variables would threaten the integrity of the original thought-experiment conditions.[4] Consider, for example, the question about the scale and commensurability of a Judgment Day account of the self. Unless there is some way in which the absolute terms of the Judgment Day account are translatable into the nonabsolute terms that would be recognized by a finite mind, it is doubtful if there would be grounds for establishing how the two levels would refer to the same thing. But to introduce into the thought experiment a translation manual would introduce a new set of variables and background conditions that would alter the initial conditions of the thought experiment. This is not a fatal problem, but it gives the thought experiment an ad hoc character.

A more realistic way to address the question about the possibility of grounding a claim to personal self-knowledge on the objective knowledge of the self is to look at an actual case in which selves are understood scientifically. This strategy yields a clearer idea of precisely what the social and cognitive sciences can and cannot supply in the pursuit of self-knowledge. The most plausible candidate here is personality psychology, the goals of which are both practical and theoretical. Unlike Judgment Day accounts of actual full identity, personality psychology is ultimately for the benefit of the person whose personality it is.

Personality psychology classifies personality according to type, by generating psychological profiles that capture prevailing patterns of personality structure. The profiles that are its end result do not have the absolute objectivity and finality of Judgment Day accounts: they are incomplete and revisable. Moreover, the fundamental theoretical principles that govern personality psychology—principles of psychological salience, characterological prototypicality, and trait differentiability—are not independent of changing cultural and historical norms. Given the proliferation of personality taxonomies across human history, from Galen to Kant to Jung to Gordon Allport, it is doubtful that any a priori limits can be set to the variety of new types of personality classification that may be generated at any one time.

With changes in the forms of social life, in the historically embedded vocabularies of sentiment and character, and in the needs of personality taxonomists come changes in the types of relevant personality classifications.[5] Any description of personality is therefore necessarily incomplete: there is always something that is left out of any ostensibly completed profile.

Despite these qualifications about its *ultimate* objectivity, personality psychology still delivers a degree of predictive, taxonomic, and explanatory rigor that appears to be unavailable in commonsense psychology, and in first-person reflective self-inquiry. This should be clear from the methodological rigor that characterizes personality assessment testing. The first stage of the testing, for instance, involves the administering of stimulus materials to subjects, in order to build up a base of relevant data: materials such as standardized self-reports and comparative self-ratings that are designed to range across large populations of subjects. Respondents are constrained to react to each question on the personality questionnaire with one of a limited number of structured choices, the goal being to rule out the excess information that comes with free-response procedures. The next stage involves scoring and coding procedures that are brought to bear on the uninterpreted data in order to minimize the role of experimenter interpretation. The uninterpreted data yielded by the subjects' responses are subjected to scale indices that have been developed progressively by clinical fine-tuning and replication studies. The final stage is the construction of robust and putatively verifiable descriptions of personality that are free of the biases of commonsense psychology.

Methodological controls such as these lend weight to personality psychology's claims to objectivity, and suggest that it might count as one of the plausible candidates for what Flanagan describes as the "enlightened version of the story of the self that emerges as science advances and first-person opacities . . . are removed." If this is the case, then personality psychology may be relevant to the pursuit of self-knowledge. Even without fine-grained detail, a personality profile could serve a number of uses in reflective self-inquiry. It could, for instance, supply me with general information about my temperament and traits to which I might not otherwise have had access; it could prompt me to explore previously overlooked emotions and motives; or it could serve as a tentative hypothesis to be confirmed, disconfirmed, or revised by further reflective self-inquiry.

There are two reasons why even these moderate uses of personality profiles are inappropriate as sources for self-knowledge. First, the subject's acceptance of a personality profile as true or accurate is no guarantee that it is in fact true or accurate. Second, personality profiles reveal more about the experimental strategies and theoretical extrapolations of the personality psychologist, and the interference caused by the testing procedures, than they do about the real contours of the subject's personality. Consider these arguments in turn.

First, personality profiles may be accepted as true by subjects for reasons other than their truth value; and the fact that they are accepted as true by subjects is not sufficient to establish the profiles as true. My acceptance of a profile as a true description of my self may have more to do with its being flattering than its being true; and my rejection of a profile as false may have more to do with its being inconsistent with my current self-concept than its being based on unconvincing evidence. There is empirical evidence to support these claims. Experiments in social psychology on the so-called Barnum effect have shown how subjects of personality tests will accept fictitious personality descriptions as containing revealing insights about themselves, as long as those descriptions are pitched at the right level of generality. The experiments have also shown how subjects will accept bogus descriptions as being just as accurate as, or even more accurate than, their genuine personality profiles.[6] The bogus descriptive statements that subjects identify as true are "one-size-fits-all" statements: for instance, "You have a great need for other people to like and admire you" and "At times you have serious doubts as to whether you have made the right decision or done the right thing."

Given these considerations, the prospects for personality profiles serving as an adequate source of self-knowledge, or even as a plausible source of tentative hypotheses, are dim. Unless the non-truth-valuable factors are screened out, subjects may ground their claims to self-knowledge on false, superficial, or distorted profiles, which have been accepted because of their emotional or aesthetic appeal, or because of the pressure of social consensus.

There is another reason personality profiles are inappropriate as a source of self-knowledge: they are inexact and poorly fitted to the contours of the self they putatively profile. This shortcoming can be traced back to the shortcomings of the methods of data acquisition in personality psychology. Methods that rely on self-reports, inventory checklists, and comparative self-rating scales have questionable "ecological" and phenomenological validity.[7] Consider, for example, how the questions that are asked of subjects in personality tests are framed. The questions are structured in such a way as to (1) systematically factor out of the subjects' responses all extraneous information about background context and complicating idiographic factors; and (2) target behavior in highly generalized or "typical" contexts. Missing from the data are the narrative elaborations and fine-grained details that are normally used for self-description in natural contexts. By placing strict limits on the kinds of responses provided by subjects, the stimulus materials can only capture a small synchronic portion of a multifaceted and diachronic reality—as if a standardized psychological cookie cutter is force-fitted upon the dynamic and highly particular contours of personality in context.

This is not the only way in which personality psychology is Procrustean. The subjects taking personality assessment tests are constrained to characterize themselves in terms more relevant to the experimental purposes of the personality psychologist than to their own purposes. This means that subjects and personality psychologists often differ in their understandings of the trait terms that are the focus of the comparative self-rating scales and inventory checklists that are the principal means of data acquisition. It is not uncommon, for example, for psychologically complex characterological terms and phenomenologically complex experiential terms to be left undefined in the stimulus materials, without clear behavioral referents, situational examples, or prototypes to supply a stabilized common meaning. This forces subjects to rely on personal interpretations, or to guess at the meanings intended by the personality psychologists.[8]

By force-fitting the subject's self-ratings and self-reports into narrowly schematic inventories, the psychological data—and ultimately the completed personality profiles—are more reflective of the categories of the experimental tasks of personality psychology than of the subject's actual personality. Thus one of the common admissions in personality psychology is that subjects never fully "match the prototypes" under which they are classified. In defense of personality psychology, it might be argued that the Procrustean character of personality profiles is simply the nature of the case, and that the demand for exacting representational accuracy where none can be had is unrealistic. The failure of personality psychology to yield a fine-grained and maximally individuated psychological portrait of subjects is not a lamentable flaw; rather, the rough to coarse granularity in the typing of personality is simply the price paid for any scientific study that seeks taxonomic generalizability across large populations.

Methodological difficulties aside, however, there are also epistemological grounds for doubting the appropriateness of personality profiles for the purposes of self-knowledge. The canonical questions in personality assessment testing take the form "Who are you and what are you like?" By contrast, the canonical questions in reflective self-inquiry and reflective self-evaluation take the form "Who am I and what am I like?" Both sets of questions appear to converge on the same object—the self—but they do so from different directions. How important is this difference in perspective and interrogative direction? Are the responses to both questions essentially the same, despite surface differences? Can they be coordinated?

One view is the following: the differences between the two sets of questions are negligible, because they supply equally valid ways of approaching the same object. Differences in investigative perspective and directionality are relatively inessential because the self remains what it is independently of who raises questions about it, and how the questions are framed. The core components of the self in question are determinate; if they were subject to some form of alteration by the questions put to it, they would not be core components. The crucial issue then is not *who* raises the questions, but whether the questions are the *right* questions. Once these are secured, then it is reasonable to suppose that there is access to information about the self that could in principle (even if not in fact) be accessed from the first- or third-person perspectives.

There are two problems with this view. First, personality assessment tests are based on artificial questions in artificial circumstances. Subjects who are the target of questions of the form "Who are you and what are you like?" are more or less passive with respect to the questions they must answer, in the same way that subjects on the receiving end of Judgment Day accounts are passive (since, ex hypothesi, these accounts cannot be challenged). The questions are put *to* the subjects by the experimenters, and this forces them to accept the experimenters' terms, to guess at the meanings of the relevant trait and behavioral terms, and to frame their answers within the narrow confines allowed them by the stimulus materials. Under no conditions are the questions used to gather data in a personality assessment test articulated *by* the subjects themselves. But it is because of this controlled and restricted degree of subject participation that the questions do not bear the mark of the subject's authorship, or the natural feelings of self-concern that characterize the posing of the first-personal question "Who am I?": the questions, in other words, do not belong to the subjects who must answer them.

Second, the questions raised on personality assessment tests for the purposes of data acquisition do not normally require subjects to adopt a reflective stance of self-criticism or self-evaluation. The questions are designed to elicit factually oriented responses, and to allow subjects to remain more or less neutral with respect to the normative moral issue of the worth or desirability of the identified traits. The general form taken by such questions is "Do traits *xyz* in fact characterize you?" There is good reason for this neutrality: without it, questions about traits would be confused with questions about self-ideals and self-images. But the factual attitude that is called for by questions on personality assessment tests is artificial, because it requires suppressing the prevailing evaluative feelings of self-regard and self-concern that characterize the first-person stance to the self. Normally, feelings of pride or shame, or approval or regret, qualify the relation of the self to itself. I approve of my generosity, but regret my temperamental shyness; I want to be more altruistic and less self-absorbed. Traits such as shyness or generosity are not regarded neutrally. I have feelings about their worth, and ideas about how they are to be cultivated or restructured in ways that are relevant to the formation of intentions and actions. Because the factual attitude is a derivative way of relating to the self, the canonical questions in personality assessment testing yield limited information.

Neither of these arguments should be taken to suggest that personality psychology is altogether devoid of relevance to reflective self-inquiry. Mere exposure to the technology of personality testing, and to the related theories of personality types, may stimulate in me greater reflectiveness, independently of the veridicality of the resulting personality profiles. With exposure to new ways of discriminating and identifying traits, I may develop a certain degree of expertise in the interpretation of personality, taking cues from my personality profiles to generate new self-descriptions, or making strong identifications with or disavowals of the character traits identified by my profile as central. But are these responses relevant to self-knowledge? Am I really in a better position to address the question "Who am I?" than before I was exposed to personality psychology?

The kind of approach to the self that is secured through personality psychology counts as one among a variety of kinds of knowledge *about* the self. It involves reporting facts about the self while keeping the role of interpretation, criticism, and evaluation to a minimum. Knowledge about self, however, does not count as self-knowledge.[9] The difference lies in the stance that is adopted toward the self. In the case of knowledge about the self, it is the stance adopted by an observer reporting on the facts of the case—even when the observer is the person whose own self is under observation. In the case of self-knowledge, by contrast, it is the stance of an agent who is confronted with the practical necessity of formulating intentions with a view to action, and with the existential necessity of having himself or herself to be.

What are the grounds for distinguishing between knowledge about the self and self-knowledge? First, the capacity for sophisticated reporting of facts about the self, whether it is derived from personality psychology or from Judgment Day accounts, is not ipso facto a sign of expertise in self-knowledge. It is possible to know about many of the facts pertaining to my character and behavior, and to use this as a base from which to construct outwardly plausible character profiles. But the mere possession of factual knowledge does not guarantee that it will be integrated into my actions and plans, or serve as a base from which I develop moral feelings of self-regard; nor does it guarantee that it will guide my acts of self-identification or disavowal to their proper target. I may for instance admit to a long-standing pattern of selfishness in my interpersonal behaviors, and outwardly identify with a personality profile that attests to this fact, but still fail to recognize in my day-to-day interpersonal relations (through simple self-ignorance or through self-deceptively motivated selective inattention) confirming instances of selfish behavior. In this case I would know certain facts about myself; but I would not be self-knowledgeable.

Knowledge about the self can interfere with effective agency as well as float free of it. The discrepancy between what I know about myself and the actions in which I engage may range from mere failure of integration of the self to active disintegration. Excessive attention to observing the self, for instance, can interfere with spontaneity of action, and can result in psychological and moral self-division. The political activist who is too busy examining the psychological motives for his or her commitment will not have the wholehearted commitment required for decisive political action. Moreover, the cultivation of expertise in psychologically sophisticated self-description may be harnessed to inappropriate ends that interfere with the pursuit of self-knowledge. I may, for instance, try to influence others with the subtlety of my introspective acumen,[10] using this as a means of distraction from the task of addressing genuinely pressing moral issues, or as a means of pretending to put an end to further self-inquiry. The effect of implementing these strategies is to create a self-contained island of knowledge about self, surrounded on all sides by self-opacity and self-deception.

Given these considerations, the distinction between self-knowledge and knowledge about self can be characterized as follows: self-knowledge is constitutive of effective agency, and of the self that acts; knowledge about self, on the other hand, is contingently related to effective agency, and to the self that acts. Characterizing self-knowledge as a constitutive relation is useful here. It makes it possible to describe persons as *being* self-knowledgeable—thereby capturing the internal relation between being and knowing, and capturing the centrality of the existential self-relation—rather than as simply *having* self-knowledge. Being self-knowledgeable is something that manifests itself systematically in the actions, commitments, and interpersonal involvements that define the self in ways that merely having true nontrivial descriptions about the self does not.

Returning now to the original problem, it is doubtful that perspective and interrogative direction can be factored out of the two sets of canonical questions, "Who are you and what are you like?" and "Who am I and what am I like?" Originating from different points of view, and approaching their target from different angles, the questions themselves make systematic differences to the self that is called into question. The first-person perspective is not one among several epistemically equivalent perspectives from which to inquire into the self, each of which support convergence on the selfsame object; it is constitutive of the self. Thus the use of external approaches to the self, such as personality profiles and Judgment Day accounts, cannot substitute for the hard work of reflective self-inquiry and reflective self-evaluation. This is something that can be taken up only by the person whose self it is.

SELF-CONCEPTS

Self-concepts provide a way of approaching the self that is easily confused with self-knowledge. A self-concept is a schematic and adaptive set of beliefs about the self that is used to represent to the person whose self it is, and to others, the character traits, values, moral feelings, desires, and commitments that are considered to define the self. A self-concept allows for automatic self-attribution in a variety of social contexts, as well as a range of behavioral and verbal presentations of self that are indispensable for the purposes of social intercourse. As with other forms of schematic representation, self-concepts are inexact, metaphor-laden, and culturally specific.

While the specific contents of self-concepts vary from person to person and from culture to culture, self-concepts are defined by a number of basic axes. A North American man, for instance, may think of himself as a husband and businessman (i.e., social concepts); as being gregarious and self-reliant (i.e., psychological concepts); as being honest and caring (i.e., moral concepts); as having an immortal substantial soul (i.e., theological and metaphysical concepts); and as being strong and tolerant of pain (i.e., somatic concepts). The trait lists of an eleventh-century French peasant, by contrast, might include reference to the humours and other entities identified under medieval psychology and medieval religious categories; but the listed traits would still be situated along broadly social, psychological, moral, metaphysical, and somatic axes. Because self-concepts originate in social life, they draw from the fund of concepts in the commonsense psychological and moral vocabulary, taking shape at our caretaker's knee, and acquiring all the marks of local cultural beliefs.[11]

Self-concepts are indispensable in thought and action. They play a central role in cognitive economizing by giving form to the way something as complex as the self is represented. They also serve to shape social behavior in ways that can be self-fulfilling, because the activities involved in self-representation have motivational and behavioral effects that are partly constitutive of the self. To the extent that self-concepts simplify and organize how the self is thought about, they can be described as having both an enabling and a limiting function: that is, they enable certain aspects of the self to be noticed, and obscure from view other aspects. This means that self-concepts preguide more explicit forms of inquiry into the self, by allowing as legitimate starting points certain avenues of self-questioning, and by excluding others.

But having a self-concept is not the same as being self-knowledgeable. There are a number of reasons for this. First, self-concepts are not essentially faithful representations of the self. Their primary role is to organize and select information about the self in the most parsimonious ways available. They do this by determining which information is attended to and how much importance is attached to it; by distorting negative information and enhancing positive information; by preventing contradictory information from being noticed; and by disambiguating ambiguous information so that it is consistent with prior beliefs.[12] But these mechanisms do not serve the ends of reflective self-inquiry, the primary goal of which is to determine the truth about the nature of the self, rather than to establish the most parsimonious way of thinking about the self. Some self-concepts might *happen* to be more or less accurate, but this is not because their original function is to track the truth. Self-concepts, in other words, are not themselves the *result* of reflective self-inquiry, but are held as unreflectively as any other adaptive cognitive generalization or idealized cognitive model.

There is another reason why having a self-concept is not the same as being self-knowledgeable: self-concepts range over significantly fewer areas of the self than veridical self-knowledge. There are many aspects of the self that are not fully accessible to the person whose self it is, and thus many aspects of the self that are not possible objects for conceptualization. At any one time there is always more about the self that can be represented from the first-person point of view than what currently has been achieved. Self-concepts capture some of the salient aspects of the self, but they neither need to, nor are capable of, capturing its full complexity. Their function rather is to organize and reduce the multilayered configuration of the self to a limited number of simple matrices, in order to facilitate the presentation of self in those social contexts where readily accessible templates for self-attribution are called for. There are a number of information-theoretic explanations why self-concepts serve this purpose: for example, compartmentalization, selective focusing, information insensitivity, and blind persistence are pressed into service to facilitate the construction of summaries of huge amounts of diverse information about the self, in order to make the problem-solving tasks associated with self-attribution easier.

Given these limitations, self-concepts can be a source of the same kinds of epistemic problems that it is their function to solve. To the extent that they filter, distort, or enhance certain kinds of information that are relevant to the self, they interfere with more accurate ways of perceiving differences and similarities in complex social situations. From within a rigid self-concept, for instance, morally significant features of interpersonal and intrapersonal situations (e.g., moral criticisms from others) might be overlooked, and a wide range of possibilities of action and expression for the self thereby closed off. In this way self-concepts can serve the ends of strategies of self-deception. However adaptive self-concepts might be, they do not lighten the burden of reflective self-inquiry: that is, calling the self, and the self-concepts that represent it, into question, with a view to increasing the awareness of the self in its relation to others.

THE STORIED SELF

Narrative provides another way of approaching the self—one that is often mistakenly identified with self-knowledge. Many of the aspects of the self that are the target of reflective self-inquiry and reflective self-evaluation can also be approached using narrative means. The answer to the question "Who am I?" often takes an elaborately storied form, with a beginning, middle, and end, plot and subplot development, characters, varying degrees of continuity and coherence, and a ready supply of literary and rhetorical devices. One way

I come to understand my desires and character traits is by situating them in a narrative life history that traces their origins, plots their development, and links them to the life stories of others. In such a narrative I am the central character as well as the author or coauthor.

These are straightforward descriptive claims about the capacity of narrative to capture those aspects of the self that are also the target of reflective self-inquiry. As such, they are more or less plausible, and enjoy broad empirical support. But they are also philosophically uninteresting claims. This is because not all cases of narrative self-understanding count as cases of veridical self-knowledge; and not all cases of veridical self-knowledge count as cases of narrative self-understanding. A robust narrative self-understanding, for instance, may be historically or psychologically false, and yet may be adaptive enough that its truth value goes largely undetected. The person who holds such a narrative may simply have a knack for generating plausible narratives; and he or she may have a weakness, attributable (for example) to an overarching pattern of self-deception, for being convinced by those narratives that seem to fit.

A number of philosophers and psychologists have defended stronger and more philosophically interesting claims than these empirical claims, as part of the theory of philosophical narrativism.[13] These include the following:

i. The self cannot be distinguished from the narrative that is woven continuously across the history of a life.

ii. Whatever unity the self possesses is a function of the unity of the narrative under which it is identified.

iii. As long as life goes on, there can be no final self-understanding, because new narrative orderings can always be discovered in situations past and present.

iv. Individual components of the narrative about the self cannot be understood unless something is understood about the narrative as whole; but there can be no understanding of the whole narrative unless there is some understanding of the individual components (i.e., the hermeneutic circle).

One of the philosophically significant claims common to most of the varieties of philosophical narrativism is the following:

v. Narrative is the *essential* form, or the central *constitutive* feature, of reflexive self-relations such as self-knowledge and self-understanding.

Flanagan, for instance, captures a widely shared version of this claim: narrative is the "essential genre of self-representation, and not merely . . . one normative ideal among others. A self is just a kind of life that has a beginning, a middle, and an end that are connected in a traditional storylike manner."[14] The idea that narrative is the essential form of self-knowledge is a principled claim: isolated empirical counterexamples do not count as potentially disconfirming instances of the claim, but instead can be analyzed in terms of it. The principled claim assumes that narrative functions as the *explanans* of phenomena such as self-representation and self-knowledge, not the *explanandum*. This, however, is not immediately obvious, given that narration is prima facie a complex phenomenon that draws upon a range of linguistic and cognitive skills that themselves require explanation. Because narrative is a higher-order skill that itself requires explanation, one of the tasks of philosophical narrativism is to establish the primitive character of narrative as something constitutive of the phenomena of selfhood and self-knowledge.

One way that philosophical narrativism makes the case for the centrality of narrative to self-knowledge is in terms of the distinction between historical truth and narrative truth.[15] Of the various statements that come to count as answers to the question "Who am I?" some (it is claimed) can be classed as statements about historical and psychological facts about the self, and others as interpretive statements about the *meanings* of these facts. The truth conditions for factual and interpretive statements about the self are not the same. The criterion of truth for statements of the former sort is correspondence with extralinguistic fact; the criterion of truth for statements of the latter sort is inter alia coherence with other statements.

In the former case, a statement about the self is true in virtue of the relevant historical and psychological facts, which exist whether or not they are noticed. Because facts are logically independent of the statements that refer to them, no amount of descriptive or interpretive manipulation can erase or alter them. The narrativist theory of self-knowledge, however, holds that factual statements about the self cannot serve as the basis for any robust form of self-knowledge. One of the arguments it uses to defend this is the coherentist one that no statement about the self is made entirely in isolation from any other statement about the self; each one forms part of a densely connected system of statements, at the core of which are certain deep-lying presuppositions about the nature of knowledge, belief, and evidence. The system is implicit in the assertion of any part of it.

The narrativist theory of self-knowledge holds that there are four singly necessary and jointly sufficient criteria of truth, the first three of which are formal, and the fourth substantive: internal coherence, external coherence, applicability, and fit with the facts.

i.   Internal coherence is the grouping together of the diverse statements constituting a self-narrative into a unified and continuous whole. This is a necessary but not sufficient condition for narrative truth, because historically and psychologically false narratives may be coherent, and incoherent narratives may be historically and psychologically true.

ii.   External coherence is the degree to which a system of statements constituting a self-narrative conforms to the narrative versions that other people hold about the self. This too is not a sufficient condition for narrative truth, because groups of knowers (such as families and communities) are not immune from laboring under collectively endorsed illusions and skewed epistemic practices; and there is no principled reason why nonconformists and hermits cannot achieve self-knowledge independently of social consensus.

iii. Applicability is the fit of a self-narrative with the pragmatic and existential exigencies of life. A self-narrative is not merely a reflective construction about the self's past but a forward-looking commitment to a broadly unified set of possible actions that express the self's orientation to the world. This too is not sufficient to establish the truth of a narrative, because it is possible that the carefully considered plans and projects that map out the self's orientation to the future rest upon coherent forms of self-deception and wishful thinking.

iv.   Empirical adequacy is the capacity of a self-narrative to assimilate a finite set of basic empirical contents that no narrative can possibly erase or otherwise manipulate. This slowly increasing fund of empirical content supplies the basic building blocks of all possible permutations of the narratives that can be generated about the self. Its function is not to uniquely determine one specific narrative arrangement, but to set broad parameters about what will first count *as* a self-narrative given such-and-such an empirical base. This too is not sufficient as a stand-alone criterion for narrative truth, because any finite set of recalcitrant experiences is compatible with two or more equally viable but conflicting narrative permutations.

Any individual statement about the self will count as true if it satisfies all four criteria. But the system of statements about the self that constitute a robust narrative will count as true only if it expresses the essential truth of the whole self, minor points of detail and small omissions notwithstanding. The extent to which the narrative is not a precise one-to-one representation of the self, accurate down to the minutest factual detail, is the extent to which it resembles an artistic expression more than it does a mirror. In painting or literature, for example, even the most faithful rendering of a subject is not simple representation. Artists necessarily employ one style from among a range of styles, which forces upon them certain decisions as to what will count as artistically and perspectively salient. But as each decision excludes a range of alternatives, with some perspectives and subject matters foregrounded at the expense of others, artistic representation unavoidably leaves out an indefinitely large amount of information. Similarly, the creation of a self-narrative involves the selection, simplification, and abstraction of narratively relevant materials, directed to the goal of creating a unique synthetic whole. An indefinitely large amount of information about the self may be left out of the narrative in order to bring to the fore certain similarities and differences in the patterns of phenomena that capture the essential truth of the whole self. As such, self-narratives enjoy a degree of interpretive flexibility. If enough coherence-preserving revisions are made, then certain factual errors, false memories, and psychologically incorrect observations about the self can be accommodated into the ongoing fabric of the narrative without its being rendered false.

The emphasis on interpretive flexibility is central to the narrativist theory of self-knowledge. But it runs into difficulty in two ways: first, in distinguishing coherent and accurate self-narratives from those that are coherent but inaccurate; and second, in distinguishing the prenarrative self from the self that is overlaid with adventitious narrative-generated artifacts. These two difficulties, while not fatal, make the identification of narrative self-understanding with veridical self-knowledge problematic. Consider them in turn.

First, the narrativist theory of self-knowledge owes an explanation of the precise degree of historical and psychological inaccuracy that can be tolerated before an otherwise accurate self-narrative devolves into an internally coherent but illusory or confabulated self-narrative. This is needed because the lightened explanatory load carried by the concept of historical truth can lead to a blurring of two distinctions that are worth preserving at all cost: the distinction between truth-telling and lying, and the distinction between expressions of personal preference and serious claims to knowledge. If these distinctions are blurred, then with enough interpretive flexibility and evidentiary malleability, and enough coherence-preserving revisions across the peripheries of the self-narrative, narrators would have the interpretive freedom to generate narratives that satisfy the criteria for internal and external coherence, and the criteria for applicability, while remaining driven by personal preference or self-deception. This would serve the needs of moral convenience by supplying a ready basis for self-centered excuses and moral exemptions: for by renarrating their life histories, narrators could correct fortune.

There is another way in which the emphasis on interpretive flexibility makes the identification of narrative self-understanding with self-knowledge problematic: the potential of self-narratives to generate overlays of psychological and phenomenological artifacts, which would not have otherwise counted as central in the configuration of the self. Narrative-generated artifacts are those psychological or phenomenological states that have the appearance of being given antecedently to their identification, but whose existence is dependent upon the presence of the narrative under which they are identified. With a sufficiently dense layering of narrative artifacts, one overlaid upon the other in an evolving series of accretions, a narrative has the potential to be self-confirming: that is, the conditions under which it is true are created by the narrative itself. Of the different kinds of narrative artifacts, two are salient: artifacts of crystallization, and temporal artifacts.

Just as volatile liquids and gases can crystallize into different determinate shapes depending on the differential causal action of external agents, so certain kinds of incipient, diffuse, or inchoate states of mind can be crystallized into different shapes depending on the differential demand characteristics of the narratives under which they are identified. Prior to exposure to narration, some desires (for example) have neither narrative structure nor determinate unity; they are plastic, and subject to alternative, even incompatible, crystallizations. The narrative confers upon them a unified morphology, in such a manner that what appears to be discovery is in fact an artifact of the narration that would not have been encountered independently.

Take for example the case of narrating the development of otherwise unfocused desires. When desires are initially inchoate or diffuse, the very activity of narrating them serves to give shape to the actions that will come to count as attempts to satisfy them. This is a kind of bootstrapping desire-action sequence, because the self-narratives that have the appearance of straightforward self-knowledge claims are also serving the ends of decision making. The truth-functional form of the narratives thus performs double duty: the narratives are truth-valuable descriptions that shape the very desires that are their referents, and at the same time they set up the determinate conditions for the satisfaction of those desires in action.[16]

Narration helps to crystallize otherwise diffuse or incipient states of mind in another way. Those who are hesitating about the desirability of their present desires in the overall economy of their long-range preferences may engage in a form of experimental narrative self-manipulation, by expressing their desires in conditional narrative form. They may try out a desire for size by integrating it into an ongoing self-narrative, and waiting to see what happens when it is treated it as if it were real.[17] This is a laborious method of determining the nature and intensity of desire, but it is a process that serves to form a desire that was genuinely indeterminate, and multiply crystallizable. While narration has a causal role in the formation of desires, the organizing fit may also go awry: crystallization may go against the grain of the incipient desire, making it difficult to determine what is really desired from what is artifactually desired.

The other kind of narratively generated artifact is temporal in nature. By regarding their past as a story that is written and rewritten, narrators are free to construe the connections between events in their pasts as connections of changeable plot rather than as connections of cause and effect. In doing this they also learn to play with different authorial voices, trying them on for size, and testing for rightness of fit, in ways that bring with them a subtle fragmentation of the unity of the first-person perspective. Narrators learn to consider themselves as authors, narrators, and characters, with the intertextual demands of these roles sometimes pulling in conflicting directions.

One of the apparent advantages of considering the past as a renarratable story is the degree of flexibility it affords in interpreting brute historical events. With enough narrative streamlining, filling in, selective emplotting and re-emplotting, and "smoothing over," simultaneity can be represented sequentially, and sequence can be represented teleologically. This is a useful sorting device that makes for narrative parsimony. But it also results in narratively generated temporal artifacts that throw reflective self-inquiry off track, because it gives to the narrative a literary character that the series of events it putatively represents does not actually have. Narrative streamlining and filling in does not adequately capture the phenomenology of the temporal grain and the temporal ambiguity of experience, because it confuses the prospective perspective with the retrospective perspective. Events in the present

moment are not normally experienced narratively in terms of plot developments linking together beginnings, middles, and ends. These are determinations that are read into events after the fact, when it is known whether
(for example) a plan was successfully realized or thwarted, or whether an
encounter was decisive or unimportant. When events are narrated, however,
they are not subject to the same constraints of temporal anisotropy. Time's
arrow is crossed backward and forward at will, allowing events to be interpreted in light of results that were not knowable at the time of their occurrence. When captured in a narrative, for example, small details that were
considered insignificant during the time of the event take on new meaning, as
signs portending a determinate development. The narration of events distorts
the phenomenology of the experience of temporal anisotropy with a layer of
temporal artifacts, because the realized future is read back illicitly into the
description of the past event, with the achieved outcome of a series of events
being used as the key to their meaning.[18] When this occurs, the phenomenological contours of the experience of time are distorted in their narration.

There are two reasons why the capacity of narrative to generate a layer
of artifacts makes narrative self-understanding unsuitable as a model for
self-knowledge: first, it introduces too much evidentiary interference into
self-inquiry; second, it distorts the truth conditions of reflective self-inquiry.

First, if there is such a phenomenon as narrative artifactuality, then the
task of reflective self-inquiry and reflective self-evaluation—to distinguish
the brute empirical facts that supply the basic prenarrative building blocks of
all possible narrative permutations from the layers of narratively generated
artifact—is rendered problematic. The density of artifactual overlay is often
such that narrators necessarily remain uncertain of the extent to which the
narrative itself—and not the self that is its putative object—has contributed
to the results of self-inquiry through the production of artifacts that merely
happen to resemble the prenarrative self. Narrative artifactuality does not
necessarily float free of the self; but nor is it governed by the ideal of convergence upon antecedently existing matters of fact. Instead, it creates some of
the very facts in virtue of which it is true. One self-narrative will crystallize
certain incipient desires, and generate certain temporal artifacts, in such a
way that they conform to the demands of the self-narrative (rather than vice
versa), while an alternative narrative will change those same incipient desires
in different ways. Once stabilized in this manner, neither self-narrative can be
described as converging on some antecedently existing set of facts about the
self that are waiting to be discovered, or that could be accessed independently

of either narrative, because they have each changed the self by overlaying it with alternative configurations of narrative artifacts. If this is the case, then narrative life histories do not conform carefully to the unique contours of the self—although this is the appearance they often give. Rather, self-narratives transform the self so that the self comes to fit them, thereby manufacturing some of the very facts about the self that they appear to uncover. Because the activity of narrating is an activity that itself generates the evidence that supports the narrative, narrative self-understanding becomes a self-confirming activity, and loses its claim to objectivity.

Thus one of the tasks of reflective self-inquiry and reflective self-evaluation is the critical one of calling self-narratives into question, with a view to determining their validity and accuracy in relation to the self. This is a complex higher-order inquiry; it involves determining the degree to which narrative self-understandings are distorted by artifacts, and the extent to which interpretive flexibility has caused narratives to drift away from the self they claim to narrate. In its critical role, then, reflective self-inquiry serves as a corrective to those forms of filling in, streamlining, artifactuality, and false individuation that occur when narrating the self loses its grounding in the historical, psychological, and phenomenological facts. Narrative self-understandings, in other words, are not the medium or "essential form" of reflective self-inquiry, but one among the many objects targeted by self-inquiry and reflective self-evaluation.

THE SOMATIC SENSE OF SELF

One of the ways of approaching the self that needs to be distinguished from self-knowledge is the somatic sense of self. This is the self as subjectively and corporeally felt, and as disclosed across a continuum of tacit feelings, moods, and somatic states of self-identification. The somatic sense of self is developmentally prior to explicitly worked-out self-understandings, and normally forms the unnoticed background of thought and action. When the proprioceptive, vestibular, or kinesthetic systems that constitute the somatic sense of self are impaired, cognitive and behavioral disorder is likely to follow. Experiences of depersonalization and de-realization that erode the primary action-guiding sense of self can accompany severe cases of visual neglect syndromes, phantom limbs, visual agnosias, spatial agnosias, anosagnosias, prosopagnosias, and other disorders of body image.

The somatic sense of self is to be distinguished from self-knowledge, because it exists whether or not the person whose sense of self it is, is self-knowledgeable. It is sufficiently independent to coexist with varying degrees of self-opacity and self-deception, as well as with increases and decreases in self-knowledge. But the fact that it can float free of the subject's awareness and understanding of centrally important historical and psychological facts about the self does not undermine its functionality.

Unlike self-knowledge, the somatic sense of self is a given, and not an achievement. It is found in incipient form in infants, and its gradual integration over time is not something that fails to happen through conscious neglect or lack of will. Although it is educable beyond the baseline condition (e.g., in the case of athletes and dancers), it is not normally something for which a person can be held responsible. But the somatic sense of self is not entirely unrelated to self-knowledge. Some of the traits, values, and desires that play a central role in the configuration of the self, and that are the object of self-knowledge, are expressed psychosomatically, through felt bodily dispositions, proprioceptive patternings, and global constitutional habits. Similarly, certain forms of self-ignorance and self-deception are expressed psychosomatically. For example, the sense of oneself as calm or nervous, active or passive, or guarded or open begins in infancy at the hands of one's caregivers, and develops across childhood as basic somatic determinations that come to be expressed in terms of posture, vocalization, and movement. At later stages of development they may come to be associated with core values and ideals, exerting pressure on the subject's self-understanding in ways that go unrecognized. An infant who experiences himself as passive, for example, and who later in infancy and early childhood fails to develop a strong subjective sense of agency, may at later stages develop attitudes and beliefs that express this constitutional passivity: for instance, self-serving beliefs about the value of the idle life, attitudes of resentment or indifference, or beliefs about the relative unimportance of conforming to conventional social norms of physical beauty.

Just as core beliefs and values may be expressed psychosomatically, so distortions in the psychosomatic sense of self may interfere with more explicit forms of self-understanding. The experience of being overweight, for example, can become associated with a diminished sense of agency, and can find expression in negative emotions of self-regard and acts of self-disavowal that interfere with the accuracy of reflective self-inquiry.[19] Experiencing one's body as shameful in the eyes of others may become associated with the felt divorce between an "inner self," regarded as the genuine center of agency, and the "outer" body, regarded as the object of explicit acts of disavowal. The face and head, for example, may be experienced as belonging uniquely to the self, while other body parts may be experienced as inessential remainders, to be disowned as "not-me," and to be characterized in object terms (e.g., "this thing in which I am encased").[20]

THE SELF IN QUESTION

There are, obviously, a variety of ways of approaching the self, not all of which are grounded upon self-knowledge, and not all of which yield self-knowledge. When I ask myself the question "Who am I?" I have at my immediate disposal a number of sources of information, ranging from externally produced personality profiles and the descriptions of my associates to my own self-concepts, self-narratives, and somatic sense of self. But reflective self-inquiry is incomplete if it relies only on these sources, and if it takes these sources at face value. Self-concepts, self-narratives, and the somatic sense of self need not be truth-tracking to be highly adaptive and plausible. Because they can coexist with states of self-ignorance or self-deception, they may supply pseudo-insights that mimic self-knowledge. If the question is to be comprehensive, I need to ask myself "Who am I, who is described by others as such and such, who is characterized by personality profiles as *xyz*, who thinks of myself in terms of this particular self-concept, who has authored this particular narrative life story, and who has this particular somatic sense of self?" One of the goals of reflective self-inquiry and reflective self-evaluation, in other words, is to determine the accuracy and probative value of these alternative ways of approaching the self.

Given that there are a multiplicity of ways of approaching the self, the framing of the question "Who am I?" can be ranged along a continuum from superficial to deep. When it is raised superficially—for instance, for the purposes of immediate social self-identification, or casual self-reports—the response it evokes draws upon a conventional self-understanding: that is, a form of self-understanding that is familiar, habitual, socially adaptive, and not itself in question. From the point of view of my conventional self-understanding, the question "Who am I?" appears to admit of a determinate answer. This is the case even if an answer is not actually forthcoming. It is a backgrounded assumption of my conventional self-understanding that the self that is targeted by the question is given, or can be given, as something accessible and relatively unproblematic. Raising the question "Who am I?" from the point of view of my conventional self-understanding is an instance of an epistemically stable inquiry. The possibility of interpretive anomalies occurring at this level of self-inquiry is kept to a minimum, because the terms in which the inquiry is framed are continuous with previously established self-understandings, which themselves have not been in question. The responses to the question that are supplied by the conventional self-understanding take the assertoric form "I am so-and-so who is X" or "I am so-and-so who does Z," which specify a range of immediately obvious desires, beliefs, character traits, and intentions. No reference is made in these statements to the configuration of deeper norms, values, and traits that they presuppose. As a superficially posed question, the question "Who am I?" has a bounded disclosive force.

When the question is posed in a more fundamental manner, however, it is not framed in the terms of the conventional self-understanding: rather, it calls these terms into question. As the inquiry moves forward, it becomes progressively independent of the investigative and evidentiary norms that were appropriate to past self-understandings. This is a fallible process. The appearance of progressive interpretive and evaluative depth is not a sure sign that reflective self-inquiry is on track. There is no point at which it is not susceptible to illusion, deception, or misunderstanding.

3

◄

SELF-DETACHMENT AND
SELF-KNOWLEDGE

►

TRANSPARENCY

One of the clear signs of an intellectualist approach in moral philosophy is commitment to the idea that knowledge is a good. One way this idea comes to be expressed is in the normative principle that knowledge ought always to be maximized if we are to live good lives. When applied to the question "Who am I?" the intellectualist approach would hold that it is both rational and self-evidently desirable for persons to maximize their self-awareness and their self-knowledge, with a view to rendering the self, and the conditions under which the self develops and flourishes, as transparent as possible. This strategy, applied consistently as a policy of moral conduct, would open up newer and more rational dimensions of thought, action, and emotion than would otherwise be available.

Stuart Hampshire defends a version of this approach to self-knowledge. He shares with Spinoza and Freud a commitment to the view that self-knowledge has the power to change the self that is its object, and even, in some cases, to liberate the self from the undesirable external and internal influences to which it is unavoidably subject as a finite part of nature.[1] His theory of self-knowledge also develops explicitly a philosophical and moral psychology that remains implicit in a number of contemporary moral theories.[2] Of Hampshire's ideal of the "man of reason" Iris Murdoch writes, "[He] is to be found more or less explicitly lurking behind much that is written nowadays on the subject of moral philosophy and indeed also of politics. . . . This man . . . is familiar to us for another reason: he is the hero of almost every contemporary novel."[3]

One of the central ideals of Hampshire's philosophical psychology is that I ought always to know what I am doing in my actions and in my motives for actions. An ideally complete knowledge of my situation, my intentions, and my psychological makeup would constitute the kind of self-transparency that is a necessary condition for rational autonomy, moral responsibility, and freedom. But what is self-transparency? What would it be like to actually *be* transparent to myself? And is it an intelligible ideal, given the motivational and cognitive limitations of human psychology?

Hampshire's portrait of the ideally self-knowledgeable person bears a number of close resemblances to the psychoanalytic ideal of the fully analyzed client. Such a person would be integrated, self-controlled, and soberly realistic with respect to how his or her intentions and desires correspond to the actual (rather than imagined or fantasized) possibilities afforded by the external situation. Achieving this level of self-transparency would involve extensive self-exploration, much of which would be painful because of its probing of habitual defense mechanisms and the volatile emotions they are designed to protect. By the end of an ideally realized analysis the client would be able to: (1) separate real autobiographical memories from false or unconsciously motivated memories; (2) distinguish real intentions from irrational wishes; (3) identify his or her present situation objectively and impartially, without the overlay of unconscious memories of the past that are characteristically projected upon it;[4] and (4) overcome the various forms of cognitive and emotional passivity that typically interfere with thought and action (e.g., self-ignorance, illusions, fantasies, neurotic obsessions, and wishful thinking).

This seems to be a burdensome—even paralyzing—degree of clarity in self-awareness, with the potential to interfere with otherwise spontaneous actions and interpersonal relations. How, after all, could I *be* myself, if I am constantly reflecting upon what is involved in, and causing, my being myself? How is authenticity possible under such conditions? But Hampshire regards the self-knowledgeable person as enjoying certain moral and practical advantages—advantages that are conducive to leading a good life—that are not to be had by those who are less self-aware: most notably, freedom. This is neither contracausal freedom nor, strictly, freedom of action and volition; it is freedom of mind, expressed as a kind of rational self-determination, and realized in everyday moral conduct by having absolutely clear intentions operating upon as many clearly conceived possibilities of action as are available.

Hampshire shares with Spinoza the view that it is primarily my ignorance about the causes of my motives and behaviors, and the formation of my personality, and not my weak will or my inherently flawed nature, that accounts for the wide variety of destructive behaviors that interfere with the realization of freedom of mind. Illusions, fantasies, and unconscious drives, the nature and causes of which remain largely unknown to me, are in actuality forms of ignorance. So powerful are these forces that they blind me to my true interests, distort my conception of the real possibilities for action, and distract me from the needs and moral claims of others. (This is a plausible description of *some* of the principal sources of individual suffering. But it is incomplete to the extent that it focuses mainly on the individual at the expense of the social and historical causes of suffering, not all of which can be reduced to cases of individual self-ignorance.)

The corrective to human ignorance, and the destructive behaviors that follow from it, is deceptively simple. It involves identifying and studying the *causes* that govern thought, action, and emotion, including the causes of the psychological and motivational makeup of the self to which thought, action, and emotion are ascribed. Why? Because psychological and psychophysical causation often go unacknowledged. I think of myself as free in what I do and what I want only to the extent that I am ignorant of the causes that are operating beneath this immediate awareness. But if this is the first step in overcoming the destructive effects of ignorance, and in achieving an adequate level of self-determination, it is incomplete. The characterization is still pitched at a general level, and it remains silent on a number of issues. It does not, for example, specify what *kinds* of causes ought to be subject to observation and analysis; nor does it explain how the mere acquisition of causal understanding can have any desirable practical consequences.

The first issue is important because of the wide discrepancies between first-person explanations of behavior and personality, and the subpersonal causal explanations of behavior and personality that are supplied by (for example) the behavioral and cognitive sciences. In the former case, what counts as causally salient includes the subject's own intentions, reasons, and feelings. In the latter case, however, these putative causal explanations would be shown, upon further examination, to be irrelevant or false, with the real causal mechanisms being framed in subpersonal or subphenomenological terms.5 One of the open-ended questions facing Hampshire's account of self-knowledge, therefore, concerns how conflicts between first-personal and subpersonal causal explanations are to be rationally adjudicated in such a way that they can be meaningfully incorporated into the subject's self-understanding. Knowing the neurochemistry of a behavioral abnormality, for example, may do little in helping the subject to alter the behavior in question. On the other hand, the subject's own understanding of the matter, framed in terms of commonsense psychological explanations that pick out causal factors that are in fact irrelevant or misconceived, may have beneficial effects on the behavior. What is clear from Hampshire's account, at this stage, is that any kind of causal understanding must take a broadly naturalized form. The self whose causal structure is the object of self-knowledge is a part of nature, and not, in Spinoza's terms, a "kingdom within a kingdom."

How is it possible to identify and explain the operation of the causes that explain thought, personality, and action, when a significant part of their operation occurs below the phenomenological surface, without the subject's direct awareness? Hampshire credits reflexive thought as the cognitive competence that supplies the necessary leverage to take this first crucial step. Reflexive thought is the capacity to "step back" from oneself, and to see oneself at a distance, as if from the outside. Everyone has this power, even if it only remains latent.6 On the basis of reflexive cognition, thoughts may always be made the object of second-order thoughts, and beliefs may be made the object of second-order beliefs or thoughts. While Hampshire's use of the metaphoric expression "stepping back" to characterize this power suggests that the reflective point of view enjoys a degree of independence from the first-order level upon which it operates that other stances to the self lack, it is not yet clear if it is genuine reflective independence, quasi-independence, or merely a *re-expression* of that first-order level.

This cursory sketch of Hampshire's account of self-knowledge raises three sets of questions. First, is the very idea of an ideally complete self-knowledge coherent? Do selves fall within the range of things that can, in principle, be known completely? If so, then under what conditions would this be possible? What shape would an ideally complete self-knowledge have? Second, is the kind of self-transparency that characterizes Hampshire's ideally self-knowledgeable person an ideal compatible with the design constraints of human psychology and cognition? Is the motivational structure it requires realizable? Or is it rather a normative ideal that sets a standard for human conduct, but that floats free of actual psychological capacities and personality structures? Third, is the acquisition of a causal understanding of the self relevant to the task of addressing the question "Who am I?" in the first place? What specifically is it about this kind of knowledge that is important for dealing with the question in a manner that is personally relevant?

REFLECTIVE DETACHMENT

If it is granted that human beings are a part of nature, and subject to the same laws of nature as all other things; and if it is granted that the goal of reflective self-inquiry is to uncover the causal mechanisms that explain the nature of personality and behavior, then it might seem obvious that self-inquiry should be governed by the same norms of objectivity that govern inquiries into the causal mechanisms that explain objects and events in the natural world. Objectivity in these inquiries is generally thought to obtain only when certain broad conditions are satisfied: for instance, when investigators suspend their personal feelings about the object in question; when the object can be observed from a variety of different perspectives such that observations can be independently confirmed or disconfirmed; and when the relevant background conditions are sufficiently stable to allow replication studies. But reflective self-inquiry and reflective self-evaluation do not appear to satisfy these conditions. In fact, they appear to violate them. This is because: (1) they are highly personal forms of inquiry in which the inquirer is both the object *and* subject of the inquiry; (2) they are inquiries that have the potential to generate in subjects strong feelings of self-regard and acts of self-identification or self-disavowal, which might easily interfere with the ideal of investigative impartiality; and (3) they are forms of inquiry in which much of the information about the self appears to be inaccessible to all but the subject in question.

But if reflective self-inquiry and reflective self-evaluation are to avoid degenerating into subjectivist self-exploration that rests on private epistemic norms, and that results in untestable knowledge claims, then the conditions of investigative objectivity must somehow be satisfied. To know who I am, I must try to secure the conditions under which I could inquire into myself with increasingly greater impartiality. Hampshire's solution to this problem is the concept of detachment. At any stage I can step back from my behaviours and current states of mind, as well as from my dispositions and character traits, with a view to observing them from a perspective that is less subject to their potentially distorting influences than it would otherwise be. The distance I gain from the immediacy of unreflective experience, and from my normally strong feelings of self-identification and self-attachment, allows me to "see around" my habitual forms of thought and feeling, almost as if I were another person watching myself from the outside. This affords a kind of intrasubjective objectivity.

The concept of detachment is suggestive and intuitively plausible. It is not uncommon, for instance, to counsel others who appear to be too caught up in their own narrow view of themselves to "step back and take a good hard look at themselves." But the metaphoric content of the concept gives a misleading impression of the degree of evaluative and critical independence that can be secured by stepping back. It is misleading because the given system of thought that serves as the starting point for the act of stepping back is presupposed in the very act of stepping back; it is not discarded or neutralized all at once. While it might seem that the detached stance allows the self to be studied *as if* from a perspective outside the self, its as-if character is not a guarantee of independence. Selves are not spatialized or compartmentalized in such a way that they have detachable parts, as objects do; nor is the first-person perspective the sort of thing that supports transformation into a second- or third-person perspective. The metaphors of detachment and stepping back might appear to have a phenomenologically intuitive basis, capturing something of the subjective character of the experiences of disassociation and noninvolvement that come with trying to maintain an impartial stance to one's behavior and personality. But the phenomenology of self-detachment is not a reliable indicator of the epistemic status of the detached perspective on the self; felt independence is not ipso facto genuine independence.

But is the concept of detachment phenomenologically realistic in the first place? Is there, as a matter of phenomenological fact, an experience of something that is like an *independent* and impartial perspective on the self? It seems not. It is a common theme in the phenomenology of Franz Brentano, Edmund Husserl, Maurice Merleau-Ponty, and Sartre that the prereflective experience targeted by self-reflection is elusive, and easily distorted by deliberate attempts to make it the object of careful observation. Brentano, for instance, noted the difficulties of trying to study impartially the phenomena of prereflective mental life as they are in themselves. In the very activity of reflecting upon them, the observer draws away the external directedness necessary for the existence of first-order intentional mental states, and in the process alters those states from what they would have been had they not been made objects of attention. Brentano's corrective is to attend to mental phenomena in their pristine condition by indirect means—out of the corner of one's mental eye—with an oblique and nonpositional noticing.[7] But this corrective is also susceptible to generating the same reflective interference that it is designed to avoid, through a kind of reflective overtargeting. In attending to elusive or inchoate states of mind, it is easy for reflection to make those reflected-upon states more determinate than they are. The very effort of trying to reflect impartially upon the unreflective, without contaminating it with interpretive overlays and theoretical expectations, has the potential to generate debris and artifacts that would not otherwise have appeared. Sartre characterizes this unwanted result as an "impure" (as opposed to pure) reflection.[8]

Hampshire acknowledges the influence of reflection upon unreflected states of mind, but regards it less as a source of evidential contamination than as an opportunity for a kind of self-directed modification of the reflected-upon states. When thoughts are made the objects of second-order thoughts, or beliefs made the object of second-order thoughts, changes take place in the first-order states. This is because the subject's beliefs about the explanation of his or her states of mind are factors that determine what those states are, even if those beliefs about the explanation are false or incomplete. "Intentional states of mind . . . are not independent objects, which remain unchanged by the subject's changing views of their nature. The subject's watching, and the conclusion of his watching in some discrimination of what his state of mind is, will be constitutive elements in his state of mind."[9]

This is a plausible account of some of the changes caused by self-reflection. But it fails to distinguish between the many different kinds of changes that follow from self-reflection: most obviously, changes that are adventitious, and that generate reflective debris, and changes that carefully articulate the reflected-upon phenomena in a manner that is consistent with their pre-reflective morphology. Reflections upon feelings and moods, for example, do not always conform accurately to the complex and shifting contours of their objects: those reflections that are off track have the potential to distort their objects, or to interfere with their spontaneous development.[10] But the effects of confounding adventitious with original states are not always obvious. False individuation, for instance, is the imposition of a false unity and artificially neat borders on the phenomena of unreflected experience, in response to the demand characteristics of the reflective point of view. My attempt to watch myself become angry while remaining detached from it may result in crudely simple syntheses replacing the less-than-unified material of my unreflected states of anger. These states are subject to "filling in" or "smoothing over" when they appear to be discontinuous or inchoate, or when they fail to conform to a unifying template. The conditions driving this form of interference are varied. There may be theoretical expectations that the phenomena display a certain degree of unity and boundedness that they do not in fact have; or the inquiry may be made easier if the phenomena are given the appearance of unity.

ALTERNATIVE SELF-DESCRIPTIONS

One of the marks of those who are rational is that they know that there are always a number of alternative ways of describing their behaviors, states of mind, and traits of character, even if those alternatives are not immediately apparent. They are aware that their current system of classification, which gives itself as unproblematically calibrated to the demands of the situation, may not be the most adequate one for their current needs and purposes; and that it may conceal more than it reveals, by oversimplifying or falsely individuating psychologically complex situations. The rational person adopts as a consistent policy of moral conduct an experimentalist stance, testing alternative systems of classification for rightness of fit and plausibility.

One of the necessary components of this strategy is the cultivation of sensitivity to the possibility of oversimplification. "There are always dangers in circumscribing a lived-through situation and in converting it into a definite and clearly stated problem. So often one thinks or says, from the standpoint of the agent: 'So much that mattered has been left out of the story; it was not quite as simple as that.'" One of the antidotes to this, Hampshire suggests, is a "sceptical nominalism."[11] This obviously cannot be the only antidote; it must also be coupled with relevant changes in conduct. The mere awareness of alternatives can supply too little or too much of what is needed for an antidote, resulting in an intellectual exercise that leaves current practices unchanged, or in a kind of paralysis of hypersensitivity to untried possibilities.

The situation of those who are rational and self-reflective is to be contrasted with that of unreflective persons, who uncritically accept their currently held self-conceptions, and the psychological vocabularies associated with them, as the schema that uniquely limn the true nature of the self. Epistemically, this is manifested as a kind of naive realism; on the corresponding personal and practical level it is manifested as a kind of egocentrism. The possibility does not occur to them that their system of classification might admit of correction, on the basis of a further understanding about how its formation has been influenced by a chain of natural causes extending far beyond their control, and far beyond their direct awareness. The self-centeredness of the unreflective person is essentially an intellectual error: "One sees the universe as revolving around oneself and one's own interests as central in it; and one cannot see past the immediate environment to the vast chain of causes that have led to the frustration of one's own desires. Like the geocentric perceiver of the sun, one ordinarily has a false perspective and a false scale, and one's emotions betray this."[12]

This is a plausible *description* of what it is like to be unreflective. But the *explanation* may be more complex. Instead of being merely an intellectual error, unreflectiveness may be a form of self-deception that has ontological origins. Sartre, as will be seen later, characterizes unreflectiveness as an inauthentic manner of dealing with the question of how to be. Its source is to be found in an incoherent desire to be ontologically determinate in the way that objects are determinate, and in a corresponding desire to flee from the anxiety occasioned by the awareness of the radical contingency of the self.

There is, Hampshire claims, more to reflective detachment than the acquisition of an expanded causal understanding. There is also a practical goal: namely, experimenting with different and more expanded forms of description for the purposes of action. "Aware of the limits to my thought set by historical conditions, I may set myself at all times to consider my own past actions, and my present intentions, from the vantage point of other systems of thought. . . . I may ask myself how [an] action, so identified, might be described in different ways by men who habitually attended to different features of situations and who classified actions by reference to different criteria. I would be trying to see all around my proposed conduct with a view to testing its rightness or permissibility. . . . This possibility of 'seeing round,' and of testing an intention by alternative descriptions in any difficult case, is itself a maxim of conduct, a part of a particular moral outlook."[13]

Experimentation with alternative systems of classification does not leave me unchanged. It opens up new possibilities of action, by revealing new perspectives on situations than were previously available from my more limited perspective. With this comes a sense of regret, because I can now look back upon my past responses to situations and see how the limits of my previous systems of classification, which to me once seemed obvious, closed off a range of possibilities of expression and emotion that might have been more appropriate. Seeing how narrowly I used to think about myself and my situation brings with it a sense of irretrievable loss. It also becomes clear to me that any attempt I may make to pretend that I have reached a final description of myself, and am therefore in a position to put an end to reflective self-inquiry, is a form of self-deception.

The experimental formulation of any new system of classification is not merely a matter of finding new names for the same objects, because states of mind change with refinements in the descriptive terms under which they are identified.[14] Systems of classification are to a certain extent constitutive of the objects they classify, rather than merely descriptive: "The range of the emotions, feelings and attitudes of mind, identified and distinguished from each other, changes as the forms of human knowledge change. We identify new emotions and attitudes that have never been recognized before. With a new self-consciousness, and with the extended vocabulary that goes with it, we discover new motives for action and new objects to which practical intentions are directed." Because the self is dynamic and evolving in this manner, it is not possible to compare how the logical and linguistic principles that are brought to bear on it through any one system of classification stand with respect to an unconceptualized reality—the self as it is "in itself."[15] Self-knowledge cannot be rebuilt upon such an ostensibly certain foundation.

The experimental formulation of alternative systems of classification is clearly an important component in any practice of reflective self-inquiry. It helps to bring to the fore aspects of the self that have been overlooked because of habit-driven ways of thinking about problems and their solutions. But can experimentation be a deliberate practice that can be formalized as a maxim of rational conduct? Can it be pursued methodically? It may be more plausible, and more in accord with the facts of ordinary experience, to postulate *imagination* as one of the primary driving forces behind experimentation. To see the self under different descriptions, and to experiment with different systems of classification for rightness of fit, requires calling upon the same mechanisms of imaginative projection that facilitate immersion into the world of a literary text, and empathetic identification with literary characters of widely differing moral sensibilities. But this is much less deliberate, and much less easily invoked, than a policy of rational experimentation.

There are two other problems with raising the strategy of experimentation to a position of prominence in reflective self-inquiry. First, it is only one relatively restricted tool in a repertoire of strategies available to deal with the question "Who am I?" Because it favors persons with strong psychological and linguistic skills, and a large dose of intellectual curiosity, it is neither an all-purpose tool, nor a tool suitable for everyone. Second, the claim that experimentation with alternative systems of classification has a degree of logical independence from the given or baseline system from which the experimentation starts is overstated. Much more remains presupposed than meets the eye. The web of unexamined beliefs, prejudices, and assumptions that are constitutive of the baseline system evolves and devolves gradually, and experimental modifications to it are always recognizably continuous with previous structures. It is no more possible to detach from it all at once, and observe its operation from an independent perspective, than it is possible to step out of our skin. The only option available is piecemeal experimentation with the system from within.

One of the arguments Hampshire uses to defend the independence of experimentation against this criticism rests on the inexhaustibility of classification. The classification and reclassification of behavior and mental states is endless, because there is no unique set of psychological concepts that is forced upon humans as unavoidable. If the objects of reference in mental life are not given once and for all, then no theoretically determinable limits can be set on the available types of classification of mental states that are objects of reference.[16] The resemblances and differences between different aspects of experience (e.g., "the same sensation," "a changed character trait") are picked out by principles of sameness and difference that are subject to change in accordance with changing interests and purposes. But while this may be true as a matter of logical and linguistic principle, in practice it attributes an unrealistic degree of plasticity to the language of mental states, as it suggests that different descriptive vocabularies can be tried on as if they were different coats tried on for size. But experimentation with alternative systems of classification does not move forward with this degree of independence with respect to the baseline system of classification. Because alternatives are not thinkable from within the given system without presupposing at least some of its fundamental principles of classification, the putative examination of the confined system of thought that is the given system of classification must itself be, to a certain extent, an act of confined thought.

Much of the difference between Hampshire's position on the relative independence of experimentation and the holist position with which it is contrasted turns on differences in emphasis. The difference can be represented by a sliding scale measuring degree of logical and linguistic independence, with complete detachment at the far end as an ideal limit, and complete immersion at the other end. Hampshire's position does not entail rejection of the basic premise of the holist position—viz., the conditioned and material character of reflective thought—but it differs on the question of the degree to which reflective thought is dependent upon the given system of classification. His argument is that once a minimal degree of detachment from the given system is achieved, a more extended form of detachment is possible, from which a still more extended form is possible, and so on. Conversely, once it is possible to look back from the perspective of a new experimentally adopted system of classification upon a recently transcended system of classification, it is possible to anticipate looking back upon the perspective from which one is currently looking back, and so on. The process of experimental ascent can be pushed further and further: "Complete rationality and full knowledge of every possibility open to us are an ideal limit at which we never in fact arrive and never could arrive. . . . We cannot suppose a man who is totally detached from every confining interest and equally open to every possibility. His self-consciousness must always operate upon a given material, the material of his own language and of its social background, and it could not operate in a void. But everyone has had the experience of coming to view some of his interests, previously accepted as inevitable, with a new detachment, as material upon which his own deliberate choice can operate."[17]

FREEDOM, SELF-AWARENESS, AND MORAL RESPONSIBILITY

Is it possible that self-detachment and self-experimentation are altogether wrongheaded as strategies for reflective self-inquiry and reflective self-evaluation? Could they interfere so much with spontaneity and naturalness—with being myself—that they systematically distort the self that is their object? This is the view of French moralists such as Sébastien Chamfort and François La Rochefoucauld. Reflection, they argued, poisons desire. The more that my feelings, desires, and traits of character are subjected to reflective scrutiny, the more they become cultivated objects, and the more difficult it becomes to distinguish the original state from the artifactual overlay that is the product of reflection. To avoid this, I ought to adopt a strict policy of unreflectiveness: I ought, in other words, to live naturally and naively, at one with my emotions and desires.[18]

This is a misleading picture of human psychology. Hampshire shares with Sartre the view that to be a person is to exist in such a way that I must take up an evaluative and action-oriented stance with respect to the question of who

I am. I am not a prisoner of my character, in the sense that I cannot but acquiesce to the limitations established by inherited dispositions, motivational patterns, and character traits; nor am I "swept along" by my immediate desires and emotions, as if I had no choice in what moves me to action and what constitutes my will. The evaluative stance I adopt toward my traits of character and my desires makes it possible for me to want to be different from who I am, and capable of deciding upon what types of things I will allow to constitute and influence my identity. Sartre, as will be seen later, develops from this model of the person a radical conception of responsibility for self, based on the claim that because persons choose themselves absolutely, they are responsible for themselves in an absolute sense. Hampshire's view is not as strong as this. But it has the effect, like Sartre's, of extending the scope of responsibility for self beyond what is normally considered tenable, and in apparent defiance of a large class of moral excusing and exempting conditions. Once I become aware of the causes that explain my personality and behavior, and become aware of why these causal determinants have the effects they do, I can no longer be considered a helpless prisoner of my character or my circumstances; nor can I try to be at one with the emotions and desires that are the effects of these newly understood causes. The acquisition of knowledge places me in a position of choice to either acquiesce to the influence of the newly identified causal determinants, or to try to change them in ways that are more consistent with my normative ideals of moral personality and moral conduct. It is at this point that "knowledge becomes decision."

Consider the following example. Suppose on reflection that I notice in my behavior a long-term trend of aggression toward an acquaintance. Hampshire's position is that once I become aware of the causal determinants that explain my behavior—through, for instance, psychoanalytic self-exploration—then I can no longer be described as behaving unreflectively and unintentionally. I am now an observer viewing my aggressive behavior from a higher-order level, as well as an agent responsible for the cessation or continuation of the behavior. This doubleness of perspective is a peculiarity of all higher-order intentional states of mind. With the advent of the new causal understanding, the aggression-triggering situations as I experience them, and those situations as they would be characterized by an outside observer, change: the complicating factor is my newly expanded self-awareness. Thus prior to the moment of self-awareness, it would have been false to describe my behavior as conscious aggression; but if the same course of behavior persists, then it becomes a true description. The dawning of awareness forces me to *try* to either accept or alter the course of my behavior, with increased moral responsibility accruing to either outcome. "I cannot escape the burden of intention, and therefore of responsibility, which is bestowed upon me by knowledge of what I am doing, that is, by recognition of the situation confronting me and of the difference that my action is making. As soon as I realise what I am doing, I am no longer doing it unintentionally. Any impartial and concurrent awareness of the tendency and effect of my own activities necessarily has to this extent the effect of changing their nature. . . . That which began as impartial observation turns into something else; the knowledge becomes decision."[19]

This is an important claim. If it were true, then self-knowledge would appear to be a difficult virtue to acquire, and an especially burdensome virtue to maintain. As more of the causal mechanisms that explain my behavior and personality come under my awareness, more responsibility accrues to me. But is this psychologically realistic? How is the ascription of responsibility possible in cases where the behaviors in question have causal histories extending far back in time, long before it was possible for the agent to exert deliberate control over the operation of external causal influences? For example, the efforts that are expended in trying to transform personality disorders through the means suggested by Hampshire (e.g., experimentation, self-observation, and self-analysis) are in some cases themselves an expression of the disorders, rather than independent operations upon the disorders that could secure the leverage needed for genuine change. Self-reflection supplies a sense of increased conscious control, but it is in fact a different way of realizing the same underlying architecture of the self.

If this is an illusory sense of freedom, then what constitutes genuine freedom? Hampshire's concept of freedom is closely tied to the concept of reflexive knowledge. The subject's reflexive knowledge of the causes of his or her current states of mind alters those states in ways that would not otherwise have occurred if they had not been thought about, and allows the subject a degree of control over the direction of those alterations. The awareness of this power "is often called [the] sense of freedom of mind in the formation of . . . beliefs, desires, and intentions." This sense of freedom is "not an absolute freedom of the will, but rather a relative freedom of intelligence."[20]

Freedom of mind is more than a purely subjective or notional sense of freedom. The subject's acquisition of reflexive knowledge about the causes of his or her states of mind is itself a determinate influence on those states, albeit an influence that is internal because it comes from the subject's own contemporary thought. Over time this internal influence can become just as powerful a factor in determining the nature of those states as the external causes (for example, childhood conditioning) that formed the original causal conditions. The reflexive feedback loop that is generated by the extra variable can also ascend to higher levels, with the subject's acquisition of reflexive knowledge about the new set of internal influences itself serving as a determinate internal influence on those newly modified states of mind, which itself serves as a factor in determining the nature of those states, and so on. The reflexive feedback loop inevitably complicates the explanation of behavior. Because the subject's acquisition of reflexive knowledge is a variable that was not included in the explanation of the original causal conditions of the behavior, a new explanation will have to be given that takes into account the new internal influences.[21]

This view derives from Spinoza, who contrasts freedom as a form of rational self-determination based on self-knowledge with bondage, which is the unchecked fluctuation of the mind responding passively to the infinitely extensive array of external causal influences to which it is subject. Spinoza's description of the passive character of prereflective life, where fantasy or obsession so often dominate, bears certain resemblances to the psychoanalytic description of neurosis: it is a state in which "we are disturbed by external causes in a number of ways, and . . . like the waves of the sea agitated by contrary winds, we fluctuate in our ignorance of our future and destiny." So powerful are passive emotions, the nature and causes of which we are ignorant, that "we say that [we are] delirious or mad": emotions such as "avarice, ambition, lust, etc. are a kind of madness."[22]

Like others in the intellectualist tradition of moral philosophy, Spinoza regards bondage not as the enslavement of the will, as it is in Kantian moral theory, but as the enslavement of the understanding. The enslaved mind is to a greater or lesser degree disintegrated because its train of thoughts is determined not by the subject's own activity but by forces outside it. Typically, the enslaved person makes the mistake of isolating as the sole source of pleasure or pain a single object, or type of object. This, Spinoza argues, demonstrates the subject's failure to understand his or her position as a finite and dependent mode within the infinite causal network of nature; and the corresponding failure to understand the complex multifactorial form that any adequate explanation of personality and behavior must take. One of the practical errors consequent to this intellectual obsession is emotional obsession: that is, loving or hating a particular thing with a typically self-destructive obsessiveness.[23]

Hampshire adopts the general outlines of Spinoza's account of freedom, extending it in a psychodynamic direction to include unconscious drives and instincts as forms of passivity of mind. Because of the domination of unconscious forces, there are many instances in which I am ignorant of what I am really doing, even though there is a broad sense in which my actions are purposeful. In these situations, I am unaware of the influences upon my conduct, and the patterns displayed in it, that may be evident to others who occupy a less subjective vantage point: influences that, originating in my infancy and childhood, exert powerful and often destructive forces over my behavior.

Neurosis, for example, constitutes one such species of mental passivity. Neurosis is a stealthy disturbance, its capacity to exist depending almost entirely on its lack of recognition. Those who suffer from neurosis are, inter alia, unable to give a coherent account of why their lives are taking the particular shape that they do. When they begin psychoanalysis, they typically offer bowdlerized editions of their past: gaps are left unfilled, sequences of events incoherent, and important periods obscure. Freud likens their life stories to "an unnavigable river whose stream is at one moment choked by masses of rock and at another divided and lost among shallows and sandbanks."[24] Given this unpromising starting point, one of the primary goals of classical Freudian psychoanalysis is to help analysands recognize and understand the causal mechanisms that explain their behaviour.[25] Whatever freedom they enjoy in changing their behaviors through an increased self-understanding is first based on identifying motives that have not been recognized before, and tracing their causal histories back to the emotional traumas of early childhood and infancy.[26]

But one of the difficulties faced by the psychoanalytic (and more broadly the psychodynamic) interpretation of self-knowledge is the problem of false insight and false interpretation. Ideally, psychoanalysis terminates with what Freud calls "an intelligible, consistent and unbroken case history,"[27] and "a picture of the patient's forgotten years that shall be alike trustworthy and complete." It is a fundamental assumption here that analysis is a valid method of personal discovery, and that with sufficient analytically oriented self-exploration analysands will have a more comprehensive and veridical understanding of the depths of their psyche than before they began the treatment. An equally central assumption is that the self-knowledge yielded by psychoanalytic self-exploration is a necessary condition for therapeutic improvement.

But psychoanalysis does not always work this way. When the process of self-exploration gets off track because of the epistemic and evidentiary interference caused by the analysand's suggestibility, or the analysand's doctrinal compliance with the analyst's treatment method and theoretical orientation, the analysis has the potential to generate coherent but false self-interpretations.[28] This does not leave analysands unchanged. In some cases, pseudo-insights about the causes of unconsciously motivated behaviors occasion temporary therapeutic improvement; they can be subjectively reassuring and adaptive. In other cases, however, they lead to iatrogenic deterioration, in the form of therapy-induced self-deception or illusion. The phenomena of false insight and false interpretation are not restricted only to psychoanalytic psychotherapy: all forms of insight-oriented psychotherapy are at risk, especially those that induce transitory regressions to earlier ways of experiencing. A number of powerful nonspecific factors that are shared by all forms of insight-oriented therapy, independently of differences in theoretical orientation and treatment method, explain how clients can be disposed to accept false interpretations and false insights as accurate: for example, the cognitive dissonance of the therapeutic encounter, the emotionally charged relationship between therapist and client, the increased suggestibility of clients, therapeutic placebo effects, social consensus about the authority of the therapist, the client's self-fulfilling expectations about the effectiveness of the treatment, and the power of therapeutic rhetoric and persuasion.[29] With sufficient exposure to these and other pressures, clients may accept as true what are in fact false interpretations; or clients' native epistemic resources, and their standards for responsible knowing practices, may be eroded and reworked to conform to those of their therapists, whose suggestive interpretations they then accept uncritically. This is not always an unwanted occasion in therapy. False interpretations may have no more explanatory power and descriptive validity than psychological sugar pills, but they may still be effective in a placebological sense: that is, they may be coherent, adaptive, and functional—even if the putative causal entities picked out in the interpretations do not refer to actual psychological or historical causes.

What do the phenomena of false insight and false interpretation mean for the problem of self-knowledge, especially in light of Hampshire's claim that psychoanalysis provides "a reflexive knowledge of the workings of the mind that fits into the philosophical definition of freedom in terms of self-knowledge"?[30] They suggest that psychoanalysis, and more broadly the insight-oriented psychotherapies, could be just as therapeutically effective supplying clients with false understandings of the workings of the mind as with accurate understandings. What is therapeutically effective is not the acquisition of veridical self-knowledge, but the creation of a *meaningful* and adaptive self-interpretation. The insight-oriented psychotherapies do not necessarily have therapeutic effects *because* they are truth tracking, and *because* they lead to veridical self-knowledge; therapeutic improvement often occurs because clients are supplied with a conceptual framework that offers a coherent explanation or rationale for their otherwise unintelligible problems. The framework need not be true to have therapeutic effects; but it must be capable of assigning meaning, and supplying labels to previously unidentified problems.

If the insight-oriented psychotherapies, including classical Freudian psychoanalysis, can be therapeutically beneficial independently of the truth value and accuracy of the interpretations and insights they yield, then pressure is placed on Hampshire's claim that it is reflexive *knowledge* of the workings of one's mind that makes sense of the philosophical concept of freedom.[31] Perhaps what is required to address this problem is a criterion that demarcates truth-tracking psychotherapies from those psychotherapies that trade in adaptive fictions and pseudo-insights. One strategy that is open to Hampshire is to ground a criterion of demarcation on the concept of detachment. The corrective to false interpretation and pseudo-insight is further detachment, more rigorously pursued and more carefully applied than in the analysis that went off track. Used as a procedural rather than substantive mechanism, detachment could supply a standard by means of which truth-tracking interpretations and insights could ultimately be distinguished from those that are false. In the midst of psychoanalysis, for instance, analysands could adopt a stance of detachment with respect to their most recently achieved insights, with a view to testing them for the presence of inaccuracies and false conclusions. The results from the most recently adopted stance of detachment would themselves be subject to the same set of corrective measures, and so on. The regress may be endless, but it is not vicious: the psychological and cognitive complexity of increasingly higher-order levels of reflective detachment ultimately forces the regress to a halt.

DETACHMENT REVISITED

What precisely is the connection between self-knowledge, intention, and responsibility for self? Is self-knowledge (1) a sufficient condition for deliberate self-directed change and responsibility for self; (2) a necessary condition; or (3) an important first step, but neither a necessary nor a sufficient condition?

Despite certain ambiguities,[32] Hampshire's position is closest to claim (2): self-determination and self-responsibility are always tied to the acquisition of reflexive knowledge, although reflexive knowledge is not a sufficient condition for these states. This is weaker than the claim that full responsibility always follows from the acquisition of knowledge, a position that is both empirically implausible and counterintuitive. It is only with knowledge and self-knowledge that I have the opportunity of deliberate change: "If I did not know what I was trying to do, no possibilities of deliberate change were open to me." It does not follow from this, however, that all cases of self-knowledge are cases where deliberate change is possible. I may have a thorough and well-tested knowledge of the causal mechanisms that explain my anxiety, for example, without thereby being able to change it in ways that I want. Hampshire also holds that it is only with knowledge that I can be held responsible for what I am doing: "Once an agent realizes what he is doing, he is no longer doing it unintentionally."[33] But it does not follow from this that all cases of self-knowledge are cases where ascriptions of personal responsibility make sense. Knowing the causes of a behavioral disorder, for example, does not, in itself, allow me to take responsibility for the behaviors that follow from it.

But does Hampshire's identification of intention, knowledge, and responsibility adequately account for more ambiguous behaviours that exhibit multiform *gradations* of knowledge and intention? There are obviously areas of behavior in which full intention and responsibility are not normally ascribed to subjects, even though it is recognized that the subjects are, in some sense, aware of what they are doing, and aware of the causes of their behaviors. Psychologically minded patients with the somatoform disorders of anorexia and bulimia, for instance, may be capable of detached reflection upon their behaviors, and capable of generating accurate causal explanations that have the outward mark of psychological insight. While this is an important achievement if it is pressed into service in the right way, their reflectiveness may also be a symptom of the underlying disorder, or a form of rationalization.

Empirical counterexamples such as this have two consequences. First, any insight-oriented psychotherapy that remains focused exclusively on uncovering the causal mechanisms that explain personality and behavior may fail to address the obvious: viz., clients' needs to understand themselves and their place in the world. Clients who are demoralized or confused may be less concerned with tracking the causal mechanisms that explain their feelings than with understanding what their feelings *mean* in a broader existential sense. Their overriding concern may be to reflect upon what their problems say about their lives, and the meanings their lives manifest. Sartre's existential approach to psychoanalysis, as will be seen in the next chapter, is designed to address these deeper problems.

Second, it would be an unforgiving form of psychotherapy that maintained: (1) that once persons with personality, behavioral, or mood disorders realize what they are doing, and why, they are no longer behaving unintentionally; and (2) that in becoming aware of their behaviors, and the causal mechanisms that explain them, they are necessarily faced with the choice either to acquiesce to their behaviors, or to try to alter them. There is a clear sense in which such persons have very limited options open to them.

It is a commonplace in the insight-oriented psychotherapies that the acquisition of knowledge in itself has little therapeutic effect. A number of conditions that are not related to the acquisition of knowledge must also be satisfied before therapeutic change is possible: e.g., the right material circumstances, the right timing of the acquisition of knowledge, the right emotional attunement, and the right therapeutic relationship. Freud, for example, was skeptical about the therapeutic effectiveness of knowledge acquisition that is unaccompanied by these other conditions: "If we communicate to a patient some idea which he has at one time repressed but which we have discovered in him, our telling him makes at first no change in his mental condition." What the patient lacks in such cases is a sense that the knowledge is his or her own: that is, self-knowledge. "If knowledge about the unconscious were as important for the patient as people inexperienced in psycho-analysis imagine, listening to lectures or reading books would be enough to cure him. Such measures, however, have as much influence on the symptoms of nervous illness as a distribution of menu cards in a time of famine has on hunger."34

The problems incurred here in explaining the role of knowledge in occasioning changes in behavior and personality reflect a deeper problem in Hampshire's concept of the person: viz., the compartmentalization and hierarchization of reason, emotion, and will. Hampshire construes the act of reflective detachment as an independent activity of the mind, one that is capable of taking the givens of character, disposition, and emotion as objects for careful scrutiny and analysis, without itself being subject to their influence. Leverage of this sort allows the reflecting self to exercise a degree of instrumental control over the range of first-order emotional, motivational, and characterological givens, with a view to weakening the effects of some and reinforcing others. The ideal form of rational self-determination is represented by those persons who are able to remake themselves by methodical and disciplined reflective action, reconfiguring the entire bundle of personality and behavior into a more integrated and harmonious whole than what they began with. The second-order agency that is required for this, and that finds its expression in reflective detachment, is clearly privileged in Hampshire's philosophical psychology as one of the distinguishing marks of persons. Compared to it, first-order desires, emotions, and traits are relatively malleable material, the primary function of which is to be receptive to the distinctive organizing imprint of a higher-order agency. Persons are defined not by these first-order givens, but by the power to disengage from them and to rationally reconstruct them at will.

The assumption here is that because there is a given dimension of human beings that is not itself the result of this second-order reflective agency, it is irrational or subrational, and therefore in need of some form of rational reorganization. But this identification is overstated. The givens of personality and behavior do not map out a dimension that mere increases in knowledge can correct or eliminate. They are essential to what humans beings are, and the connections to the world and to others that they supply are no less real and no less significant than those supplied by more purified forms of reflection. If the compartmentalization of reason, emotion, and will is psychologically unrealistic, then there are also grounds for doubting the characterization of reason as an impartial and independent faculty in dealing with the givens of emotional and volitional life.[35] Hampshire's theory, which pictures persons as divided up into a composite of reason (which gives us knowledge of our tendencies), will (which is the capacity to decide about our tendencies), and emotion, "refuses to allow that feelings might put pressure on reason in a way that couldn't be controlled by the will. For [Hampshire] wishes to keep reason intact and uninfluenced by anything outside itself. Or rather, if it is influenced by anything outside itself . . . he wants to say that reason can step back and make a new assessment of this total situation, and that in light of this assessment the will can make a new decision. But is this realistic?"[36]

Sartre's philosophical psychology, as will be seen, errs in the opposite direction, rejecting compartmentalization as a strategy in philosophical psychology in favor of radical holism. Sartre rejects the kind of epistemic independence that Hampshire ascribes to reflective detachment, and the kind of leverage such independence is supposed to have in effecting transformations of the self. One of the central arguments of Sartre's existential ontology is that human beings cannot step back from the movement of their *existence*, to view the event of their existing, and their relation to that event, as if from a detached point of view. This argument Sartre bases on one of the fundamental claims of the existential approach to phenomenology: viz., that existence is not the kind of thing that can be suspended or bracketed in order that it may be studied, qua phenomena, with impartiality. So tightly wound is my connection to existence, and so thoroughly personal is this connection, that any attempt to detach myself from it always and already presupposes it. Thus the existential criticism of Hampshire's account of self-knowledge is that: (1) construing reflective self-inquiry as reflective detachment is too narrow; and (2) self-detachment does not yield the relevant ontological depth that is needed to work out the question "Who am I?" in a fundamental manner. The proper target of reflective self-inquiry and reflective self-evaluation should be pitched at a level deeper than that of mental states and their causes: viz., at the level of the agent's way of being in the world; and the proper access to this target will require something other than a stance of reflective detachment.

Here the existential-phenomenological account of self-knowledge takes a broadly transcendental turn, away from the naturalism of Hampshire, Spinoza, and Freud. What Hampshire construes as the basic determinants of thought and action, and as the basic building blocks of the self, are according to Sartre already aspects of a basic world design, or a framework of meaning, which functions as a fundamental background in terms of which the particular causal mechanisms that explain psychology and behavior make sense. This does not deny an explanatory role to causal mechanisms; rather, the series of causes and effects that explain mental states and traits of character is enmeshed in a larger "meaning-matrix," or a project, in terms of which they are intelligible. Sartre argues that it is this global underlying structure that makes possible the causal influences of the past on the present. Thus my relation to my past is not uniquely determined by events such as infantile and childhood traumas, but by the horizon within which I experience and make sense of these factors.[37] The horizon, however, is not of the same logical order as the particular events and experiences which it renders intelligible. To make this horizon the target of reflective self-inquiry and reflective self-evaluation requires that we inquire into the deep structures of the *being* of human beings. Self-knowledge, in other words, must be ontologically grounded.

4

◀

A MYSTERY
IN BROAD DAYLIGHT

▶

IDENTITY AND "BEING IN QUESTION"

Jean-Paul Sartre's existential philosophical psychology, as developed in *Being and Nothingness* and several other early and middle works, is most notable for its emphasis on freedom. Its central theoretical claim is that persons are free, in a morally and existentially important sense, to be as they want to be: free, that is, to choose who (but not what) they are, and to lay out the ground plan of a way of life, within a range of given determinants and situational constraints. Persons are also free within certain bounds to remake themselves, and the assumption of alternative ways of life and life plans always remains a living option, even if it is never actualized. To this is added the claim that regardless of whether persons actually remake themselves, they are always and already completely responsible for their actions and their way of being in the world. The freedom they enjoy consists in an autonomous and creative agency, and not, as many critics of Sartre have charged, in radical indeterminacy or causelessness.

It might seem obvious that if persons were radically free to determine who they are, then they would also be knowledgeable about their radical choices, and the deeper structures of the self they have chosen to be. But Sartre denies this. Instead, he holds that the deep-lying structures of the radically chosen self are hidden from the first-person point of view, almost as if they are located behind a blind spot: they are lived but not known as such. There are a number of explanations for the self's elusiveness. One is the overwhelming anxiety that comes with owning up to the radical contingency and ground-lessness of the self they have chosen to be, and the creative disavowals of authorship and self-responsibility that typically follow from this. Most human behavior falls into one of several basic patterns of flight from truths about the self and its existence: for example, bad faith, the "spirit of serious-ness," or the attitude of psychological determinism. Ontologically, then, per-sons are self-divided and self-diremptable beings, aware of themselves at a certain narrowly ontic or thing-oriented level that targets straightforwardly empirical aspects of the self, but opaque at the ontological level, which targets what it means to be and not to be. Lucidity and existential self-awareness are prized virtues in Sartre's philosophical psychology, but they are hard-won, and generally tend to elude the more deliberate attempts to secure them.

Sartre's concern in *Being and Nothingness* with tracing the connections between self-knowledge, agency, and selfhood departs in critical ways from Hampshire's account. One of the central differences revolves around the con-cept of self qua agent. Sartre's analysis is not directed at the self qua psy-chophysical ego, which he argues is a synthetic by-product of "impure" objectifying reflection; nor is it directed at the self in so far as it is a causally complex configuration of character traits and states of mind. Sartre does not deny the existence of the ego or the psychophysical self (although he denies the existence of the unconscious as a causal mechanism that explains the self); but he claims that there is more to the self qua agent than what can be captured at this ontic level of description. The self is not a thing or entity. What the ontic level of description of the self presupposes is a much more fundamental level, which it is the goal of existential phenomenology and existential psychoanalysis to explore: viz., the *being* of the person to whom an identity or self is ascribed. If the self qua agent is to be understood in onto-logical terms, then what is called for is a method that penetrates more deeply than the methods appropriate for inquiries that focus principally on uncover-ing causal mechanisms.

Like Heidegger, Sartre argues that what is distinctive about human beings is not simply that they *have* selves, but that they have the special capacity to *take on* selfhood. If having this or that actual self is possible only on the basis of the capacity to assume a self, then it is incomplete to think of selfhood as fixed, or as tied to determinate character traits and a determinate psychological and motivational makeup; it is rather an ongoing issue that is always confronting the human being whose self it is: it is, existentially and morally, "in question." It is not the case, in other words, that human beings are what they are *simpliciter:* they have themselves *to be.* Selfhood is best viewed as a kind of ongoing project that serves as a response to the question of how to be; and it is best viewed as answering to a range of fundamental possibilities of being, or life possibilities. To understand how the self as agent is to be construed in ontological terms therefore requires construing the concept of being in such a way as to avoid the reification or substantialization that occurs when ontic modes of inquiry are taken as the model for ontological inquiry. Being, in other words, must be construed as a transitive verb, and not as a substantive noun.

One of the consequences of this repositioning of selfhood in relation to an ontological and temporal ground is that the capacity to assume a self lies well beyond the scope of a reflective self-inquiry that targets only de facto character traits, behaviors, and states of mind, and the causal mechanisms that explain them. Thus one of the central goals of self-knowledge is the understanding of being as it pertains to selfhood. But achieving a degree of lucidity with respect to one's "ownmost" possibilities of being meets with a number of investigative and phenomenological obstacles, not least of which is the fact that existing is not something from which one can step back and observe as if from a detached and independent perspective. From Sartre's ontological point of view, one of the principal shortcomings of Hampshire's account of self-knowledge is that it does not adequately account for the *being* of the person whose self it is. It is restricted to an ontic level that targets the causal structure of the self as a kind of thing or entity but it overlooks the ontological dimension (viz., the "being-in-question" of the agent) in terms of which this causal structure is itself possible.[1]

To see the self in ontological terms as constituted by possibilities is to see the self as presupposing a prior relation or stance—what Sartre calls a radical choice—to fundamental possibilities of being. This prior relation is not itself the result of a series of causes and effects; nor is it built up over time by the accretion of particular experiences. Rather, it is what makes such configurations possible in the first place.

Once the target of reflective self-inquiry is construed in ontological terms as a dynamic and ongoing project-to-be, it becomes much more difficult to articulate and analyze. There are a number of reasons for this, all of which can be traced to the peculiar fact that being is not an object or thing, but rather a kind of event. First, the project is a moving and changing target, requiring me to remain vigilant in my reflective self-inquiries about premature closure and finalization. Second, the project is a globalized target, not a specific configuration of psychological, characterological, and dispositional constituents. In order to interpret it I must try to identify something that has the character of an elusive overarching horizon, but from a perspective that is internal to the horizon. Third, my access to the project is unavoidably interpretive; it is not a matter of "reading off" facts, but layer-by-layer interpretation that involves me in a complex hermeneutic circle that changes with changes in the interpretive strategies adopted. Reflective self-inquiry is not guided by a determinate object that simply awaits discovery.

Sartre's philosophical psychology has strong Kantian underpinnings in the way it conceives persons as the source of their own moral authority and moral being, in its defense of freedom as the condition of possibility for moral responsibility, and in its elevation of persons (qua moral agents) above the realm of nature and the empirically determined. The general form taken by Sartre's explanation of agency and moral personality is transcendental, in the tradition of Kant and Husserl. Before turning to Sartre's account of self-knowing, it is essential to sketch the broad outlines of the self that is its target: that is, the self as agent.

In his early and middle work, Sartre is committed to the view that persons are not prisoners of their character, past, unconscious desires, or biology; and that their reasons and choices are not merely rationalizations for behavior in which they would nevertheless engage. There are a number of ways this idea might be construed, but the approach adopted by Sartre holds that qua selves, persons are capable of determining themselves by their own reasons and choices. The existentially relevant determinants of identity are internal to persons in a way that physical causes and antecedent conditions (including unconscious forces) are not. This means that persons can determine who they are from the inside, without being fully influenced by alien (external or internal) forces. Persons are, within bounds, authors of their identity, because they contribute through their own choices to the making of what, qua agents, they are.

Typically, however, the conventional moral and religious beliefs in terms of which persons understand themselves dissimulate this dimension of freedom, giving the impression that persons are thinglike and externally determined. The existential self-understanding that is the goal of reflective self-inquiry is a kind of "dark enlightenment," because of the disorientation it occasions in revealing this otherwise consoling belief as ungrounded, repressive, and existentially inauthentic. Sartre and Heidegger share the view that it is entirely up to persons to determine what kind of being they are going to be. Unlike objects, persons do not exist in a straightforward de facto sense. It is not the case that persons are, and can only be, what they are; it is more accurate to say that they have themselves to be, and that they have their own existence to *assume*.[2] The distinction between an existent and its existing (i.e., the ontological difference) means that it is the responsibility of persons to work out what they are going to do with the fundamental life possibilities confronting them at any one moment, and what basic orientation they are going to take in the face of existence.[3] Becoming aware of the concrete moral consequences of the ontological difference is one of the goals of reflective self-inquiry.

Sartre can be seen to follow Kant in defending the view that persons are capable of determining themselves by their own choices and reasons, and the view that identity-shaping choices are not themselves caused by antecedent or external conditions. But this does not commit him to the radical libertarian view that choice is a matter of chance or a random break in the causal network. This view he emphatically rejects.[4] His argument, rather, is that persons enjoy a special kind of agency, wherein the *ultimate* determinants of their actions and identity are their own choices. By postulating the existence of a special internal source of agency, Sartre, like Kant, believes that some of the fears created by naturalistically oriented accounts of the self (such as those defended by Hampshire and Freud) about diminished responsibility can be allayed; for then a distinction can be made between behaviors determined by causal factors that are alien to the self (including certain internal forces and motives), and actions determined ultimately by the self and for the self.

The idea that the ultimate determinants of action and identity are the self's own choices can be articulated in a different way. At a certain depth, human agency is explained by itself, and no further explanation is possible. The explanation of a particular action, for example, will refer to certain desires in a given situation, the explanation of which will refer to a larger frame of attitudes and beliefs, which in turn will refer to a larger framework of projects. Ultimately this chain of explanation terminates—not in something external and antecedent to the agent, but *in the agent*. Whatever lies at these depths, Sartre argues, must be fundamental; that is, it must consist of the most basic set of terms by means of which persons understand themselves and shape their way of being in the world; and it must not be derived from anything external to it. In Kantian terms—and Sartre's argument has a clear Kantian bearing here—it must be the condition of possibility of personal experience. But trying to target these deep-lying conditions of possibility in reflective self-inquiry, and to subject them to reflective self-evaluation (as, for example, valuable, worthy, or authentic), is especially difficult. It is much easier to remain within the familiar ontic terms at hand, and to rely on conventional but ultimately mystifying self-understandings.

Before continuing, it is worth pointing out two problems that hinder Sartre's account of self-knowledge and the self. The first is its uncritical acceptance of the incompatibility of freedom and determinism, and its defense of the idea that an absolute *ligne Maginot* must be established to protect human agency from causation. The assumption here is that human agency cannot be built up from some initially unfree or nonagential material. The second is a problem of infinite regress in the chain of explanation: even if actions are explained by some deeper agency, then what explains this? However many levels of agency are postulated, there will still be a level inviting the question "What explains it?" To be consistent, the source of agency must in turn be explained, and this ultimately must terminate in something external and antecedent to it—unless one holds the implausible thesis that the self, like a god, is its own ground and source of being.

THE FUNDAMENTAL PROJECT

What is the nature of this special source of agency that Sartre reserves only for persons? In virtue of what am I ultimately self-determining? And can I ever attain a degree of transparency about the ultimate determinants of the self that I have chosen to be, or am I left foundering in the dark? Sartre's views on this source of agency are much less rationalistic than Kant's, and much closer to Nietzsche and Heidegger's views, because he emphasizes (1) the deeply futural, contingent, and self-divided nature of the capacity for self-determination (viz., the radical choice of self and the fundamental project) and (2) the cognitive inaccessibility of the ultimate determinants of the self.

Sartre argues that the identities of persons are not ready-made or imposed from without; nor are they wholly products of conditioning or unconscious forces. Instead, they are shaped by means of a choice that persons make regarding their ultimate ends. The way this choice is realized across many years of experience is best characterized as a kind of project; that is, as a long-term endeavor of constructing a self. Sartre likens the agent's capacity to freely choose his or her self to the creation of an artwork: for example, the relation between a sculptor and a block of marble.[5] In both cases order must be created from a raw material that underdetermines the final form, and thus requires a certain intervening constructive activity from the sculptor-agent. In both cases the sculptor-agent must evaluate, criticize, and deliberate about the ongoing process of the creation and its fit with his or her intentions. Finally, in both cases there is a tendency for the sculptor-agent to underestimate (or be deceived about) the real extent of his or her creative freedom. (The analogy would clearly be misleading if restrictions were not placed upon the plasticity of the raw material, and upon the constructive powers of the sculptor-agent.)

Like sculptors, persons shape their identities by projecting themselves toward the future. This does not take the form of an aggregate projection, one comprised of a series of smaller separate projections that overlap one with another, like the chain links of a fence. All the actions and experiences of which lives are comprised "derive their meaning from an *original* projection" that persons make of themselves.[6] Given this strong futural organization, the identity of persons is best characterized as a coherent long-term project that exhibits an inner dynamic and intelligibility, rather than as a series of events strung loosely together, in response to external causal forces and antecedent conditions. Projection toward the future is the way in which a highly organized and unified *meaning* is created from the "raw" psychological and historical material of life; it is the way a future is fashioned. Merleau-Ponty captures a sense of this: "One day, once and for all, something was set in motion which, even during sleep, can no longer cease to see or not to see, to feel or not to feel, to suffer or be happy, to think or rest from thinking, in a word to 'have it out' with the world. There then arose, not a new set of sensations or states of consciousness, not even a new monad or a new perspective . . . [but] a fresh possibility of situations. . . . There was henceforth a new 'setting,' the world received a fresh layer of meaning."[7]

The explanatory power Sartre attributes to the concepts of the choice of self and the fundamental project is vast, and the claims he makes about them have a clearly transcendental import. The project is "the original relation which the for-itself chooses with its facticity and with the world." It concerns "not my relations with this or that particular object in the world, but my total being-in-the-world." Again, it is the "primary project which is recognized as the project which can no longer be interpreted in terms of any other and which is total." Finally, in distinctly Kantian terms, he claims that "what makes all experience possible is . . . an original upsurge of the for-itself as presence to the object which it is not."[8]

To complicate matters, Sartre makes a number of puzzling claims about responsibility for self and moral desert, which reflect his conviction that because persons choose themselves absolutely, they must be responsible in an absolute sense. Persons are, he claims, totally responsible for themselves, including the things that befall them;[9] they are responsible for all aspects of their situation; they always have the sort of lives they deserve; and there are no accidents in the lives they have chosen to lead. The assumption that makes such extreme claims intelligible is that unless persons make themselves absolutely, they could not be responsible at all. To clarify some of these sweeping claims, the concepts of the choice of self and the fundamental project will be explored in greater detail, and then examined vis-à-vis the question of self-knowledge.

Sartre conceives the fundamental project in strongly holistic terms as a densely interconnected system of relations between all the components of a life. Every aspect of a person's life—profession, emotions, works, choice of friends, habits—expresses a "thematic organization and an inherent meaning in this totality."[10] The fundamental project displays a kind of intrinsic intelligibility: with the right method, the structure of the project can be discerned in a single act or gesture within it, however insignificant.

Despite various descriptions of the fundamental project as the "transcendent meaning" of each concrete desire, and as the "center of reference for an infinity of polyvalent meanings," Sartre rejects the idea of the transcendental ego—that is, a transcendent pole to which all experience must necessarily refer, or to which it must belong. The unity of the fundamental project does not flow centrifugally from a determinate center, as if it were an anchor holding the parts of the self in place, but is a function of the relations *between* the different parts. Even the psychophysical ego, which might be taken as the natural center for character predicates, and as the seat of psychic unity, is merely a synthetic and ideal construct. It is an object *of* conscious experience, but not a real structure that is coextensive or autochthonous with conscious experience.[11]

Sartre characterizes the fundamental project as something that is actively constructed across the period of a whole life. The numerous antecedent conditions that in empirical psychology are construed as having a causal influence in the formation of selves affect persons not for what they are *in themselves*, but for what persons make of them in so far as they project

beyond them, confer meaning upon them, and construct from them a signi-
fying situation. Unlike Hampshire, then, Sartre grants to causation only an
attenuated role vis-à-vis the constituting or meaning-conferring activities
that are brought to bear upon it. The environment, for example, "can act on
the subject only to the extent that he comprehends it; that is, transforms it
into a situation."[12]

The idea that persons do not passively submit to external causation, but
define themselves by their projects beyond it, does not mean that the choice of
self occurs in a vacuum. I do not choose my parents, language, and historical
era, or my biological and neurophysiological makeup; I find myself "thrown"
into a situation, and endowed with certain brute characteristics. But facticity
underdetermines the many ways in which I *assume* it, find meaning in it, and
take it up as part of a way of being. One of the illustrations Sartre provides
here is the case of assuming a physical disability, and making from it a meaningful situation: "Even this disability from which I suffer I have assumed by
the very fact that I live; I surpass it towards my own projects, I make of it the
necessary obstacle for my being, and I cannot be crippled without choosing
myself as crippled. This means that I choose the way in which I constitute my
disability (as 'unbearable,' 'humiliating,' 'to be hidden,' 'to be revealed to all,'
'an object of pride,' 'the justification for my failures,' etc.)."[13]

What this means is that I alone create the meaning of the ensemble of fac-
tical conditions that root me in a particular situation: I am the being who
transforms my being into meaning, and through whom meaning comes into
the world.[14] Sartre's indebtedness to the Kantian and Husserlian theory of
transcendental constitution and meaning-giving is plainly evident here: the
creation of meaning is not itself something that can be explained in causal
terms. It is an ontologically primitive process. Curiously, however, I am also
unaware of the fact that I am the source of this meaning. Prereflective experience tends naturally toward self-dissimulation, covering over its own
meaning-giving activity in the very act of conferring meaning. Naive realism,
complicated by a tendency to self-deception and "seriousness," is the default
condition of my prereflective life: that is, the uncritical assumption that my
thought pictures a world and a self that are always and already divided up at
their true joints, as if the meanings I find in things are there as mind-
independent givens. If I can ever achieve it, an authentic existential self-
understanding undermines this consoling but false view of the world.

Sartre is careful to divest his claims about the fundamental project from
any hint of foundationalism. The choices persons make regarding the

question of how to be—"that by which all foundations and all reasons come into being"[15]—are not themselves founded, and can in no way serve as a source of existential, epistemic, or moral certainty. As a kind of "groundless ground," or contingent foundation, the radical choices that define the self are fragile and always diremptable. As paradoxical as this idea may sound, it brings out the sense in which there is nothing deeper than the radical choice of self that might in turn define or condition it, and give to it the authoritative ontological justification that it lacks. It functions as the unsupported bedrock of a whole complexly interrelated way of being in the world. This explains Sartre's claim that the "absolute event or for-itself is contingent in its very being"—even if it is "its own foundation *qua* for-itself."[16] Sartre's rejection of all forms of essentialism and foundationalism means that the hold I have over my identity is much more tenuous than I normally (or self-deceptively) think. Nothing concerning my identity is immune to change; and nothing about my identity is clearly labeled and awaiting discovery. This is one reason why Sartre characterizes human beings as "in question" in their very being.

THE RADICAL CHOICE OF SELF

Major life changes are common phenomena. Persons find themselves at crossroads in their lives, often not knowing what they really want, who they really are, how their self-conceptions fit their experiences, or in what direction they should endeavor to go in order to live good lives. Over time, they may develop into morally better or morally worse persons, or undergo conversions, or adopt new religious or moral beliefs, or break free of destructive emotional patterns. If, as Sartre argues, the fundamental project that describes the basic architecture of the self is not grounded, then are the changes persons undergo across the history of their lives changes from one project to another, or changes *within* a single project? To what extent can persons actually control these changes through deliberation or choice? To what extent can these changes be made the object of reflective self-inquiry and reflective self-evaluation?

Some of these questions might be clarified by considering in greater detail Sartre's account of what constitutes the bedrock of the fundamental project. The metaphor of bedrock is a felicitous one, because it evokes a suggestive image of autonomy: bedrock is that upon which other things rest, without itself resting upon anything. The choice of self is autonomous in roughly this sense: a fundamental project is constituted ultimately by the choices persons make regarding the question of how to be, and this does not rest upon or presuppose anything more fundamental. The choice is apprehended, Sartre claims, "as not deriving from any prior reality"; it is so deep-rooted and autonomous ("*selbständig*") that it "does not imply any other meaning, and . . . refers only to itself."[17]

These are transcendental claims. The idea that the most fundamental relation persons have to being is not cognitive, epistemic, or rational, but one which these relations *themselves* rest upon, and which makes them possible (viz., choice and projection), is a transcendental claim in the sense that it identifies something that is basic to all human experience; it refers to the whole of the *form* of human experience, and not to any particular content within experience. The relation, in other words, is not an empirical one in the sense that it is built up piecemeal from accumulated particular experiences. It is, rather, a *constitutive* feature of experience, and therefore it is not something that from within experience, or on the basis of experience, can become grounded. However, developing an explicit and clear understanding of this dimension of the being of persons, rather than the ontic dimensions that presuppose it, is a particularly difficult task.

One way to clarify these transcendental claims is to consider how they are instantiated in everyday practice. The efficacy of moral reasoning in ordinary decision-making procedures provides a good test case, because it involves such activities as deliberating about conflicting courses of action, engaging in moral discussion with others, and seeking to rationally justify one's choices. Sartre grants that within a way of life, when means and not ultimate priorities are in question, choices about conflicting courses of action may be guided by deliberation, reflective self-inquiry, and moral argument. The controversial point he makes, however, is that these activities have significance only insofar as they presuppose a prior commitment to a way of being in the world, which is not itself a commitment that has been arrived at through these means. That is, my commitment to a whole way of being makes possible certain kinds of moral argument and justification for a number of normative issues that are internal to that way of being, but it is not itself an appropriate subject of argument and rational justification.

Sartre's restriction of the scope of moral reasoning to project-internal concerns reveals just how primitive he considers the chosen commitment to a way of being to be. His claim that the choice of self entails a choice of what will first *count* as reasonable and unreasonable means that it is up to me to choose which rules of argumentation, and which moral conflict-resolution procedures, I will be bound by;[18] and, more fundamentally, that it is up to me to carve out what will count as a relevant moral concern from among the vast spectrum of possible normative concerns. The choice of self is "that by which all foundations and all reasons come into being."[19] Such is its depth that it is "prior to logic"; it is a "pre-logical synthesis" that "decides the attitude of the person when confronted with logic and principles." Thus "there can be no possibility of questioning it in conformance to logic."[20]

These are strong claims, and appear to lend to Sartre's philosophical psychology an antirationalist air. They fail to explain how persons can raise such questions as "Who am I and what really matters to me?" in a non-question-begging manner. Normally, questions like these are intended to be questions *about* the agent's project and way of life. The reflective self-inquiry and reflective self-evaluation they call for is not intended simply to *presuppose* the fundamental project, or to express it in a different dimension. The framing of the questions proceeds on the assumption that answers to them can be established on more or less lasting and independent grounds. Moreover, the questions arise in a state of genuinely felt puzzlement; they put the self in a new light, thereby revealing previously undisclosed possibilities. But Sartre's claim that the choice of self is a choice of the very kinds of foundations and reasons that will be countenanced in framing and answering questions of *any* sort seems to deny just this. Sartre's point, however, is not that my attempts to work out these probing questions are futile; or that the questions are unanswerable, and that I am left in the dark about who I am. It is rather that in the process of working out these questions, the choices I make about how to be cannot be determined entirely on objective and rational grounds independent of my narrow first-person perspective. Eventually, the search for justification, and the moral reasoning that it involves, comes to an end, and I am thrown upon my own finite and fallible resources. Here, action begins where reflection leaves off.[21] It is at this stage, as Heidegger and Sartre argue, that the basic questions of existence can be worked out only by existing.

Limitations such as these are not only symptoms of cognitive shortcomings, the poverty of rationality, or (as Hume would argue) the preponderance of emotional, affective, and habitual factors in the psychological makeup of human beings. They reveal something about the ontological structure of the identity of persons: viz., questions of moral and rational justification are necessarily *internal* to a person's fundamental project and way of being in the world, but *as a whole*, a person's way of being does not afford external rational justification nor independent investigation (of the sort defended, for example, by Hampshire). This is another way of arriving at the idea that the radical choice that underlies the choice of self, and that serves as the target of the question "Who am I?" is a groundless and elusive ground.

This view is not without problems. While Sartre clearly wishes to avoid underpinning his philosophical psychology with an unchecked subjectivism, it is still not clear precisely where he allows reflective self-evaluation and the rational justification of choices to leave off, and radical choice to take over. The idea that there is both an objective and a subjective side to self-inquiry, self-evaluation, and self-determination is not deeply controversial; what is, however, is the question of the scope of the subjective and irreducibly decisionistic element that comes into play when persons exercise a choice with regard to their fundamental possibilities of being.

SELF-KNOWLEDGE AND THE FUNDAMENTAL PROJECT

Sartre further develops his picture of persons as finite, situated, and cognitively limited beings in his account of self-knowledge. It seems obvious that being self-knowledgeable is an essential component of the stance I must take up when I am confronted with my fundamental possibilities of being; and that it is an essential component of authenticity and existential responsibility, and in overcoming self-deception. Sartre's view, however, greatly complicates this picture, and in doing so encounters a number of difficulties. The basic architecture of my identity—the choice of self and the fundamental project— is lived but not known; and if it comes to be known, it is known not from the first-person perspective but from a distanced and relatively impoverished third-person perspective. The fundamental project is the presupposed background of my experience, but as such it cannot be made explicit as an object of conceptualization, as the objects of ontic studies can be. It is hidden because of its very familiarity and pervasiveness.

It is in his discussion of existential psychoanalysis that Sartre most clearly develops the idea that the knowledge I can acquire about my fundamental project is primarily objectifying and external, rather than practical, integrative, and existential. Sartre argues that what I come to know about myself cannot be squared with how I am *for* myself, because knowledge is acquired from an external perspective; conversely, how I am for myself cannot properly be made an object of knowledge, because knowledge is of necessity analytical and objectifying. (The sharp either-or nature of this dichotomy, characteristic of many of Sartre's conceptual and phenomenological distinctions, resembles the perspectival dichotomy illustrated in the duck-rabbit figure.)

If, from an epistemic point of view, there is something elusive and unnameable about the ontologically deep properties of my way of being, then the question "Who am I?" must be approached from a different angle. Sartre's suggestion is that it must be worked out primarily by *existing* (e.g., by radical choices and situationist responses), and only derivatively by more deliberate stances such as reflective self-inquiry and reflective self-evaluation. The arguments he provides to establish the distinction between knowing and being clearly reflect his Heideggerian critique of epistemology, and his suspicion of "the primacy of knowledge." Epistemology, he claims, unjustifiably privileges knowing over being.[22] To right this imbalance, one of the goals of the philosophy of existence is to show that knowledge is (in Heidegger's terms) only a "founded mode of being," which is not privileged in revealing to human beings the nature of existence. Unlike Heidegger, however, Sartre also relies on a theory of consciousness to generate his critique of the role of knowledge. This approach clearly has antecedents in the Kierkegaardian view that all knowledge concerning the subjective is false knowledge; and that subjectivity as concrete reality is a kind of "non-knowledge."

The problem here, however, is that Sartre purchases the primacy of pre-reflective experience over knowledge and self-knowledge only at the cost of an attenuated model of knowledge, and only by invoking an implausibly sharp distinction between the lived and the known. At the same time, he is forced to give the concept of pre-ontological comprehension an explanatory load that it cannot bear, in order to make up for the lost ground that results from weakening the explanatory load that should have been carried by the epistemic relations of knowledge and belief.

The Fundamental Project as Unnoticed Background

Epistemically, every attempt I make to work out the question "Who am I?" in a fundamental manner is limited and revisable. The very nature of the subject matter targeted by the question—that is, the ontological structure of my fundamental project—imposes these limitations. The global architecture and the deeper meaning of my most basic relation to being is elusive and easily overlooked, not because it is hidden like a dark secret in the soul but because it is too pervasive and too close to me. It is the always presupposed background (or horizon) of my experience, but as such it cannot be made explicit as an object.

Placing restrictions on the representability and cognitive accessibility of the horizon of thought, action, and perception is a familiar phenomenological theme, defended variously by Husserl, Heidegger, and Merleau-Ponty. In order to inquire into and know something, a number of things must be presupposed that are not themselves inquired into and known. Behind thought lies a nonrepresentable pretheoretical background, which for Heidegger consists of skills and tacit know-how, and for Merleau-Ponty consists of "pre-predicative" perceptual experience. But this background is not itself something that is known explicitly; it constitutes part of the structure of being in the world, and as such it is presupposed in every cognitive act. Sartre applies this fundamental phenomenological insight to his philosophical psychology. The nonrepresentable background is located at the very heart of the experience of the self, in my relation to my own fundamental project. With its elusive horizon-like character, the fundamental project that is the target of reflective self-inquiry and reflective self-evaluation is a "mystery in broad daylight,"[23] always and already familiar to me, but always obscured by a blind spot. "If the fundamental project is fully experienced by the subject and hence wholly conscious, that certainly does not mean that it must at the same time be known by him; quite the contrary."[24] Although nothing about the basic architecture of my way of being is hidden from my view by means of an opaque barrier, in the way that it would be if it were hidden in the unconscious, it is not something that I know clearly and explicitly.

From a phenomenological point of view this is a plausible description, because it captures a number of aspects of what it is like to be in the midst of an ongoing historical event, and to embody (and be borne along by) its deeper meanings without simultaneously having an explicit awareness of them: what might be called "perspectival internalism." Immersion in prereflective life precludes that detached perspective on life that would reveal it as an intelligible dynamic whole: "One can't take a point of view on one's life while one's living it."[25] Sartre's account of the elusiveness of the project is also plausible from a psychological point of view. Even if they do not serve the ends of existential authenticity, self-ignorance, oversight, or lack of perspective may be more psychologically and socially adaptive than ontological lucidity about the ultimate groundlessness and contingency of identity.

Pre-Ontological Comprehension

Despite the restrictions placed on knowledge and self-knowledge, Sartre's perspectival internalism does not entail the view that there is no first-person access of any kind to the fundamental project. If I am a "being of distances" with respect to my being, I am not ipso facto a stranger to myself: I always and already *comprehend* my project and my radical choice of self, though not clearly, and not in a way that can be captured in propositional form. The deeper patterns and the latent ontological meanings of my project are always vaguely grasped and embodied—even if they are not known as such. This is the upshot of Sartre's view that one of the defining characteristics of being human is the possession of an implicit and prethematic grasp of being. Following Heidegger, who follows the *verstehen* theorists, Sartre calls this grasp "pre-ontological comprehension," and construes it (mostly without argument) in ontological rather than epistemological terms; it is not a form of knowledge or representation but a way of being that finds its expression in a variety of ends-oriented projects. Pre-ontological comprehension is neither analytical nor inferential. It is an immediate and tacit grasp of the meaning of human events, including the event of being, and the event of choosing and taking up an identity.

The significance that Sartre attaches to construing comprehension onto-logically rather than epistemologically cannot be stressed strongly enough. Because pre-ontological comprehension is the original character of the *being* of human life, it follows (Sartre claims) that it is not a contingent or learned skill, or an item of knowledge that comes "from without": to be is to dwell bodily in the comprehension of being. Understanding is my very mode of existing—so, unlike the epistemic relations of knowledge and belief, it is not something that I can properly fail to have, although I can fail to articulate it.[26] Pre-ontological comprehension thus conveniently provides me with an endlessly fertile and mostly accurate source of information about existing, while at the same time blocking skepticism about the very possibility of onto-logically oriented self-understanding. "The human reality which is myself assumes its own being by understanding it. . . . I am, then, first of all, a being who more or less obscurely understands his reality as a man, which means that I make myself a man by understanding myself as such."[27]

To compensate for the weakened explanatory role assigned to the concepts of knowledge and belief, Sartre attributes a significant degree of explanatory power to the concept of pre-ontological comprehension. In doing so he also weakens the plausibility of the concept. Human beings, he claims, have a truth-bearing though tacit pre-ontological comprehension of some of the most fundamental characteristics of human reality: of being, nonbeing, the futility of sincerity, the criteria of truth, the existence of the Other, the human person, and the fundamental project.[28] Nothing of ontological significance falls outside the range of pre-ontological comprehension. With such a wide range, Sartre is able to preserve the phenomenological intuition that to be a person is to be pretheoretically attuned to the latent meanings of the world. It is not possible to be *radically* mistaken about our most basic relation to being, and yet our comprehension of being (including our own being) is so pervasive in thought and experience that it can never be fully spelled out.

Prereflective Self-Awareness

If Sartre's claims about the elusiveness of the fundamental project amount only to the claim that many aspects of the self as agent never come into full view, then he has rightly captured what might be called the underprivileged access to self that typifies the first-person viewpoint. There is always more about my self than can be represented at any one time; and the ways in which I represent myself to others and to myself do not always pick out the most salient aspects of the self. But this construal of the project's elusiveness is not the view Sartre defends. The fundamental project is in some respects already in full view, Sartre claims, because I always and already *fully experience* my project.

Unlike Heidegger, who avoids invoking the concept of consciousness to explain *Dasein's* relation to being, Sartre links his account of pre-ontological comprehension to his account of prereflective consciousness. To be is to understand being pre-ontologically—as well as to *experience* it. This emphasis on experience follows from the increased scope Sartre attributes to the concept of prereflective consciousness, coupled with the strong holistic thesis that the structure of a person's way of being in the world can be discerned from any single part of it. Every act, from the most insignificant gesture to the most life-transforming decision, is an *experienced* but densely compressed manifestation of the whole ongoing dynamic movement of the project, at once expressing and constituting "the total relation to the world by which the subject constitutes himself." Because the fundamental project is fully experienced by the person whose project it is, there is no need, from the first-person point of view, to search the depths "without ever having presentiment of its location, as one can go to look for the source of the Nile or the Niger."[29]

Again, Sartre preserves the general phenomenological intuition that all prereflective experience—including the prereflective experience of the fundamental project—is accurate, but as it is highly compressed and difficult to spell out, it tends to yield both too much and too little of what is needed for an adequately scaled self-knowledge. On the one hand, it is tacit and undeveloped, and effaced by the external objects of awareness. As with other forms of prereflective awareness, it is "non-thetic" and "nonpositional." The self-relation is such that the experiencing subject is not originally an object for himself or herself, and does not posit the self as a possible object for attention. On the other hand, the prereflective experience of the fundamental project is an awareness of everything "all at once," in a state of extreme indifferentiation, "without shading, without relief. . . . All is there." Like the famed cube upon which Husserl and Merleau-Ponty trained their phenomenological attention, too much in the prereflective experience of the fundamental project is given all at once—an inexhaustibly rich reality that overflows all perspectives on it. But the idea that everything is given does not mean that everything about a person's way of being is laid out clearly as an intelligible whole. The price paid for such a total delivery is high: if *everything* is given all at once, it is also unavoidably subject to a certain confusion and "syncretic indifferentiation,"[30] rather like the compression experienced by Leibnizian monads in their reflection of the rest of the universe of monads.

To complicate measures, and to further reinforce the distinction between knowing and being, Sartre places tight restrictions on the scope of reflexive knowledge by drawing a sharp distinction between knowledge *(connaissance)* and consciousness *(conscience)*. His purpose in doing this is to show that while the fundamental characteristics of a person's way of being in the world are fully experienced, they are not objectively known as such. This is not an empirical claim. The argument is not that it is simply a matter of empirical fact that the fundamental project is overlooked; nor that it is a matter of empirical fact that the tools necessary for identifying and conceptualizing truths at the ontological level are not normally available without the special intervention of an inquiry such as existential psychoanalysis. Sartre's claim is a stronger one about the logic (or the phenomenological logic) of epistemic practices that bear on prereflective experience. The knowledge I acquire about my fundamental project through practices such as existential psychoanalysis can only reveal my project from an external perspective—and this is a perspective which of necessity fails to capture the *meaning* of my experience of the project. Knowledge cannot adequately represent my project from the inside—that is, how I am *for* myself. It can only represent the project from the standpoint of an external observer, which is a standpoint deprived of what Heidegger calls the sense of "mineness" *(jemeinigkeit)* and what

William James calls the "warmth and intimacy" of the first-person perspective. Thus self-descriptions and self-analyses are invariably impoverished. There is, Sartre claims, no mediation or "table of correlation" between my prereflective experience of my project and my knowledge of the project that comes from reflective self-inquiry and reflective self-evaluation. (Similar epistemic constraints apply to my knowledge of my body.)[31] "[We] are always wholly present to ourselves; but precisely because we are wholly present, we cannot hope to have an analytical and detailed consciousness of what we are. Moreover this consciousness can be only non-thetic."[32]

Neither the logical nor the phenomenological construal of the claim that the fundamental project is lived but not known entails the stronger claim that the project is intrinsically unknowable. The project qua lived reality is elusive, but it is not a *ding an sich* that is beyond all possible experience. The fact that the project resists analysis and conceptualization in so far as it is lived resembles the fact that the eye cannot simultaneously see itself seeing. But the eye is not invisible. With external means it can become an object within the visual field, like any other object. The same is true of the fundamental project: with external means (viz., the methods of existential psychoanalysis) it can be known from the outside, in the same manner that another person might know it. Still, the external perspective allows only an imperfect and objectifying apprehension of a reality that is intrinsically non-objectlike. Thus Sartre claims that "what always escapes these methods of investigation [viz., existential psychoanalysis] is the project as it is for itself, the complex in its own being. This project-for-itself can be experienced only as a living possession; there is an incompatibility between existence for itself and objective existence."[33]

From an epistemic point of view, then, I suffer a blind spot to my fundamental project, which I apprehend "only by living it."[34] Only an infinite intellect can know me perfectly both from the inside and the outside—but this is a perspective, Sartre argues famously, to which no sense can be attributed.

AUTOBIOGRAPHICAL BLIND SPOTS

The reflexive blind spot that is built into the first-person perspective comes to insinuate itself in the self-ascription of psychological attributes and character predicates (e.g., "ambitious," "sensitive"). Self-ascription is possible only on an *inductive* basis, through observation of the conditions under which the relevant terms are applied by others in appropriate social contexts; but it is, strictly speaking, impossible to internalize these predicates and *live* them without becoming a kind of quasi-object to oneself—a transformation of self that, Sartre argues, is a species of bad faith. Character predicates are not "soluble" in prereflective experience, because they represent the other's perspective on the self: they are "unrealizable." Character therefore is for other people; it is not something that is experienced from the first-person point of view.[35]

Sartre likens the restricted nature of self-ascription to the hypothetical sphere described by Jules Henri Poincaré, in which the temperature of the sphere decreases with the move from the center to the surface. Living beings try to "arrive at the surface of this sphere by setting out from its center, but the lowering of the temperature produces in them a continually increasing contraction. They tend to become infinitely flat proportionately to their approaching their goal, and because of this fact they are separated by an infinite distance."[36] Similarly, self-ascription is liable to generate oversimplified syntheses, false continuities, and reflective artifacts.

Sartre's application of the distinction between knowing and being to self-ascription clearly constrains his own efforts at reflective self-inquiry. *The War Diaries* record his attempts to engage in dispassionate self-observation, with the goal of analyzing his deeper motives and feelings, and ultimately his fundamental project. But the price Sartre pays for making what is experienced prereflectively the target of investigation is too high. Under his gaze, his feelings and desires lose their spontaneity, appearing eventually "like dried plants in a herbarium." As a result, Sartre writes, "there was something missing in me . . . a certain way of dwelling in oneself: of being an integral part of oneself." At one point fed up with "constructing tireless spotlights" to shine upon himself, Sartre imagines an idealized opposite—a person "hesitant, obscure, slow and upright in his thoughts. . . . I saw him, for some reason, as a worker and hobo in the Eastern USA. How I should have liked to feel uncertain ideas slowly, patiently forming within me! How I should have liked to boil with great, obscure rages . . . !"[37]

Self-observation such as this is not the kind of reflective self-inquiry and reflective self-evaluation that is needed to work out the question "Who am I?" because it has disintegrative results, and tends too much toward narcissistic focusing. It is as if the only option in Sartre's self-inquiry is between a paralyzing lucidity that distorts the prereflective experience it targets, and an unreflecting spontaneity that altogether disallows perspective-taking and exact description. Sartre's autobiography *The Words* continues with this problematic approach, pursuing an unsentimental and ironic existential-psychoanalytical self-analysis that uses the same method and explanatory categories deployed in his biographies of Genet and Flaubert:[38] philosophical themes, for instance, of contingency, freedom, bad faith, seriousness, the look, being-for-others, and playing at being.

In general, Sartre claims, the goal of existential psychoanalysis is to "bring to light, in a strictly objective form, the subjective choice by which each living person makes himself a person; that is, makes known to himself what he is. . . . [What] the method seeks is a *choice of being* [and] at the same time a being." The guiding methodological principle of existential psychoanalysis is that a person is a unity and not a collection of disconnected parts. A person "expresses himself as a whole in even his most insignificant and his most superficial behaviour. In other words, there is not a taste, a mannerism, or an human act which is not *revealing*." However, because the subject of existential-psychoanalytical *self*-analysis (as in the case of *The Words*) is both analyst and analysand, the analysis must operate upon an unfinished and changing totality. The analyst-analysand confronts some of the same problems that are confronted by historians writing contemporary history, when the dust of events has not yet settled: viz., a constantly growing body of evidence the meaning of which is liable to change retroactively with new evidence, ongoing uncertainty as to what counts as evidentially salient, and a precarious proximity to the subject matter of the inquiry. This is further complicated by the fact that the analyst-analysand does not enjoy any privileged access to the fundamental project that is targeted by the analysis. Existential self-analysis requires of the subject the adoption of the third-person point of view. It involves "a strictly objective method, using as documentary evidence the data of reflection as well as the testimony of others. Of course, the subject *can* undertake a psychoanalytic investigation of himself. But in this case he must renounce at the outset all benefit stemming from his peculiar position and must question himself exactly as if he were someone else."[39]

The major shortcoming with Sartre's self-analysis is that it fails to capture his fundamental project as it is for himself: this can only be experienced as a living possession. While the self-analysis allows him to formulate as knowledge what he already understands (or pre-ontologically comprehends) in an inarticulate experiential way, there is something about his reality as an existent that eludes even the most exacting analytical self-descriptions. The impossibility of bridging the gap between knowing and being ultimately constrains Sartre's attempt to address the question "Who am I?" By the end of the autobiography Sartre claims to have uprooted many of his illusions, and to have rendered his project transparent to a degree that was not available to him before. But the self-analysis he pursues in the autobiography suffers from the very illusions of self-objectification he claims to have overcome. In depicting a lifelong struggle with idealism and the illusion of retrospection—a struggle that ostensibly results in liberating insight—the autobiography itself comes to suffer from the same idealist storytelling and retrospective illusion it tries to excise. Referring at the end of the autobiography to the sheer difficulty of trying to make sense of himself, he admits: "So try to figure it out. As for me, I can't."[40]

Much of Sartre's autobiography focuses on his childhood as an only child raised by his widowed mother. He traces to his childhood the motivational origins of the illusions and self-deceptions from which he suffered his entire life, and which were inspired by quasi-religious sentiments that once provided metaphysical consolation: the illusion of the retrospective perspective, the illusion of verbal idealism, and the illusion of the moralist. Sartre interprets his aspiration to be a great writer, for instance, as a desire to transform every aspect of experience into words, which as a child he regarded as more real than anything else: "I regarded words as the essences of things. . . . [T]he Universe would rise in tiers at my feet and all things would humbly beg for a name; to name the thing was both to create and take it. Without this fundamental illusion I would never have written." To uncover the origin of this metaphysically precocious desire, Sartre eschews traditional psychological explanation ("the great explanatory idols of our epoch—heredity, education, environment, physiological constitution")[41] in favor of ontological analysis. The young Sartre's desire to be a writer was not the outcome of causal forces operating upon a relatively plastic organism. It was, he claims, a solution to the problem of being—a problem he had first encountered as a child when he experienced disturbing ontological moods that left him feeling superfluous and insubstantial.[42] Sartre's response was to try to be by being a writer. He believed that complete identification with the role of writer—being a writer in the same manner of being that an inkwell *is* an inkwell, thereby satisfying the principle of identity[43]—could supply him with the feelings of solidity and self-identity that he inwardly lacked. If successfully realized, this strategy would justify an otherwise superfluous existence. The little Sartre thus played with the role of writer in order to realize it, adopting the behaviors of writers so convincingly that the play-acting became indistinguishable from the reality. "The liar was finding his truth in the elaboration of his lies. I was born of writing. Before that, there was only a play of mirrors. With my first novel I knew that a child had got into the hall of mirrors. By writing I was existing." At the same time, however, the young Sartre also had vague intimations that no amount of posturing could eliminate his ontological insecurities and supply him with the determinate identity he so acutely lacked. Sartre's analysis of his decision to be by being a writer is unforgiving; it is the mature adult's philosophical evaluation of the child's prephilosophical beliefs. He characterizes his project as "the mad enterprise of writing in order to be forgiven for my existence"; and as a way of being that involves a permanent stance of derealization, because it required him to "kill himself in advance" in order to "enjoy immortality." "I chose as my future the past of a great immortal and I tried to live backwards. I became completely posthumous."[44]

One of the related illusions Sartre claims in *The Words* to have finally eradicated through existential self-analysis is the moralist's desire to expose in others the self-deceptive stratagems by means of which they avoid owning up to their existential freedom: "I was not on earth to enjoy things but to draw up a balance-sheet."[45] The irony here is twofold. Sartre's first-order motive to uncover self-deception in others is itself a kind of self-deception, because it is founded on a strategy to create a determinate identity that would annul the radical contingency by which he constantly feels threatened. Sartre again traces this particular "imposture" back to his childhood, to the time when he deceived himself into thinking that it was his destiny to reveal humankind's lack of destiny, and that he would achieve salvation by exposing the impossibility of salvation. But his second-order goal of eradicating the first-order self-deception through existential self-analysis is itself in jeopardy of being a self-deception of a higher and more complex order. Motivating the outwardly honest self-evaluation of *The Words* is the lingering desire for salvation: "I sometimes wonder whether I'm not playing loser wins and not trying hard to stamp out my one-time hopes so that everything will be restored to me a hundredfold." By pursuing such sobering self-analysis, "he's secretly waiting for his reward."[46]

Sartre's description and analysis of his childhood is framed in the terms of a mature philosophy. This is problematic, because when the adult Sartre reads into the experience of the child sophisticated philosophical distinctions in sentiment and intention that were not available to the child, the description of childhood becomes overstylized and ordered.[47] This is a symptom of the very retrospective illusion that it is Sartre's goal in the autobiography to overcome—that is, smuggling known outcomes into the description of sequences of events in which the outcomes were not yet known. The retrospective illusion has the effect of smoothing over the contingencies and loose ends of life history, and giving to it the appearance of a linear and forward-looking development to which each inconsequential moment ultimately contributes. "I have committed the mad blunder . . . of taking life for an epic." But Sartre's disavowal of epic storytelling is framed in terms of a life story that bears the marks of epic that he wishes to reject, with themes of alienation, liberating insight, and redemption: "The retrospective illusion has been smashed to bits; martyrdom, salvation, and immortality are falling to pieces; the edifice is going to rack and ruin; I collared the Holy Ghost in the cellar and threw him out; atheism is a cruel and long-range affair: I think I've carried it through. I see clearly, I've lost my illusions. . . . For the last ten years or so I've been a man who's been waking up, cured of a long, bitter-sweet madness." These claims are made with a false sense of finality to which Sartre is not strictly entitled, as well as with an illusory retrospection that smoothes over the contingency of the past. The life Sartre recounts displays a progressive development in which every stage contributes to the final goal of existential lucidity. Disavowing all forms of idealism, and all forms of salvation, his self-analysis nevertheless adopts the style and terminology of the drama of a secularized existential soteriology: "My sole concern has been to save myself—nothing in my hands, nothing up my sleeve—by work and faith. . . . Without equipment, without tools, I set all of me to work in order to save all of me."[48]

A "FOUNDED MODE OF BEING"

Sartre's distinction between knowing and being serves as a corrective to the intellectualist bias of Hampshire's account of self-knowledge. The emphasis on the historical and internalist nature of perspective-taking in reflective self-inquiry has a degree of phenomenological realism lacking in Hampshire's account of reflective detachment, which construes reflective self-inquiry as an independent and impartial activity of the self with respect to the self. The situation of self-inquirers resembles that of Neurath's mariners, who must rebuild their ship while it is afloat on the open seas, without the benefits of dry dock, and with only limited materials at hand. Since self-inquirers are always and already in the midst of ongoing life histories, their efforts to fathom the deeper meanings and the global architectures of their lives are themselves part of those life histories, and constitutive of their architecture.

There is no independent perspective on a life in the making, just as there is no dry dock for Neurath's mariners.

But Sartre's account of reflective self-inquiry and reflective self-evaluation also lacks a certain degree of phenomenological realism to the extent that it transforms the *distinction* between the lived and the known into a sharp either-or *dichotomy* that effectively restricts inquiry to oscillating between the first-person and third-person perspectives. This overstates the differences between the two perspectives, and fails to account for the input of the second-person perspective. Reflective self-inquiry, as will be argued later, is more of a socially interactive process between the self and the other than a monologically restricted self-analysis. It is bound up in the web of argument, in the confrontation of the first-person perspective with the second-person perspective, and in the moral and emotional give-and-take of face-to-face dialogue.

Sartre is forced to his conclusions because, inter alia, his model of knowledge *(connaissance)* is too narrow, and his phenomenological account of the structures of experience too restrictively dichotomous. While the dichotomy between consciousness and knowledge serves to protect the phenomenological principle of the primacy of prereflective experience, it does so at the expense of accounting for the integrative and self-transformative potential of reflexive forms of knowing. Sartre characterizes knowledge as, for instance, "thetic" and "positional"; and as presupposing "reliefs, levels, an order, hierarchy."[49] To know that something is the case is to stand in a subject-object relation with respect to the object of knowledge, and this involves "positing" the object, and apprehending it from the outside. While the overriding intent is clear—to show that knowledge is only a "founded mode of being"—the existential-phenomenological model ignores a number of different forms of knowledge, not all of which are analytical or dualistic (e.g., perceptual knowledge, practical knowledge, moral knowledge).[50]

Perhaps aware of the epistemic restrictions placed on self-knowledge by the dichotomy between the project-as-lived and the project-as-known, and still wishing to allow room for a form of self-knowing that would have far-reaching existential consequences, Sartre introduced the possibility of "purifying reflection":[51] that is, a self-reflection that would serve as a nonobjectifying realization of pre-ontological self-understanding. But because the demands on the notion of purifying reflection were so high, and because the dichotomies between the reflective and the prereflective were so sharply drawn, it remained an undeveloped theme in *Being and Nothingness:* it was a promissory note rather than a theory.

One of the strengths of Sartre's account of the problem of self-knowledge is that it takes life as a whole as the basic unit of empirical significance. This allows him to avoid abstraction and oversimplification, and to describe more faithfully the phenomenology of moral life. Those theories of self-knowledge that fail to do this tend to force-fit the problems into manageable form, but at the cost of remaining true to the complexity of the relevant phenomena. However, Sartre's denial of the efficacy of moral reasoning, his holist approach to life architecture, and the restrictions he places upon self-knowledge create a number of problems for the explanatory scope of his philosophical psychology—most notably problems in accounting for the different forms of psychological and moral development, and the self-understandings accompanying them, which occur across life history. Rather like the theory of incommensurability and meaning variance that accounts for large-scale changes in scientific paradigms, Sartre's account of the elusiveness of the fundamental project commits him to holding that changes in the way persons shape their lives are discontinuous and ultimately unjustifiable. New ways of being do not evolve from previous ones, as articulations of a single underlying reality; nor are they formed gradually as a result of increasingly penetrating reflective self-inquiry and reflective self-evaluation. The clearest example of Sartrean self-transformation is the radical conversion, which involves a total break with the past, a complete reinterpretation of the meaning of past events and present situations, and the adoption of a new meaning framework. A global flip-flop like this is liable to happen in an instant: "These extraordinary and marvelous instants when the prior project collapses into the past in the light of a new project which rises on its ruins and which as yet exists only in outline, in which humiliation, anguish, joy, hope, are delicately blended, in which we let go in order to grasp and grasp in order to let go—these have often appeared to furnish the clearest and most moving image of our freedom."[52]

The problems with this view of self-transformation are clear: it is too extreme—"a grandiose leaping about unimpeded at important moments"—and it results in what Sartre was later to call a "revolutionary and discontinuous catastrophism."[53] The architecture of personal identity is at once too rigid and too fragile. With no middle ground between change and constancy, the integration of the fundamental project stands precariously balanced against its complete disintegration. Moreover, the price of changing the project is too high: given its tight interconnectedness, if any part is to change, everything must change. But the fact that the fundamental project can only sustain transilient changes that are global rather than gradual, reflectively driven, or rationally governed is contrary to Sartre's stated aim of interpreting human agency in terms of existentially self-aware self-determination. What results, paradoxically, is a kind of determinism by the fundamental project. Once chosen, I am virtually locked into my project, and my voluntary or reflective efforts to change its basic structures are futile. When I deliberate about alternative ways of life, the "chips are down." All that I can hope for is a radical conversion—but even this hoping is an expression of my current project.[54]

These restrictions on rationality and self-knowing have the unwanted consequence of rendering self-determination an unintelligible and nonrational achievement. Without recourse to noncircular self-inquiry and self-evaluation, and to the rationally guided formulation of choices between different ways of life, the question "What is best for me?" is not rationally decidable. The history of identity changes is thus a history of unintelligible facts. There are, as existential psychoanalysis reveals to me, no lasting and project-independent reasons why my life takes the form that it does, and why certain life changes occur and others do not. Beyond the biased and revisable self-interpretations I formulate from within my current fundamental project in response to the question "Who am I?" I must accept these facts as ultimately inexplicable—or as absurd. But this clearly undermines the idea that human beings are self-determining, morally self-aware, and the authors of their lives.

Given the perspectival internalism that characterizes my relation to my fundamental project, there can be no lasting and independent grounds upon which to distinguish between the better and worse choices that I make in determining who I am and what way of life I want. Sartre's internalism does not allow for the possibility that there is a better choice of life possibilities that *would* be evident to me in light of greater knowledge and self-understanding. But this is precisely the point of defending a philosophical psychology that holds that I am in question in my being, and capable of making choices that concern the deepest level of my being. For when the practical question "Who am I?" is raised in a fundamental manner, I am keenly aware that I can make mistakes, or be misled, or self-deceived, and can therefore fail to lead a life that is meaningful. Moreover, I am fully aware that in light of greater knowledge, maturity, and wisdom, I actually could work out this question with increasingly greater clarity and justification.

5

◀

"THE MAN WITHOUT QUALITIES":
IRONY, CONTINGENCY, AND THE
LIGHTNESS OF BEING

▶

THE SELF "WELL LOST"

Both Hampshire and Sartre hold that there are certain determinate facts about the self qua agent that it is the task of reflective self-inquiry to explore, even if these facts are systematically elusive because they are modified by the very attempts to explore them. Hampshire regards the structure and the causal determinants of the self as existing independently of and antecedently to the subject's reflexive knowledge about them. While the acquisition of reflexive knowledge has the potential to modify these facts, their identity is not, at least initially, logically or causally dependent upon the subject's awareness of them. Similarly, Sartre regards the principal structures of the fundamental project as antecedent to and logically independent of the subject's explicit reflective awareness of them. So deep-lying is the project that the subject's self-interpretations can be regarded as expressions of its core structures, rather than as independent reflections upon them. In both cases, the self that is the object of self-knowledge is, at least to a certain extent, *discovered;* in both cases, moreover, there will always remain certain facts about the self that do not come into full view for the subject whose self it is.

Richard Rorty's view is markedly different. Self-knowledge, he argues, is not a matter of discovering antecedently given facts, and it is not validated when descriptions and interpretations about the self display some degree of correspondence with the putative facts to which they refer. If talk of facts is to be countenanced at all, it should be rephrased as talk of theory-laden facts or facts-relative-to-a-framework. Rorty regards reflective self-inquiry not as oriented toward the *discovery* of the self, but as the *construction* of a self through textualist means, such as the development of a "personal vocabulary." It is not merely the case that the basic categories in terms of which I understand myself cannot be objectively grounded, if by this it is meant that such categories must serve as faithful mirrors of my self as it is "in itself," independent of all conceptual frameworks; there is, he claims, no *need* for such categories to be grounded in this manner in the first place. The goal of discovering my "true self" is a fiction; and the self that would ostensibly legitimate such a search is a self "well lost."

Rorty's account of the relation between self-knowledge and the self, representing a version of the postmodern decentering of the self, is influenced by a variety of unlikely sources, including Nietzsche's aestheticism, Sartre's theory of radical contingency, Heidegger's existential hermeneutics, and Wittgenstein's philosophy of language. He begins his account with the holist claim that the pursuit of self-knowledge necessarily occurs against the background of an entire language and web of practices, which supply the robust vocabularies of personality and sentiment of everyday discourse. The precise formative role of this background in the generation of self-interpretations goes largely unnoticed. The background is receded, and dissimulated by a kind of naive realism that accepts uncritically that the similarities and differences specified in the vocabulary-embedded descriptions of selves are indicative of their real nature.

The fact that there is no other available source of raw materials means that both the form and content of any particular self-understanding are ultimately limited by the range of possible permutations that vocabularies can undergo as they evolve and devolve over time in response to changing environmental pressures and social needs. "Such vocabularies contain terms like *magnanimous, a true Christian, decent, cowardly, God-fearing, hypocritical, self-deceptive, epicene, self-destructive, cold, an antique Roman, a saint, a Julien Sorel, a Becky Sharpe, a red-blooded American, a shy gazelle, a hyena, depressive, a Bloomsbury type, a man of respect, a grande dame.* Such terms are possible answers to the question 'What is he or she like?' and thus possible answers to the question 'What am *I* like?' By summing up patterns of behavior, they are tools for criticizing the character of others and for creating one's own."[1]

Without further qualifications, however, a holistic account of the background conditions of self-understanding is compatible with commitment to epistemic objectivity as a regulative ideal. This would be incompatible with Rorty's antifoundationalist project of deconstructing the transhistorical "Philosophical" metanarratives that threaten to "freeze over" culture. Rorty's strategy is to block this move by arguing that the very idea of uninterpreted facts that could get some purchase on epistemic objectivity—facts about the self that could ground self-interpretations—is incoherent. It is senseless to suppose that there is some extralinguistic factual basis that would justify privileging one vocabulary of the self over another, on the grounds that it delivers a truer or better insight into the self, or a better moral map. There simply are no such facts.

This move has curious consequences. It appears to militate against anything counting as an adequate and lasting answer to the question "Who am I?" But this is precisely the point of trying to raise the question in a fundamental manner. If my conventional self-understanding only has the resources to supply superficial answers to the question, and if my previous attempts to work out the question have fallen short because they have not been pushed far enough, then I will approach the question with a sense of uncertainty, puzzlement, or dissatisfaction. My goal in pursuing an activity as difficult as reflective self-inquiry will be to arrive at an answer that is lasting and personally significant; that is, one that will not change with the latest fad in the vocabulary of selves, or with temporarily recalcitrant experiences.

But if Rorty's claim that the only source of ideas about selves are relatively transient vocabularies is valid, then the question "Who am I?" could only admit of answers that are as lasting as the vocabularies in which they are embedded. Whatever insights into the self I might gain through reflective self-inquiry would inevitably evolve and devolve with changes in my vocabulary, with the durability of any one convincing insight being underwritten largely by noncognitive and pragmatic considerations. I could not expect to uncover deep and lasting truths about myself; and I could not reasonably expect such a thing as a veridical or "objective" answer for my question "Who am I?" to emerge in the long run. But this would be highly unsatisfactory. Tracking the truth is crucial to reflective self-inquiry, because I care about who I am, how my life is going, and how I am perceived by others; and because I am aware of how ruinous it could be for me, and for others who care about me, if the question is answered incorrectly, or if its exploration is contaminated with self-deception or fantasy.

Even more unsatisfactory, however, would be coming to grips with the fact that my primary action-guiding sense of self, that in virtue of which I understand myself as myself, is radically contingent. This would mean that whatever results my self-inquiry *appears* to deliver—lasting insight, therapeutic healing, or the overcoming of self-deception—are not *in fact* a matter of progress or convergence toward the truth. They are yet another stage in the evolutionary drift of vocabularies, with new vocabularies of the self and "new forms of life constantly killing off old forms, not to accomplish a higher purpose, but blindly."[2] This, as Sartre recognized, is a dizzying view, and one that could be expected to lead to a kind of existential anxiety, and a disturbing sense of the uncanniness surrounding the fact that I am myself and not someone else. But these, as will be seen later, are not the characteristic ontological moods Rorty thinks would be experienced by persons who have realized in thought and action abstract philosophical truths about the constructed (and deconstructable) nature of the self.

Rorty regards all problems, topics, and distinctions, especially as they pertain to the self, as language-relative, because they express a prior choice to use a vocabulary of such and such a kind. The choice, like the Sartrean choice of self, is radical; that is, it is not governed by overarching standards of rationality that are external to it, and it is not dependent upon any more fundamental choice that might condition it. No single vocabulary of the self can be rationally evaluated (as a whole) as deeper or more primordial than any other, because there is no neutral metalanguage from which such comparison could be meaningfully accomplished. Rorty thus suggests that the metaphors of depth and primordiality used to qualify vocabularies according to "Philosophical" norms of objectivity should be discarded altogether—as should the epistemological metaphor of the mind as a mirror of nature and itself—on the grounds that they are no more than misleading cultural constructions.

But what does it mean to say that all problems and distinctions are language-relative? Does this not lead to a form of linguistic idealism about the self? The notion that vocabularies about the self cannot be compared with unmediated reality is certainly not unambiguous. It can be interpreted in at least two ways, one of which preserves a version of the Kantian dualism of scheme and content, and the other of which rejects that dualism as incoherent.

If it is construed in the first way, then access to reality (such as the self as it "really is") could *in principle* be achieved by means other than those that are contingently available to humans. This would make it possible to talk intelligibly about grounds for rational comparison of the validity of alternative conceptual schemes and alternative vocabularies of the self. The fact that humans cannot have access to the real as it is in itself is simply a function of obstacles in their given cognitive or conceptual endowment; but these are not necessarily obstacles that differently constituted creatures might encounter. The existence of constitutional limitations, in other words, remains compatible with the ontologically robust notion that there is one determinate way that reality is, accessible if and only if constitutional mediation were to be factored out.

The second interpretation, by contrast, holds that the very idea of a non-conceptualized reality that might supply grounds for rational comparison of alternative conceptual schemes is incoherent. This is Rorty's view, which he applies to self-description and self-interpretation. His suspicion of the idea that there might be some ideal external perspective that could be taken with respect to the self, the attainment of which would present the right conditions for putting an end to reflective self-inquiry, derives from the more general antirealist view that sense cannot be given to the notion that there is one absolutely correct meaning for basic ontological concepts such as "existence," "object," and "fact" that is uniquely specified by a determinate mind-independent reality. By first deconstructing the entire "Philosophical" vocabulary of mirroring, including the idea that particular statements are true *of objects,* Rorty is able to reject the realist view that holds that the relation between self-knowledge and the self is a vertical relation between statements and nonsentential facts, some of which statements are more privileged than others. The realist view is unnecessary. There is no need to suppose that a privileged group of sentences in my repertoire of valued self-descriptions must be true of something—my "self," or my actual full identity, or my fundamental project—in order to be considered basic. They simply need to display a greater degree of functionality, and a greater degree of coherence with other sentences in my self-interpretation, than other sentences. Talk about the basic sentences of a self-interpretation is therefore best construed in terms of horizontal relations between sentences and other sentences, with some sentences happening to be grouped more parsimoniously than others, and some groupings happening to display more adaptive consequences than others. The realist's concept of a determinate thought-independent reality—a "hard, unyielding, *être-en-soi* which stands aloof, sublimely indifferent to the attentions we lavish upon it"—is a philosopher's fiction.[3]

But is this plausible? The concern it raises is that all of our ways of talking about the self are *equally* cut off from the reality they are ostensibly about, because whatever is counted as real is whatever the vocabularies we have chosen to use say is real. But merely saying that something is real does not make it real. Moreover, some ways of talking about the self are undeniably worse than other ways, not merely because of noncognitive considerations such as maladaptivity or empirical inadequacy; it is because they are contaminated with self-deception, self-ignorance, or false consciousness. Can the distinctions these self-relations rest upon—for instance, being deceived about the self versus being knowledgeable—be given up without violating common-sense psychology and the phenomenology of moral experience?

One way to preserve a weakened version of realism is to hold that some vocabularies are more in touch with the real because they are more successful than others at predicting, controlling, or adapting to the vicissitudes of the environment. This view is intelligible on the assumption that comparison-establishing terms such as *better* or *worse* can be applied across alternative vocabularies of the self without question-begging assumptions about criteriological validity. Along these lines it could be argued that the vocabulary that pictures the mind as an information-processing system is more in touch with the real nature of the mind than a demonological vocabulary, because it is better at predicting and coping with the phenomena of mental disorders. On similar grounds, it might be argued that a self-description that is the product of rationally guided and consensually supported self-inquiry is more in touch with the real nature of the self than one that is driven by private fantasy, historical revisionism, or self-deception, because it is better at coping with the immediate social environment. The noncognitive criteria to which these comparative evaluations might appeal in establishing what counts as better or worse levels of coping include the vocabulary's theoretical economy, its consistency, its intuitive plausibility, and its internal coherence.

To be fully consistent, however, Rorty cannot allow that such operators as predictive success and coping are sufficient to establish one vocabulary as "closer to the real" than any other vocabulary. This is because the criteria that establish what counts as successful (versus unsuccessful) coping are themselves internal to the vocabularies in question, which in turn are uniquely fitted to the action demands of the social environments they serve. Sense can be made of these operators only in terms of a particular vocabulary and the set of practices embedding it; but it is senseless to suppose that there is some external vantage point that affords comparison of "language-as-a-whole in relation to something else for which it is a means to an end."4 While it is a natural temptation to regard the most recent vocabularies for making sense of selves as "better in the sense that they *seem* better than their predecessors," the appearance of progress is neither necessary nor sufficient to establish their transhistorical validity. But the problem with criteriological internalism such as this is that while it allows vocabularies a very significant degree of autonomy, it is only at the cost of granting to them an unwanted degree of uncriticizability. Very little could count as a non-question-begging criticism of an alternative vocabulary's standards of coping, thereby raising concerns about the very possibility of distinguishing between better and worse vocabularies.

Applied to the self, Rorty's position might be called "constitutive textualism": that is, the vocabularies that are adopted to make sense of internal and external environments are constitutive of the self, rather than representations that either converge upon or diverge from an antecedently given self. This has important implications for the concept of agency. If the changes that vocabularies undergo occasion changes in the selves they constitute, then it seems reasonable to suppose that some forms of self-transformation can be initiated from the inside simply by the deliberate adoption of new vocabularies. Rorty suggests as much: a human being is "a self-changing being, *capable of remaking himself by remaking his speech*." This textualist conception of agency is intended to fill in the space once occupied by the concept of substance in early modern philosophy, and by the concept of the abstract moral agent in Kantian and Rawlsian moral theory. Persons are perpetually self-weaving webs of beliefs and desires, but there is neither a substantial self nor an abstract moral agent "behind" these webs, to which ownership could be imputed in the same way that properties are ascribed to substance, and by means of which the identity of persons over time could be underwritten. A person "is a network that is constantly reweaving itself in the usual Quinean manner—that is to say not by reference to general criteria (e.g. 'rules of meaning' or 'moral criteria') but in the hit-or-miss way in which cells readjust themselves to meet the pressures of the environment."5

It might seem that this characterization of persons as *self*-weaving webs of beliefs and desires is circular, because it smuggles in the very concept of self that it is Rorty's goal to establish: *who* or *what* carries out this weaving, if it is not the self? Such would be the view of a traditional "Philosophical" interpretation: there must be a self—or a "master weaver"—that remains distinct from the materials undergoing reweaving. But this, Rorty argues, is a distinction (and a collection of metaphors) that serves no purpose. The self is *only* a network that weaves and reweaves itself; there is nothing behind or above the activity of weaving—no substrate-self or transcendental self—that initiates the weaving without itself being implicated in that activity. This point is crucial to Rorty's deconstruction of traditional "Philosophical" conceptions of the self, but it is counterintuitive and, as will be argued later, phenomenologically unrealistic. One of the prevalent distinctions in commonsense psychology, as well as in phenomenological psychology, is the distinction between the self as agent and the passing states, actions, and traits of character attributed to the self. Generally, the self is regarded as something more unified and stable than the aggregate of particular states that configures and reconfigures over time; it is that in virtue of which these states belong to something or someone, and that in virtue of which they are more or less unified. One reason this distinction has taken hold in commonsense psychology is the phenomenon of reflexive agency. Selves have the capacity to identify with or disavow some of the states attributed to them, while selecting and organizing them in ways that were not originally given. Selves, in other words, are agents, because they are constituted in part by their actions upon themselves, and by the awareness they have of those actions as their own.

Rorty's concept of the self, however, undermines the commonsense conception of agency. His view is that selfhood is something that *happens* blindly and passively to organisms: the weaving and reweaving that make selves what they are occurs in "the hit-or-miss way in which cells readjust themselves to meet the pressures of the environment."[6] This is problematic. It fails to explain how the more or less unified sense of agency that is a central component of the phenomenology of selfhood can be developed from such an unpromising starting point as a transient and passively formed nexus of beliefs and desires. If this were an accurate account of the origin of human agency, then it could be expected that in conditions in which the external pressures of the social and natural environments are themselves transitory and conflicting, the resulting selves would be transitory and conflicting. Selves would develop into amoeboid creatures, merely reflecting the external influences of the changing environment, and failing to develop the robustly articulated structures of character, motivation, and cognition that give to selves a well-defined inner cohesiveness. But with certain exceptions, selves remain more or less integrated despite the external pressures that would fragment them.

There are two further problems compounding this one. First, if selfhood is something that happens passively to organisms, then it is unclear what conditions would have to hold in order for agent-designating moral concepts such as responsibility and blame to be ascribed to selves. Networks that merely adjust passively to their environments are no more regarded as satisfying the conditions for the ascription of agency and moral responsibility than are amoebas adjusting to the haphazard pressures of their immediate environments. One of the necessary conditions for the assignment of moral responsibility to an agent includes the conscious performance of an action; another condition is the recognition that an action is one's own. Under these conditions, persons who are acting by chance, or unconsciously, or in passive response to the environment, are not held fully responsible for what they do. In the face of this criticism, one strategy Rorty might adopt to preserve some degree of compatibility between the concept of the passive self and the concept of responsibility for self would be to hold that talk about responsibility is itself just one more vocabulary for coping with the environment. Self-ascriptions of responsibility and blame do not refer to deep moral properties; they represent yet another way in which networks of beliefs and desires can readjust themselves in random cell-like ways to meet the pressures of their immediate environments. This leveling move, however, would weaken the concept of responsibility for self to a point where it could simply be dropped for reasons of moral convenience.

Second, if selfhood is something that happens passively to organisms, then it is doubtful if Rorty's normative ideal of self-enlargement is realizable. A self whose configuration is so extensively dependent upon the vagaries of environmental pressures would not be capable of the kind of deliberate and self-directed experimentation with new forms of self-weaving that is the mark of authentic self-enlargement. If this experimentation were itself the organism's manner of passively adjusting to its environment, then any accomplishments in self-understanding would amount to after-the-fact rationalizations for what would *happen to* selves anyways. What would appear to be the active experimentation on the self by the self would in fact be the passive adaptation of a cell-like network to the vicissitudes of the environment.

IRONISM AND SELF-ENLARGEMENT

Despite their differences, Hampshire, Sartre, and Rorty share the view that the self is more like an open-ended process than a determinate object. They also share the view that the ways of describing the self are inexhaustible. To suppose that one form of description enjoys a privileged authority in relation to the question "Who am I?" is to fall prey to what Nietzsche calls a craving for metaphysical comfort, and what Sartre calls the spirit of seriousness: viz., a desire to finalize inquiry, to close off potentially destabilizing challenges, and to be bound by a privileged set of descriptions. Where Hampshire, Sartre, and Rorty differ, however, is on the question of the appropriate stance that should be adopted toward the open-ended nature of self-knowledge. What reflective attitude and character ideal, to be implemented in matters of moral conduct and practical reasoning, would be consistent with the fact that there is no way to underwrite the ongoing and self-modifying nature of reflective self-inquiry in terms of a transhistorical account of the self?

Rorty considers the "syncretic, ironic, nominalist intellectual" as the ideal of such a moral personality. This is a person who is "ironic, playful, free and inventive in [his or her] . . . choice of self-descriptions," who treats all vocabularies of the self as tools rather than as mirrors, and who moves fluidly between different vocabularies with the awareness that none delivers a final truth about the self. If the ironic intellectual can be described (without inconsistency) as committed to any stance, it is to experimentalism combined with aestheticism. The ironic nominalist satisfies three conditions: "1) She has radical and continuing doubts about the final vocabulary she currently uses because she has been impressed by other vocabularies, vocabularies taken as final by people or books she has encountered; 2) she realizes that argument phrased in her current vocabulary can neither underwrite nor dissolve these doubts; 3) insofar as she philosophizes about her situation, she does not think that vocabulary is closer to reality than others, that it is in touch with a power not herself."[7]

Irony and playfulness are unusual attitudes to adopt in response to the open-ended nature of the self, and to the inexhaustibility of self-description. First, they would be difficult attitudes to implement as logically self-consistent policies of thought and action, given that the ironist's radical doubts about all vocabularies should apply also to the vocabulary in which those doubts are themselves formulated. But this would result in a doubt that cancels itself out. Rorty might evade this difficulty by construing the ideal of the ironic intellectual not as a substantive ideal that mirrors some deep truth about the human condition, but as a formal ideal requiring a highly refined sense of reflexivity; that is, an ideal requiring the ironist to be ironic even about the ironic outlook, and to consider the vocabulary by means of which the ironic stance is actualized as yet another tool that might be dropped, rather as one might throw away a ladder after climbing it. This would meet the demands of logical consistency, but it would also leave the ironist without a satisfactory reason as to why such an ideal (rather than any other) ought to be adopted in the first place.

Second, it would be more psychologically realistic, and more consistent with the tradition that views self-knowledge as critique, to suppose that the realization of the absence of any finality in reflective self-inquiry has the potential to occasion a certain degree of existential confusion or despair. But the ironist remains ironic and playful in the face of such hard truths. In reflecting upon the question "Who am I?" the ironist celebrates the fact that what currently counts as "normal" discourse about the self is no more than a transitory moment in an ongoing conversation that has no transhistorical significance. The ironist's goal is "self-enlargement" for its own sake, rather than for the sake of extrinsic goals such as virtue, authenticity, or freedom. It is the goal of multiplying vocabularies, playing with self-descriptions, and refusing in the spirit of ironic detachment to identify with any single self-description as the final story of the self.

The concept of self-enlargement is Rorty's neopragmatist interpretation of Nietzsche's radical revisionism. Both Rorty and Nietzsche regard fundamental religious, moral, and metaphysical beliefs—including those that have a central role in shaping the self—as no more than temporary tools for coping with the world; and both regard these beliefs as likely candidates for revision and replacement with other equally temporary tools. But Nietzsche, unlike Rorty, remains concerned about the ever-present possibility of self-deception and self-alienation that follows upon the realization of hard truths such as these: for example, escaping into metaphysically consoling practices of secular salvation that mimic otherworldly salvation. In this regard his views are more psychologically realistic than Rorty's, highlighting as they do the importance of existential and moral courage, and the various forms of cowardice and flight that such realizations tend to occasion.

Where Rorty considers the occasion for revision of any one vocabulary of the self to be no more than the ongoing movement of the conversation of humankind, Nietzsche considers it to be the corrosive effects of the passage of time, particularly in light of the realization of the truth of the eternal recurrence. However deeply committed I am to a particular vocabulary of the self, there will always be some future vantage point from which I can look back upon it and regard it as inconsequential, in the same way that as an adult I look back with mild amusement upon the childhood toys I once coveted so fiercely. But the relinquishing of the toys of childhood is not a kind of epistemic ground-clearing work that serves as preparation for convergence upon some higher truth: it is simply a matter of picking up newer (but not necessarily better or more truthful) toys in an ever-renewed spirit of playfulness, with the awareness that the serial progression of toys marks out not some form of progress, but more drifting. Nietzschean wisdom consists in rediscovering and revaluing the seriousness I had as a child, at play.[8] "Perhaps the day will come when the most solemn concepts which have caused the most fights and suffering, the concepts 'God' and 'sin,' will seem no more important to us than a child's toy and child's pain seem to the old—and perhaps 'the old' will then be in need of another toy and another pain—still children enough, eternal children."[9]

Like Rorty's ironists, Nietzsche's free spirits delight as much in the proliferation of new perspectives as do children in the proliferation of new toys. But there are significant differences between the two ideals, especially in the attitudes they adopt toward the ultimate ontological groundlessness of the entire process of rediscovery and revaluation. First, Nietzsche refuses to give up the idea that some forms of life, and some kinds of self-formation, are better or worse than others. His exhortation "Become who you are!" which prefigures the existentialist's concern with authenticity, presupposes some form of distinction between a true self and a false self. With the overwhelming forces of herd morality, and the intoxicating forms of life denial associated with retreat into the otherworldly, there are for Nietzsche many ways to become lost from the self that one is or can become.[10] The distinction between alienated and unalienated selves is not unproblematic in Nietzsche's philosophy, given his rejection of the substantialist and essentialist concepts of self, but it is clear that Rorty's rejection of *any* form of distinction between a higher and lower self, and his rejection of all forms of "self-purification," are not compatible with the Nietzschean distinction.

Second, Nietzsche is skeptical about the value of irony as a stance worthy of cultivation by free spirits who have embraced a postphilosophical spirit of playfulness. The ironic attitude that is for Rorty an ideal of personality is for Nietzsche a failure of courage in the face of the difficult task of self-creation that follows upon owning up to the truth of the eternal recurrence.[11] Ironic detachment is an attitude that leads to a clever but ultimately egoistic outlook that undermines the vital life forces that are needed to take decisive action. By regarding all higher ideals as transient and ultimately contingent constructions, the consistent ironist will not be able to engage in projects of self-creation with the commitment that is necessary for carrying them through to completion. "An age acquires the dangerous disposition of irony with regard to itself, and from this the still more dangerous one of cynicism: in this, however, it ripens even more into clever egoistic practice through which the vital strength is paralyzed and finally destroyed."[12] The free spirits that are Nietzsche's ideal are beyond irony. They pursue new self-interpretations not for the sake of the pursuit itself, or for the sake of keeping the conversation going, but for the sake of achieving a mode of life that is the best for them. Because so much is at stake in their pursuit, and because there are so many ways they may go wrong, they are unable to remain ironic and detached. The distinction between better and worse forms of life, and better and worse self-interpretations, is operative in Nietzsche's account of the self in a way that it cannot be in Rorty's account.

AUTHENTICITY AND SELF-PURIFICATION

Rorty's account of self-knowledge faces similar difficulties in its attempt to appropriate existential philosophy's theme of radical contingency while dropping its distinction between authentic and inauthentic forms of life: viz., a psychologically unrealistic account of the subject's reaction to hard existential truths, and an underestimation of the forces that lead to self-alienation.

By rejecting vertical metaphors of depth, integration, and centering in favor of horizontal metaphors of play and proliferation, Rorty attempts to distance himself from Sartre and Heidegger's ideal of authenticity, which rests on the distinction between authentic and inauthentic modes of existence, and the possibility of the eradication of bad faith and "seriousness." Rorty describes this ideal as falling within the tradition of the ethics of "self-purification," which, like the Platonic model of the self from which it is ostensibly derived, is an ideal devoted to "identifying our true, human self and expelling, curbing, or ignoring the animal self." Self-purification is "a desire to slim down, to peel away everything that is accidental, to will one thing, to intensify, to become a simpler and more transparent being."[13] This is a misleading characterization, because it conflates a number of important claims that in existential philosophy are kept distinct. First, the distinction between the so-called true self and the animal self is unlike the distinction between authenticity and inauthenticity, which marks out possible modes of *existing* rather than determinate kinds of selves. Inauthentic modes of existence are characterized inter alia by conformity, distraction, a sense of directionlessness, and the systematic evasion or cover-up of ontologically significant issues. An authentic existence, by contrast, is characterized by lucidity about the real nature of the choices that one is always and already exercising with respect to one's fundamental life possibilities. This brings with it an integration of one's project, an intensification of one's relation to existence, and a greater degree of clarity about one's responsibility for self. Authenticity, in other words, is not the discovery of a "higher" or "true" self but the lucid acceptance of fundamental ontological truths about the relation between having a self and having to be.

Second, it is misleading to characterize the existential self-determination that is expressed in the radical choice of self as a form of simplification (e.g., "slimming down, peeling away") when weighed against the manifold anxieties that come with the assumption of existential responsibility. In many respects the development of a lucid awareness of the possibilities of being is a more complex and more demanding form of existence than an existence based on self-deception and bad faith; there is more at stake, and more that can be lost, than what is given in the inauthentic mode of existence, which characteristically levels down and oversimplifies all that is outstanding. Despite the mischaracterization of existential self-determination, Rorty's point in using the image of self-purification is clear: it is to sharpen its contrast with the ideal of self-enlargement, while refusing to allow that self-knowledge can be an existentially destabilizing force. Self-enlargement is "the desire to embrace more and more possibilities, to be constantly learning, to give oneself over entirely to curiosity, to end by having envisaged all the possibilities of the past and of the future. . . . [It is] the life that seeks to extend its own bound rather than find its center."14

Rorty thus rejects the idea defended by Sartre and other existential philosophers that the fundamental character of the relation of human beings to their existence involves a struggle for integration against the forces of disintegration and self-alienation. There are only different vocabularies and different forms of self-weaving, some more expansive than others and some less. The existential vocabulary represents only one more way of coping with the vicissitudes of the environment, but it is no more privileged in giving us an account of the human condition than any other vocabulary. This is a leveling move. What for the existentialist is an inauthentic mode of being manifested in moral conduct as evasiveness, flight, and distraction, is for Rorty one experiment with self-descriptions among others. The crucial operators in the existentialist vocabulary that serve as the high point of existential ethics—authenticity and lucidity—are for Rorty no more than tools around which certain contingent practices are constituted; they do not point beyond themselves to certain deep facts about human beings or the human condition. A human life is not something that can attain a degree of authentic wholeness or integration, because there is nothing to complete or integrate: there is only a web of relations to be woven and rewoven, "a tissue of contingent relations, a web which stretches backward and forward through past and future time." A human life is not "something capable of being seen steady and whole."[15]

Rorty's rejection of the distinction between authentic and inauthentic forms of self-understanding has a number of problematic moral consequences regarding responsibility for self, a concept that for Sartre and other existential philosophers has paramount importance. Because Sartrean selves exist without appeal to or grounding from any authority higher than their own, they carry the full burden of responsibility for their actions and way of being, including those events that befall them. This is accompanied by the anguishing awareness that there are no legitimate exempting or excusing conditions to which they can appeal to ease their burden. By contrast, Rortyean selves are free to reconfigure or evade the burden of responsibility by experimenting with alternative vocabularies that allow them to redescribe the conditions under which moral responsibility and blame can be ascribed.

By relativizing the truth criteria for self-descriptions to personally chosen vocabularies, the logical and referential stability of agent-designating moral concepts such as responsibility, desert, and punishment is undermined. If there is no independent backdrop against which to assess the rival truths of alternative self-descriptions, then the self-ascription of responsibility or blame can become a matter of moral convenience. Consider for example what happens when I reflect on the meaning of a sequence of actions in which I engaged as a young man—say, my engaging in civil disobedience to protest an unjust war. Was this, I ask myself now, an act of youthful idealism, an act of courage, or sheer folly? The point of reflecting on my past self is to discover what really happened, and to describe as faithfully as possible my actions, reasons, and motives as they were at the time of their occurrence. If Rorty is correct, then the goal of isolating the original actions and intentions from later interpretive overlays, which are necessarily framed in terms of a particular vocabulary, is incoherent. The meaning of the actions can only be determined in the present, with reference to my current vocabulary; there is no further fact to which I might appeal to

settle conflicting accounts. But this means that the description of the original actions suffers a kind of referential indeterminacy, because with enough
adjustments in the relevant vocabulary, I am free to redescribe the actions in
such a way that they happen to fall outside of the continuum of blamewor-
thy or praiseworthy actions: they become morally neutral events. But this
places the practice of experimental self-description on the same epistemically slippery slope as Stalinist history writing: the redescription of the self,
like the rewriting of the Soviet Encyclopedia, permits me to correct fortune
by remaking history. If the force of these moral distinctions is to be
preserved, then answers to such questions as "What really motivated me at
the time?" and to broader questions such as "Who was I then?" cannot be
framed on the basis of personally convenient epistemic practices. The
answers must be geared to the discovery of my actual, rather than notional
or textual, identity.

THE MOST DISENCHANTING OF SCIENCES

It should be obvious that Rorty's view that every form of self-understanding
is simply one more variation in an endless series of self-weavings has pro-
nounced leveling effects in ethics, psychology, and social and political philosophy. It should also be obvious that while it is critical of conventional ways of
making sense of the self, it seeks to avoid the negative psychological and existential destabilization that accompanies more traditional forms of philosophical critique. The combination of deconstructive leveling and psychological
preservation is particularly evident in Rorty's interpretation of classical psychoanalytic psychotherapy, another area in which the pursuit of self-
knowledge has immediate and pressing practical consequences.

Freud, as is well known, considered psychoanalysis to be "the most disenchanting of sciences,"[16] its disturbing discoveries about the weakness of the
conscious self vis-à-vis the forces of the unconscious locating it in the same
tradition of conceptual decentering as the discoveries of Copernicus and
Darwin.[17] Self-alienation, according to Freud, is a given of human psychology: humans are neither masters of their own house nor transparent to the
motives driving them to act as they do. "In every case . . . the news that
reaches your consciousness is incomplete and often not to be relied on. Often
enough, too, it happens that you get news of events only when they are over
and when you can no longer do anything to change them. Even if you are not
ill, who can tell all that is stirring in your mind of which you know nothing

or are falsely informed? You behave like an absolute ruler who is content with the information supplied him by his highest officials and never goes among the people to hear their voice. Turn your eyes inward, look into your own depths, learn first to know yourself!"[18]

Rorty rejects the interpretation of the unconscious as a source of self-alienation. Instead, he interprets Freud's partitioning of the self into conscious and unconscious dimensions as an anti-essentialist way of talking about minds in terms of multiple person-analogues, each one of which consists of internally coherent clusters of beliefs and desires.[19] "Each of these quasi-persons is . . . a part of a single unified *causal* network, but not of a single person (since the criterion for individuation of a person is a certain minimal coherence among its beliefs and desires)." While the notion of minimal coherence remains ambiguous, Rorty's intention is to leave open the possibility that the same human body can play host to two or more numerically distinct persons, thereby violating the commonsense equation that holds that there is one self per one body per one person. But what is the point of this reinterpretation of the unconscious? The point is to demonstrate that the conscious self is no more the true or higher self than the unconscious self is the false or lower self. Rorty replaces the traditional view of the unconscious as a destructive hidden economy of irrational instinctual energies with the view of the unconscious as a witty "conversational partner" that consists of "one or more well-articulated systems of beliefs and desires, systems that are just as complex, sophisticated, and internally consistent as the normal adult's conscious beliefs and desires." To be divested of the distinctions between a higher and a lower nature, and a rational versus irrational center of agency, requires seeing our unconscious selves not as "dumb, sullen, lurching brutes, but rather [as] intellectual peers of our conscious selves, possible conversational partners for those selves."[20]

This allows for an unusual reinterpretation of the psychoanalytic concept of self-knowledge. Hampshire, it will be recalled, regards the ideal of self-knowledge in the practice of psychoanalysis as the acquisition of a veridical insight into the causes of destructive neuroses. The more that subjects come to learn about the unconscious forces governing their lives, the more they are in a position to control them. By contrast, Rorty regards psychoanalytically driven self-knowledge as no more than the enlargement of the conversation one has with oneself, with the unconscious standing in as a newfound interlocutor to help carry the conversation forward. Psychoanalytic psychotherapy is not a matter of achieving a degree of rational self-control through veridical self-knowledge, but "a matter of getting acquainted with one or more crazy quasi-people, listening to their crazy accounts of how things are, seeing why they hold the crazy views they do, and learning something from them. It will be a matter of self-enrichment."[21]

There are two difficulties with Rorty's interpretation of the unconscious as a "sensitive, whacky, backstage partner who feeds us our best lines."[22] First, it underestimates the degree to which the unconscious is a source of suffering and inner division. A Rortyean refitting of the clinical dimension of psychoanalysis, transforming clinical work from an intense struggle over the psychological well-being of the analysand into a tame pursuit centered on the witty bickering of conversational partners, trivializes the intense need felt by analysands to overcome their suffering and replace it with some degree of inner harmony. Rorty's conception of the goal of psychoanalytic self-enlargement is more egalitarian than the traditional therapeutic goal of controlling one part of the self, the unconscious, by another, the conscious. It involves treating the different accounts told by the conscious self and the unconscious as *equally* intelligible and internally consistent stories. Neither one provides a privileged answer to such questions as "Why am I acting this way?" or "What really did happen to me in the past?" To accept this revision is to recognize that "the choice of a vocabulary in which to describe either one's childhood or one's character cannot be made by inspecting some collection of 'neutral facts' (e.g., a complete videotape of one's life history). . . . [To] say that all the parts of the soul are equally plausible candidates is to discredit the idea of a 'true self' and the idea of 'the true story about how things are.' . . . Maturity will, according to this view, consist rather in an ability to seek out new redescriptions of one's own past—an ability to take a nominalistic, ironic, view of oneself."[23]

It is doubtful if this view of psychoanalytic psychotherapy can be applied in clinical practice without inducing iatrogenic effects. Psychotherapy of any form is a volatile enterprise. In psychoanalytic psychotherapy in particular, powerful psychological pressures are deployed to break down the analysand's habitual coping mechanisms and defenses. The introduction of ironist and nominalist ideas as part of the treatment method adds another layer of complexity to the analytic process, and another layer of powerful emotional and intellectual stressors. For analysands who do not have well-integrated selves, exposure to these ideas may exacerbate latent tendencies toward psychological fragmentation.[24] For analysands with well-integrated selves, the cultivation of these attitudes must be weighed against the risks of promoting highly intellectualized rationalizations of underlying behavioral or psycho-logical problems. With suggestible clients, for instance, the risk of ideational overlays—overlays that masquerade as insight into the groundlessness of self-interpretation—might result in false memories or temporarily reassuring self-misinterpretations that interfere with genuine therapeutic improvement. In the psychoanalytic context, analysands are vulnerable and their successes fragile. Powerful nonspecific mechanisms and pressures (e.g., placebo effects, client suggestibility, self-validating insights, emotional involvement, and seduction by a technical discourse) are already at work before the effects of any specific theoretical framework have been felt. To complicate an already volatized situation with an ironist framework is to increase exponentially the number of ways of falling into the trap of therapeutically induced self-deception and illusion.

PLAYING WITH IDENTITY

Urlaub vom Leben: *The Psychology of a Master of the Hovering Life*

The leveling effects brought by Rorty's theory of the self to the existential theory of contingency, and to the psychoanalytic theory of the unconscious, raise an important question: what would it be like to *be* a syncretic, ironic, nominalist intellectual—that is, not simply to elaborate an abstract theory about an ideal form of personality, or to adopt an "as-if" stance toward prac-tical reasoning, but to instantiate the ideal in the context of engaging in everyday moral conduct, participating in interpersonal relations, and formu-lating intentions with a view to action? There are grounds for thinking that the cultivation of a thoroughgoing sense of ironic detachment would gener-ate complex psychological and phenomenological artifacts that would not otherwise have occurred, which would result in the development of an artifactual self that is overlaid upon and fused with the pre-artifactual self in much the same way that confabulated memories are overlaid upon and fused with original memories. The phenomenology of the artifactual self would appear to be just as real as the phenomenology of the preartifactual self, but it would instantiate the phenomenology predicted by the theory, such that cer-tain experiences would conform to the contours of the psychological theory that explains them through mimicking the theory's *explananda*. The degree to which the phenomenology of the artifactual self is confounded with the phenomenology of the preartifactual self is often such that it is not possible to distinguish clearly what is antecedently given from what is adventitious.

Some aspects of the artifactual self would also display unusual properties that tend to go against the phenomenological grain: notably, a sense of the lightness of being oneself (i.e., a sense of disconnection, and a fading of the feelings of self-regard and self-identification), and an unrealistic sense of the fungibility of lived time (i.e., a sense of the revocability of all events). These are theory-driven artifacts, rather than basic properties of the experience of being a self in time; and they are derived from and intelligible in terms of the more primordial experience of self-ownership. An evocative literary portrait of how some of these artifacts come to be produced by the cultivation of an ironic attitude is found in Robert Musil's novel *The Man without Qualities*. Ulrich, the novel's central character, satisfies most of the conditions of Rorty's ideal: he is reflective, detached, and ironical; he has materialist and nominalist leanings; he is skeptical about the unity and substantiality of the self; he experiments with different forms of self-understanding; and he makes himself highly suggestible or autosuggestible through his reflexive experimentation.

Ulrich's first appearance in the novel is symbolic of the experimentalist outlook. Standing at the window of his house, he is engaged in a "time-and-motion" study of the patterns of traffic flow and pedestrian movement on the street below him. "For the last ten minutes, watch in hand, he had been counting the cars, carriages, and trams, and the pedestrians' faces, blurred by distance, all of which filled the network of his gaze with a whirl of hurrying forms. He was estimating the speed, the angle, the dynamic force of masses being propelled past."[25] From the point of view of the person in the street the scene is a familiar and meaningful environment, but to Ulrich it is the place where law-like patterns of nature are instantiated. The glass window through which he looks symbolizes his detachment from the world, and his inability to reconcile scientific objectivity with human-scaled meanings.

The first part of the novel traces Ulrich's attempt to take what he calls a leave from life *(Urlaub vom Leben)*, an experiment in which he tries to live as if he were not actively engaged in life, and as if all the actions he initiates are equally revocable. It is a "life between intellectual brackets," a "hovering life,"[26] much like the life of Rorty's ironic intellectual who experiments with new vocabularies without becoming attached to any single one. It is through this experimentation that a number of identity-constitutive artifacts are generated that, from his perspective, appear to reveal the real nature of the self, but which are in fact no more than the psychological and phenomenological residue of his theoretical outlook. Predictably, the experiment eventually comes to a halt because of the psychological crisis it provokes.

The experiment takes its inspiration from Ulrich's nominalist belief that the concepts of sameness, unity, and identity are constructions imposed by the mind upon phenomena that are in actuality constantly conjoined and numerically distinct.[27] This is not a theory he merely happens to hold as an intellectual commitment: he believes it is true of the concepts of self and character—including, precisely, his own self and character. During the experiment Ulrich actually experiences himself as arbitrary and centerless. When he utters the word "I," he feels it refers only to temporary complexes of memories, moods, and feelings, contingently affixed to a particular body, and displaying only a relative constancy over time. Because it is only a matter of chance that he is identified by this particular configuration rather than any other, he feels that his experiences do not "belong" to him in quite the right way: a sense of ownership is missing. "There has arisen a world of qualities without a man to them, of experiences without anyone to experience them, and it almost looks as though under ideal conditions man would no longer experience anything at all privately and the comforting weight of personal responsibility would dissolve into a system of formulae for potential meanings."[28]

Ulrich attempts to supply some justification for his unusual experience of self by appealing to modern physical science, which he believes has demonstrated that human personality is no more than the shifting sum total of the effects of external and subpersonal causes impinging blindly upon loosely organized organisms. "The personality is losing the significance that it has had up to now as a sovereign issuing edicts from on high. We are coming to understand its evolution according to the pattern imposed upon it, we are coming to understand the influence its environment has on it, the types according to which it is constructed, its disappearance in moments of intense activity—in short, the laws regulating its formation and its behaviour. Just think—the laws of the personality . . . ! For since laws are . . . the most impersonal thing there is in the world, the personality will soon be no more than an imaginary meeting-point for all that is impersonal, and it will be difficult to find for it the honourable standpoint that you don't want to do without."[29]

The arbitrariness of personality is revealed to Ulrich during certain moods of uncanniness, when he becomes aware of the stark contingency of existing, and the contingency of the fact that he is himself and not someone else.[30] In these moods he experiences himself as light and insubstantial. Sensations and thoughts cross his field of awareness without his feeling toward them any

sense of ownership. They weave and reweave themselves in endlessly config-
urable ways, without a central anchor point. Similarly, character traits such as
"shy" or "generous" have for Ulrich only an apparent permanence, changing
with changes in external circumstance, and with changes in the descriptions
under which they are identified. Subjectively, he feels that he is "as far from
all the qualities as he [is] near to them, and that all of them, whether they had
become his own or not, in some strange way were equally a matter of indifference to him." As there is no single set of fixed traits that Ulrich calls his
own, which would serve to ground emotions of self-regard and feelings of
self-identification, he lacks a sense of "ownness" *(eigenschaft)*. Like Rorty's
ironic nominalist intellectuals, who regard themselves as the placeholders for
changing vocabularies, Ulrich thinks of his identity as nothing more than a
placeholder for transitory configurations of floating particles of sensation and
emotion. "To his own way of feeling he was tall, his shoulders were broad, his
chest expanded like a filled sail from the mast, and the joints of his body fas-
tened his muscles off like small links of steel whenever he was angry or quar-
relsome. . . . On the other hand he was slim, lightly built, dark, and soft as a
jelly-fish floating in water whenever he was reading a book that moved him
or was touched by a breath of that great homeless love whose presence in the
world he had never been able to fathom."[31]

Ulrich's experience contrasts sharply with the phenomenology of the prereflective and preartifactual experience of the self, one of the core components of which is the phenomenon of self-ownership. The experience of
being a self is constituted by the experience of one's body, sensations, and
thoughts as one's own, as if there is a constant and tacit "adhesion" of the self
to its various parts and states.[32] It is in virtue of this self-relation that there is
never any need, when experiencing events or initiating actions, to think "X is
happening—but I wonder if it is *I* who am experiencing it?" Normally, it is
only in moments of depersonalization or "proprio-blindness"[33] that the
bonds that connect me to my primary action-guiding sense of self are
thinned, and I experience myself in a passive and derealized mode. But the
phenomenology of disconnection can also be generated by theoretically
driven experimentation of the sort performed by Ulrich, resulting in complex
phenomenological artifacts and reflective debris. Ulrich's sense of himself as
traitless is a function of a notional self that has been overlaid upon his preartifactual self in a way that makes it seem that the experiment is uncovering
significant truths. But these results are so contaminated with the nominalist

theory of the self to which they conform that some of the artifacts vanish with the cessation of the experiment.

The sense of self-ownership that Ulrich acutely lacks is not the result of thought or reflection. It has its source in bodily sensation, kinesthesis, and proprioception, somatic dimensions of experience that are not originally linguistic in nature and that do not presuppose mastery of any form of vocabulary.[34] Beginning in infancy, proprioception and kinesthesis provide the basis for accurate bodily self-awareness, boundedness, and a sense of somatic self-ownership. Phenomenologists from William James to Maurice Merleau-Ponty, describing the variously nuanced configurations of the phenomenology of self-ownership, have identified a fundamental difference between seeing the body from the outside, as one object among the range of objects in the world, and the feeling of its being one's own. Ulrich's uncanniness about being himself is a function of his seeing and treating his body as if from the outside, as if it were an object. He lacks what James calls the feelings of "warmth," "familiarity," and "appropriation" that constitute the sense of personal identity, and that come to the fore only when they encounter some form of breakdown.[35]

THE LIGHTNESS OF BEING IN TIME

One of the curious phenomenological artifacts resulting from the cultivation of ironic detachment is the altered experience of the passage of time. Ulrich's sensitivity to the permanent possibility of redescription of all events gives him the feeling that no single episode in his life is inscribed absolutely onto the face of time. He experiences a sense of the *lightness* of being in time, and this contributes to his inability to identify wholeheartedly with any single project of lasting duration. With the inexhaustibility of description comes a certain relativization of the described events vis-à-vis one another: none can be accorded privileged status as, for instance, turning points, terminations, starting points, or "moments of truth." As can be expected of Rorty's ironists, Ulrich's experimentally driven narratives are amorphous and endlessly erasable.

The experience of the fungibility of time can be understood on the analogy with playing a game. In some games, moves can be taken back, suspended, or replayed without affecting the game's momentum and buoyancy: the moves do not obey the principle of temporal irrevocability. Similarly, ironists who experiment with their identity experience the events that constitute their lives as revocable, and subject to indefinite erasure or redescription. Subjectively, it is as if moments brush by them lightly, without the protentional pull of the future and the retentional pull of the past, and without leaving indelible imprints. This is the case for Ulrich, who does not experience the urgency that attaches to action in the world, but rather has a constant sense of floating lightly over the succession of present moments, while remaining equally distanced from each one. "We infinitely overvalue the present moment, the sense of the present, the Here and Now. I mean, the way you and I are here together now in this valley, as though we had been put into a basket and the lid of the moment had fallen shut. We overvalue that. . . . The world itself isn't so very whole-heartedly what it's pretending to be at this moment. . . . The feeling of having firm ground underfoot and a firm skin all round, which seems so natural to most people, is not very strongly developed in me."36 Ulrich has reshaped his experience of time in such a way that he has overcome the need for timely answers, and the need for closure, that normally accompanies the awareness of being in a finite period of time, with an ever-dwindling fund of moments. It is as if he is unaware that the life he is leading is the one life that is his to lead; and that with each step forward into his life history he is directly or indirectly working out the questions "Who am I?" and "How do I want to live?"

Ulrich's attenuated sense of being in time is most clearly illustrated in his attitude to Moosbrugger, a deranged murderer whose trial he has been following with curiosity. Moosbrugger displays precisely the kind of primordial intensity of moment-to-moment experience that Ulrich lacks. Ulrich examines the murder and Moosbrugger's motives from a number of perspectives, each time viewing them under alternative descriptions. But as each description cancels out the other, he ends up feeling neither anger nor pity toward Moosbrugger, nor compelled to do anything for or against him. His views, he tells himself, are merely speculations, not objective facts; and as no view emerges as truer, or better, than any other view, the conditions under which he could engage in definite action are systematically canceled out.

From a phenomenological point of view, however, Ulrich's experience of the fungibility of time is more an artifact of a highly reflective experimental attitude than a fundamental structural feature of the experience of time. It is no less real as an experience, but it would not have arisen independently of the experimental stance he has adopted in trying to live a hovering life; and the ostensible truths it reveals about the nature of time are in fact no more than the residue of the theoretical outlook, which distorts the more primordial dimension of the experience of the nonfungibility of time. The events constituting a life cannot be taken back or replayed differently, as moves in games can be.[37] Once they occur, they are permanently inscribed on the face of history, and remain resistant to decomposition or erasure. Neither the passing of time, nor ex post facto redescription, reduces once-occurrent events to nothing, or to something less than real; nothing has the power to make them not have been. Thus the mere cessation of an event, and its passing from all memory, does not affect the fact of its occurrence. If the once-occurrent events of life are absolute within the movement of history, then the most that redescription or experimentation can do, as Ulrich's experimentation shows, is create an artifactual overlay that masks the prereflective experience of time as nonfungible. Merleau-Ponty captures a sense of the transhistorically absolute character of the elapsed past: "If time is the dimension in accordance with which events drive each other successively from the scene, it is also that in accordance with which each one of them wins its unchallengeable place. To say that an event takes place is to say that it will always be true that it has taken place. Each moment of time, in virtue of its very essence, posits an existence against which the other moments of time are powerless."[38]

This literary example gives some indication of what it might be like to actually be an ironic nominalist intellectual. It shows how the cultivation of the stance of ironic detachment can occasion a wide-ranging alteration of a whole web of feelings of self-concern and feelings of self-identification that have a temporal orientation. Ulrich's experiment, like the experiments with alternative vocabularies performed by Rorty's ironists, has the power to reshape the phenomenological surface, but in ways that distort the phenomenological grain.

RADICAL CHOICE REVISITED

Rorty's theory of the self is based on an unusual linguistic interpretation of the Sartrean theory of radical choice.[39] For Sartre's talk about the radical and criterionless choice of self, Rorty substitutes talk about the radical and criterionless choice of descriptive vocabularies of the self; and for Sartre's talk about the freedom that is manifested in the radical conversion from one fundamental project to another, Rorty substitutes talk about the freedom that is manifested in stepping from one vocabulary into another. But is the concept of choice as a formal ideal of self-enlargement a genuine choice? What turns on it? Without independent constraints on self-description, and independent constraints on the choice of criteria by means of which vocabularies could be judged as lending themselves to bona fide self-enlargement, I would find myself confronted with a limitless array of discursive and textual possibilities, but without a framework to evaluate the relative merits of conflicting options in a non-question-begging manner. Whatever choices I make would be a matter of arbitrarily opting for one particular vocabulary over another, considerations of coping and functionality notwithstanding. But this would incur the same set of problems incurred by Sartre's theory: viz., it would make self-determination an unintelligible and nonrational achievement. If I remake myself by remaking the vocabularies under which I describe myself, then the history of vocabulary changes I undergo is ultimately a history of unintelligible facts. But this stands in sharp contrast with my concern to form self-descriptions that tally with who I am rather than with what my vocabulary says I am, and with my concern to achieve some degree of self-directedness that is more than the mere expression of the transient preferences and biases of my current vocabulary. There can be no lasting reasons for my identity to take the shape that it does, other than those always-revisable reasons supplied from *within* my current vocabulary. Ultimately, then, these facts must be accepted as inexplicable. But this view undermines the idea that I am self-determining, and that I would be capable of making better choices than I have made, or am currently making, in light of greater self-knowledge.

Curiously, there is in Rorty's model of the radical choice of vocabularies a kind of intellectualist subjectivism not unlike that of the Enlightenment project of foundationalist philosophy that is the ultimate target of his deconstruction. Ironic intellectuals (such as Ulrich, the man without qualities) are solitary and disengaged subjects who are set over and against a world that has no intrinsic connection to their sense of self. Their stance toward others, the world, and themselves is one of hovering. Whatever social and material conditioning their personalities and behaviors might have incurred are regarded as accidental features from which they can detach themselves at will, simply through choosing different vocabularies. Nietzsche diagnosed this as the "ascetic ideal." It is as if the only freedom worth wanting for the ironist is the freedom to wear the world like a loose cloak, capable of casting off custom, tradition, and authority at a moment's notice.[40]

6

◀

DIALOGIC
SELF-KNOWING

▶

SOLITARY SELVES

One of the obvious components missing from the three accounts of self-knowledge that have been explored so far is the social and interpersonal dimension of reflective self-inquiry and reflective self-evaluation. Hampshire, Sartre, and Rorty tend to regard the acquisition of self-knowledge as an individual activity: that is, as a struggle of the self with itself, with the goal of casting light either on the causes that make the self what it is, or on the self's relation to being, or on the self's textual nature. In none of the three accounts is the acquisition of self-knowledge viewed as a process involving the self in social activity, such as seeking the advice and feedback of friends, gathering together the character reports of others, cocreating a narrative, or engaging in some form of shared exploratory dialogue. The acquisition of self-knowledge is seen primarily as an activity *of* the self, *by* the self, and *for* the self. It has more in common with a monologue of the self with itself than it has with a dialogue of the self with the other.

The individualist bias here is not altogether implausible. On the surface at least, it seems that nothing could be better known to me than my own self.

No one has better access to the bulk of relevant information about my desires, beliefs, and traits of character than I do, even if there are some truths about me that others see more clearly than I. This is not because I enjoy privileged access to my contemporary states of mind; it is because I enjoy a privileged starting point compared to that of others, because I am both the inquirer and the subject matter upon which the inquiry is directed. The tools that I bring to the task of reflective self-inquiry and reflective self-evaluation, unlike the tools used by others who might claim some expertise in the matter, have the virtue of being similar in kind to the very materials upon which they operate. There is, moreover, no one who is in a better position to raise the question "Who am I?" than I am, because I stand to benefit or lose the most from the success or failure of my self-inquiry.

In addition to these considerations, there are a number of negative reasons why the involvement of others in such an inquiry should be regarded with caution.

First, interpersonal perception is often wildly inaccurate. The other person's perception of me is freighted with cognitive biases, interests, and pre-suppositions. What others take as salient in response to my question "Who am I?" reflects their own strategies in the interpretation of persons and senti-ments; and what they take as carefully considered biographical reports may be unwittingly constrained by the state of the relations currently existing between us. The simplest form of empirical evidence for this is to be found in those cases where different persons describe me in different ways. To one acquaintance I am generous to a fault, to another frugal and reserved; to one acquaintance I appear to be contented with my lot in life, to another I am unhappy and resentful. While it is possible that conditions can be estab-lished under which conflicting descriptions can be adjudicated for their truth value, so that an overall best description may emerge in the long run, the empirical likelihood of agreement is slim. Despite agreement about the skele-tal outline of relevant historical facts, for example, few biographers produce qualitatively similar biographies of the same subject.

Second, the information about me to which other persons have better access than I myself is not always immediately relevant for the purposes of addressing the question "Who am I?" This is because of differences in the level, scale, and scope in which the relevant information is framed. My inquiry is for me and about me, and the terms in which it is pitched are scaled appropriately to my situation and needs. Knowing that others regard me as displaying such-and-such character traits, or that they understand my behavior in (for example) psychoanalytic terms as exhibiting such-and-such patterns, may be helpful to me in understanding my psychology as others understand it: but theirs is the second- or third-person point of view, and without further translation it remains knowledge *about* my self.

A large body of evidence from social and cognitive psychology bears out this point, and casts doubt on the accuracy of the trait ascriptions that persons make about themselves and others in explanatory contexts. While other persons may serve as sources of information about my attitudes and sentiments, what they reflect back to me is subject to entrenched and systematic cognitive biases. One of the most prevalent of these is the so-called fundamental attribution error: that is, the systematic discrepancy between first-person and third-person viewpoints in the explanation of behavior. Generally, an observer's explanation of my behavior tends to emphasize the role of internal causes such as character traits and dispositions, while under-emphasizing the role of situational factors and the first-person subjective experience of agency. This tendency is evident in trait attributions, biographical sketches, and commonsense psychological explanations of behavior. By contrast, the first-person explanation of the same set of behaviors tends to underemphasize the role of internal causes, while emphasizing the role of situational factors and subjective agency. How I explain my actions from the inside, from the first-person point of view, is not coordinated with how my actions are explained from the outside, from the third-person point of view.

Given these considerations, it would seem that reflective self-inquiry and reflective self-evaluation are optimally pursued when the epistemic interferences of the social dimensions of everyday life are kept to a minimum. While it is inevitable that I participate in a form of life with other persons, and draw from it robust vocabularies for making sense of the self, the pursuit of self-knowledge requires a certain turning away from the outer world, precisely in order to get a better and less mediated view of myself.

This is a captivating picture, but it is false. There are a number of reasons why it is false.

First, the self is too complexly configured to be accessible to a single finite mind inquiring into itself by itself.[1] Nothing in the self's resources can adequately compensate for the investigative leverage supplied by jointly pursued inquiry. Second, the understanding of the self is incomplete without an understanding of the social and interpersonal conditions influencing the self's moral and psychological development. Third, the accuracy or inaccuracy of self-understandings has direct effects on the well-being of others. It is in the interests of social adaptivity and social harmony to preserve accurate self-understandings, and to correct those that are inaccurate or subject to self-deception. Fourth, learning about the social dimension of the self—how one is in the eyes of others, and how one's actions and traits of character affect others—is not possible without actually having participated in the appropriate kinds of social relations in which the interpersonal attitudes and reactive behaviors of others are also manifest: that is, social relations in which the effects of others' actions and traits of character upon oneself are clearly perceivable. Fifth, there are truths about the self that can only be gained through certain kinds of dialogue with others—dialogue that involves feelings of participation, morally reactive attitudes, and mutually responsive emotions.

Together, these five considerations suggest that the means to self-knowledge, and the content of self-knowledge, have a clear social dimension; more specifically, that they presuppose standing in certain appropriate kinds of social relationships. But what is the nature of this social dimension? How basic is it? Is it merely an *instrument* for the acquisition of self-knowledge? Is it the case that it provides access to truths about the self that could in principle be acquired by nonsocial means such as solitary self-reflection? Or is it the case that self-knowledge is in some manner *constituted* by complex and highly coordinated ways of interacting with others?

There are three views that supply answers to some of these questions:

i.   self-knowledge is made possible by participation in communities of like-minded persons;

ii. self-knowledge is made possible by truth-tracking intersubjective agreement and consensus; and

iii. self-knowledge is made possible by dialogic encounters with other persons.

Each of these views captures part of the truth. Each is broadly compatible with the others, to the extent that they share the view that the conditions of acquisition of self-knowledge, and the content of self-knowledge, involve some form of interlocutive encounter with others. But there are also significant differences between them on the question of the nature of the interlocutive encounter insofar as it bears on reflective self-inquiry, and on the identity of the interlocutive other. One of the primary differences, as will be seen, focuses on the question of the *otherness* or the *sameness* of the other person in the interlocutive relation. View (iii) takes the strongest position in this regard, and (i) the weakest.

LIKE-MINDED COMMUNITIES

One of the conditions under which I come to know who I am, what I hold valuable, and what I want to do with my life is participation in a community of persons who are like me in respect of basic beliefs and moral practices. This is the view defended by Michael Sandel. To be capable of an understanding that goes beyond the awareness of immediate wants and desires, I need to live in a community defined by "a common vocabulary of discourse and a background of implicit practices and understandings within which the opacity of the participants is reduced if never finally dissolved."[2] I know myself, and the facts of my life, with the help of others with whom I concur on certain basic metaphysical and epistemological beliefs, behavioral standards, moral norms, and nonmoral valuations. This kind of like-mindedness does not require strict one-to-one convergence on each basic belief; but however much I differ from my cohorts on specific issues, my project of reflective self-inquiry and reflective self-evaluation presupposes the ability to wield a communally shared fund of concepts and contrastive distinctions, and to do so while standing within the horizon they establish. This is the strong like-mindedness claim.

The dependence of self-knowledge upon a shared background of practices naturally places constraints on the contents of the insights that can be yielded by reflective self-inquiry. One of these constraints, Sandel claims, is the understanding that "others made me, and in various ways continue to make me the person I am."[3] The suggestion here is that I cannot entertain the thought of myself as a social atom without failing to understand certain obvious truths that are presupposed in the very holding of this thought. To think of myself as a social atom is to systematically downgrade the massive evidence of intersubjective constitution supplied by family upbringing, historical setting, and cultural milieu.

Sandel's view is clearly incompatible with the Rortyean ideal of experimentalist self-enlargement. Among the many social arrangements that would be needed to sustain the implementation of the Rortyean ideal would be the protection of discursive space for multiple vocabularies, as well as wide tolerance for divergent and transgressive discursive practices. Sandel regards pluralist societies such as these as antithetical to the conditions required for like-mindedness to flourish. Within such societies, the possible forms of self-understanding would be so diverse that any single achievement in self-understanding could be made to look parochial against some other available option.[4] The development of self-understanding requires not the proliferation of discursive possibilities but the cultivation of the social conditions that allow for respect for individual differences within the broader framework of like-mindedness; it therefore has more in common with a collective project of digging patiently in one place, with the collaborative input of others, than it has with visiting a marketplace that displays a vast array of goods to be compared and chosen at will, and then ultimately discarded in favor of newer goods. Because self-understanding occurs within a stable background of tacitly agreed-upon norms and shared traditions, those who are self-knowledgeable have "confidently situated selves" rather than ironic and detachable selves.

What makes the strong like-mindedness condition implausible, however, is that it favors as social conditions of like-mindedness small and homogeneous nation-states with limited ties to the rest of the world, rather than large pluralistic societies that are without traditional linguistic and historic centers. But there is no reason to suppose that members of large pluralist societies are, as a group, somehow less capable of robust self-understandings than their counterparts in more homogeneous communities; and there is no reason to suppose that nonconformists who live on the margins of homogeneous communities are less capable of robust self-understandings than those who are "confidently situated" within them.[5]

There are two other problems facing the like-mindedness claim. First, moderate degrees of like-mindedness have the potential to interfere with the range and depth of reflective self-inquiry, by reinforcing an uncritical acceptance of the shared values that it is the very goal of the inquiry to call into question. Like-mindedness is thus double-edged; it may encourage penetrating reflective self-inquiry, or it may serve as a disguise for intellectual myopia, or as communally sanctioned resistance to disturbing or transgressive forms of inquiry. Selves that are too confidently situated may be too confident of themselves to raise the question "Who am I?" in a fundamental manner, in such a way that they break out of the circle of limiting presuppositions. Sandel rejects this criticism on the grounds that it is not like-mindedness that leads to intolerance but certain forms of cultural heterogeneity—particularly those that lead to the disruption of traditional forms of life. "In our day, the totalitarian impulse has sprung less from the convictions of confidently situated selves than from the confusion of atomized, dislocated, frustrated selves, at sea in a world where common meanings have lost their force."[6] But historical cases in which atomized and dislocated selves are found side by side with the totalitarian impulse only demonstrate the presence of a correlation, not causation; many factors other than the existence of atomized selves may have led to such historical situations.[7]

The second difficulty is that satisfaction of the like-mindedness condition offers no guarantee of veridicality in reflective self-inquiry. Those social arrangements that satisfy the condition, and therefore seem to be good candidates for generating robust forms of self-understanding, are just as susceptible to epistemic failure as those that do not satisfy the condition. In both cases epistemic norms and criteriological practices can become systematically skewed in such a way that like-minded subjects remain unaware of the distortions affecting their knowing practices. Under these circumstances, self-inquiry with others who are like-minded is less likely to remove self-opacity as it is to complicate it with newer and more complex distortions, including shared forms of self-misunderstanding and self-deception.

Sandel gives as an example of one of the conditions of like-minded self-inquiry the case of friendship: "Where seeking my good is bound up with exploring my identity and interpreting my life history, the knowledge I seek is less transparent to me and less opaque to others. Friendship becomes a way of knowing as well as liking. Uncertain which path to take, I consult a friend who knows me well, and together we deliberate, offering and assessing by turns competing descriptions of the person I am, and of the alternatives I face as they bear on my identity."[8] But this is not enough. Friendship is not a guarantee of veridicality in reflective self-inquiry, because deliberations between friends are no more immune to the generation of false, deceived, or superficial self-understandings than inquiries that do not satisfy the like-mindedness condition; nor are they immune to the progressive and undetected relaxation of epistemic standards. To avoid this, the deliberations need to take place within a framework of critical and truth-tracking inquiry. But this requires an element that goes beyond the like-mindedness displayed in friendships: viz., the moral confrontation of the self by the other person. That in virtue of which I understand myself is so familiar and easily overlooked that it requires the shock of the encounter with the *otherness* of other persons—rather than the encounter with the *sameness* of other persons—to be brought to light. The otherness of the other person is not a function of the other's disagreement with the self, since disagreement is compatible with like-mindedness on other more basic beliefs. Nor is it a function of empathy. One of the central claims of the dialogic philosophy of Emmanuel Levinas and Martin Buber is that the other person by whom I become self-knowledgeable and morally self-aware is other in the sense of being an ethically provocative force who calls me into question, and who destabilizes my otherwise perva-sive loyalty to myself.[9]

Despite these problems, there are two important ideas worth preserving from Sandel's account, both of which serve as building blocks for the follow-ing accounts of the social dimension of self-knowledge. The first is the idea that knowing oneself as a person with a particular life history and particular character traits is both more complicated than knowing one's immediate wants and desires, and considerably less private than it might initially seem. The second is the idea that the pursuit of reflective self-inquiry requires some form of close interpersonal contact; and that this contact is constitutive of self-knowledge, rather than an instrument that contingently leads to it. But the precise nature of this contact, and the conditions under which it is possi-ble, still remain to be determined.

CONSENSUS AND INTERSUBJECTIVE VALIDATION

Because the satisfaction of the like-mindedness condition does not rule out the possibility of reaching agreement with like-minded others about beliefs that are in fact illusions or falsehoods, one of the further conditions that must be satisfied if self-knowledge is to be possible is the commitment to truth. To know who I am in any robust sense, I must stand in those kinds of social rela-tions in which truth matters. But for this to be possible, I must first have an understanding of what it is to be in cognitive agreement with others; that is, to be in agreement on issues pertaining to truth and falsity. But to have an understanding of this presupposes an understanding of a number of other conditions: an understanding, for example, of what it means to describe a belief as true or false; an understanding of what counts as evidence; an under-standing of the standards by which to evaluate evidence as adequate or inad-equate; and an understanding of how to apply the concepts of truth, evidence, and justification in public contexts.

Self-knowledge, in other words, is dependent upon relations with other persons in which some form of cognitive agreement has been (or can be) reached; and this requires an understanding of the relevance of truth and falsity in claims to self-knowledge. The social relations in question, however, are not necessarily relations of like-mindedness, empathy, or friendship, although it is possible that these kinds of relations are vehicles for some of the relevant conditions. They are, essentially, relations in which claims to self-knowledge are grounded on the possibility (if not the actual achievement) of intersubjective agreement between the self-knower and other knowers with similar cognitive interests and cognitive practices. The mere presence of intersubjective agreement of this kind is not a sufficient condition for truth, since consensually endorsed beliefs may be false; but intersubjective agreement of the right kind is a necessary condition for truth. But what counts here as agreement *of the right kind?* *Who* must agree? And how many persons must reach agreement?

Ernst Tugendhat, whose account of the intersubjective nature of self-inquiry attempts to steer a middle course between individualist and consensualist approaches, develops one plausible answer to these questions. Tugendhat defends two claims that initially appear to be incompatible: first, that every path of reflective self-inquiry, and by implication every path of self-determination, must be an individual one; and second, that an essential criterion of the correctness of any individual path is that it would have to meet with the approval of "those who understand something of the matter."[10] Despite the apparent tension, these two claims are compatible.

Tugendhat's goal is to show that the exploration of the questions "Who am I?" and "How do I want to be?" can be linked to the question of truth without being pushed toward the individualist subjectivism of Heideggerian and Sartrean existential philosophy. He does this by showing how the exploration of these questions *answers to* something other than the resources, choices, and epistemic standards of the subject who is raising the questions: viz., to the subject's actual identity, and to the critical feedback and evaluations of other persons who are sufficiently experienced in such matters. The concept of "answering to" is an important one here because it is designed to supplant Heidegger and Sartre's decisionist orientation, according to which the relation of "answering to" is an entirely internal one between the self and itself. If the existential approach is valid, then the criterion of the correctness of my path of self-inquiry and self-determination is something that I myself establish. In addition to being both the inquirer and the very subject of my inquiry, I am also the standard of inquiry and that by which the standard is applied. In working out the question "Who am I?" I answer to myself, or to my existence—not to something or someone other than me. But if the path of reflective self-inquiry and reflective self-evaluation is not delineated with clear-cut markers declaring that I am on the right track, then how am I to know whether I am getting closer to my target, and not straying into false territory? The existential approach denies that there are any grounds independent of my own decisions and carefully considered judgments to which I can appeal in order to identify the convergence of my inquiry upon its proper target. Determining this is entirely up to my own reckoning and choice, and my capacity to wholeheartedly affirm this special fact about my investigative solitude and to make it a part of my reflective self-inquiry (rather than to evade it by appealing to the normative standards of my community) is itself constitutive of my authenticity. The self's inquiry into itself is measured by the self, and not by something other than the self.

The importance of Tugendhat's strategy of underwriting objectivity in reflective self-inquiry and reflective self-evaluation with some form of intersubjective consensus becomes clearer when it is placed side by side with Charles Taylor's account of self-reflection, which is also based on the rejection of existential decisionism. Taylor's account, like Tugendhat's, defends a broad realism about the self, but it still remains within the individualist framework of existential philosophy insofar as it attempts to underwrite objectivity in *intra*subjective rather than intersubjective terms. With Hampshire and Sartre, Taylor defends the view that the practices of reflective self-inquiry and reflective self-evaluation both reveal their objects and at the same time shape them and their modes of evidence. This does not mean that the self is a plastic object. The possibilities of shaping the self are constrained by a reality that exists antecedently to the reflective stance adopted toward it, and this means that self-interpretations can be assessed as "more or less adequate, more or less truthful, more self-clairvoyant or self-deluding." But it is always possible in this endeavor to follow the wrong path and to stray into false territory. When my self-interpretations fall short or far afield of this antecedently existing self, the self does not remain unchanged. Incorrect self-interpretations, powerful enough to shape the self they are wrong about, are forms of self-distortion and self-transformation. Thus "we don't just speak of error but frequently also of illusion or delusion."[11]

But how do I know that I have not followed the wrong path, and that the self I am evaluating has not been contaminated by misinterpretations that nonetheless have the appearance of being veridical? One strategy would be to check my inquiry against the interpretations of others who are in a position to comment upon the matter. This is Tugendhat's view. Another strategy would be to pursue *further* reflective self-inquiry. This is Taylor's view: I determine if I am on the correct path by reevaluating the results of my previous self-evaluations, with the goal of distinguishing those that are truth-tracking from those that are convincing misinterpretations. This would involve, for instance, reassessing the train of reasoning that I followed from my starting point to my most recently achieved stage of self-understanding, reassessing the evidence, and reassessing the relevant epistemic norms, interpretive strategies, and evidentiary criteria used along the way. The process moves forward, Taylor suggests, with such questions as "Am I right about my most basic evaluations?" "Have I really understood what is essential to my identity?" and "Have I truly determined what I sense to be the highest mode of life?"12

But the reevaluation of previously achieved evaluations is not intrinsically reliable, because there is nothing preventing me from being misled in this higher-order pursuit. A series of successive reevaluations can drift imperceptibly further afield of its target, while appearing nonetheless to offer plausible correctives for previous evaluations. At a certain stage in the reevaluation of my previous efforts at reflective self-inquiry, for example, I may come to the conclusion that I had been laboring for years under entrenched illusions about my abilities, which I now believe I see accurately. Because this new outlook seems to explain much more convincingly a number of frustrated projects and dashed ambitions that before had appeared anomalous, I might conclude that my self-inquiry is converging on its proper target. But this conclusion is uwarranted. I still have no assurances that my newly won evaluations are not themselves misinterpretations masquerading as truth-tracking reevaluations. I may be misled in this regard because the grounds to which I am appealing to establish the correctness of my reevaluations are not independent of my own carefully considered judgments about the matter, which themselves may be skewed by those very illusions. I am still measuring my inquiry by resources internal to the self that is the very object of the inquiry.

Tugendhat's strategy to block this kind of interpretive drift is to appeal to social consensus: that is, to move the touchstone of objectivity for reflective self-inquiry from the epistemic resources of the reflecting self to the epistemic resources of the other who stands in some appropriate relation to the self. Taylor's strategy, by contrast, is to underwrite objectivity by appealing once again to the investigative resources of the self, and in particular to its capacity to *radicalize* the process of reevaluation. Taylor holds that most reevaluations of previous attempts at reflective self-inquiry and reflective self-evaluation, however carefully pursued, are carried on within the terms of a "language which is out of dispute." But when reevaluation is radicalized, as it can always be, "the most basic terms, those in which other evaluations are carried out, are precisely what is in question. It is just because all formulations are potentially under suspicion of distorting their objects that we have to see them all as revisable, that we are forced back, as it were, to the inarticulate limit from which they originate." But how is radicalized reevaluation to get started, given the fact that any starting point is dependent upon something prior and given, which it takes as its target while simultaneously originating in it? If the starting point of radical reevaluation is not independent of the very formulations that are undergoing reevaluation, then it appears that it must assume the very formulations that are its target. To avoid the threat of circularity, Taylor appeals to the hermeneutic concept of openness: "How then can such re-evaluations be carried out? There is certainly no metalanguage available in which I can assess rival self-interpretations. If there were, this would not be a radical re-evaluation. On the contrary the reevaluation is carried on in the formulae available, but with a stance of attention, as it were, to what these formulae are meant to articulate and with a readiness to receive any gestalt shift in our view of the situation, any quite innovative set of categories in which to see our predicament, that might come our way in inspiration."[13]

The concept of openness is intended by Taylor to supply some form of *intra*subjective objectivity. But does it offer me any reasonable assurances that my radicalized reevaluations are not straying into false territory? Taylor addresses this question by likening radical reevaluation to situations of conceptual innovation in philosophy, where intractable problems that are generated by traditional distinctions eventually lead to the development of new languages and new sets of categories with which to formulate alternative approaches. The radicalization of reevaluation follows a similar pattern: it involves trying to "reach down to [my] deepest unstructured sense of what is important," in order that I may "see reality afresh and form more adequate categories to describe it. To do this I am trying to open myself, use all of my deepest, unstructured sense of things in order to come to a new clarity."[14]

But appeal to the stance of openness is unavailing unless it can be shown that openness is exempt from the same kinds of shortcomings that hinder less than radical forms of self-evaluation. Just as I may try to be "open" to an artwork—to "use all of my deepest, unstructured sense of things in order to come to a new clarity"—and yet be misguided with respect to what the artwork is saying, so a stance of openness may reiterate the very formulations that are undergoing reevaluation; or it may serve as the unwitting vehicle of entrenched forms of self-deception. Taylor acknowledges the difficulties of cultivating a stance of openness: "It may take discipline and time. It is difficult because this form of evaluation is deep in a sense, and total in a sense that the other less than radical ones are not."[15] But this only postpones the problem, because the adoption of a stance of openness as a way of correcting the process of reevaluation does not give me access to tools that are independent of my own fallible resources.

The difficulties faced by Taylor's account suggest that resources internal to the self are not sufficient to underwrite objectivity in reflective self-inquiry and reflective self-evaluation. The convergence or divergence of reflective self-inquiry with respect to its target is not established *by* the self and *for* the self: it is established in the relation between self and others. Reflective self-inquiry runs up against something other than the very self that is in question; in Tugendhat's terms, it *answers to* other persons. But what does this mean?

Tugendhat's first move in clarifying the concept of answering to is to suggest that reflective self-inquiry must aim to establish true beliefs about the self in question. This is a tall order: what makes some beliefs true and others false, and how are they to be distinguished from one another? Tugendhat's position, like Taylor's, is broadly realist. True beliefs about the self are not true because they are said to be true; nor are they true because they are chosen to be true. They are true in virtue of the facts of the person's self, life history, and character. Without this factual backdrop to which all claims about the self must answer, it would not be possible to assess the validity of claims to self-knowledge; nor would it be possible to separate out illusions and self-deceptions from accurate self-knowledge. Reflective self-inquiry is not self-creation ex nihilo, answering to nothing and turning on nothing.

This position is intuitively plausible, but it fails to address an obvious hermeneutic objection that is raised in defense of the very existential position it rejects: viz., how it is possible to get at the facts of the self to which claims to self-knowledge ostensibly refer. Whatever claims might be made about the self necessarily take a propositional form: that is, they take the form of sentences such as "I am X" or "I believe that I am Y." But when these propositions are evaluated for their truth or falsity, they are not compared directly to unadulterated nonpropositional facts but are referred to other propositions that make certain claims about the self that are not themselves immediately in question, which are themselves tested by referring to other propositions, and so on. Brute facts, if there are such things, are not used to test knowledge claims, which are of a different order from the facts themselves. Any claims about the self must be given propositional form, and brought into relation with an ongoing fund of previously established knowledge claims. It does not follow from this that there is no given element in knowledge claims about the self, and that it is "interpretation all the way down"; but whatever is taken as factual in regard to the self is already and always interpreted. Prior decisions have been made about what the facts actually are, what particular facts (of a wide range of facts) are going to count as relevant, and what kind of propositional form will be given to the relevant facts.

Tugendhat's second move in clarifying the concept of "answering to something" is to argue that the results of reflective self-inquiry need to answer to the possibility of rational justification: that is, they need to be supported by well-founded evidence, by consensually endorsed evidentiary criteria, and by a followable chain of reasoning that makes clear the progression from starting point to conclusions.[16] Without this support, no single conclusion about the self would carry any more weight than any other conclusion. This is a plausible requirement, especially in those situations in which I am involved in deliberations regarding projects and life plans, and need to have an accurate account of my life history, my values, and my traits of character. In such cases there is a great deal at stake, and there are many ways I can go wrong. If my deliberations were based on nonrational choices, or on subjectivist self-experimentation, for instance, they would carry no force over time; they would be held in place only by the inertia of personal and historical circumstance, and by the epistemic preferences and habits that currently structure my knowing practices. Nor would they carry force before the criticisms of others who are helping me to deal with these issues. But Tugendhat adds to this a much stronger condition: reflective self-inquiry and the self-determination to which it leads must be answerable to the ideal of determining what is *best* for me, and what sort of life would be best among the possible alternatives. What counts as best here is not entirely up to me. There are "objectively justifiable" preferences, and the way they are identified is through a process of careful reflective deliberation.[17]

But is the addition of this condition compatible with the idea that every path of reflective self-inquiry is ultimately an individual one? If my view about the best way of life, and the best form of self-understanding relevant to that way of life, conflicts with the views of others, or the views that I have held in the past, then how could these differences be rationally resolved?

How can I be reasonably assured that what I now take as the best way of life, and the best form of self-understanding, have more than a transient plausibility, one that will not vanish at some later stage of reflective self-inquiry?

Tugendhat's resolution of this problem involves distinguishing between the different logical stages of the process of reflective self-inquiry. When I ask myself the question "Who am I?" and the related question "How do I want to be?" I necessarily begin from within the boundaries marked out by conventional norms and ready-to-hand self-understandings. As long as the starting point of my inquiry presupposes this large fund of beliefs and values as something unquestioned, the burden of choice rests on something other than me. But this is only the first pass at reflective self-inquiry; it does not fully call me into question. What I need to do is aim for a level of inquiry in which I call my existence as a whole into question, without appealing to conventional self-understandings. Reaching this level requires "leaving all pregiven substantial criteria for the determination of my being aside, and...focusing the choice upon my being as such; and this means nothing other than, 'Who do I want to be?' " At this stage, rational deliberation loses its traction. The process of finding reasons and adducing grounds comes "to an end when decisions about one's life are at issue." All I can do then is stake my ground and declare "This is how it is, and this is how it shall be!" When this stage is reached, what counts as my best course of action (and with it my best form of self-understanding) is constituted precisely by my wanting it so, which does not in the final instance rest upon reasons.[18]

The distinction between the penultimate and ultimate stages of reflective self-inquiry is a useful one for the purposes of clarification, but it has a limited usefulness elsewhere. The distinction is more accessible to the philosophical logician, who has the advantage of occupying the observer's point of view, than it is to the subject whose inquiry is situated at one stage or the other, and who must alone determine whether the process of reflective self-inquiry has terminated. Because the distinction does not show up in experience in such a way that it is clear that one stage has been surpassed and the next stage attained, the subject is still left without a clear answer to the question "How do I know that I have finally arrived at the best way of life, and the best form of self-understanding?"

The distinction seems to place Tugendhat's solution in the same theory of existential decisionism that it is his intention to reject. His claim that self-determination "is grounded in the question of truth even though it can not be fully resolved in this question"[19] leaves open the possibility that a certain element of arbitrariness can contaminate the final stage of the inquiry, when deliberation comes to an end. It is precisely at such a point that self-deception can enter in under the guise of insight. Tugendhat tries to block this possibility by showing how in the ultimate stages of reflective self-inquiry the subject must still answer to the feedback of others. Not only does the justification of the validity of the results of self-inquiry necessarily occur in an intersubjective context; the results must also be aimed at achieving consensus with other rationally minded interlocutors who understand something of the matter.[20] Consensus among those with some degree of moral expertise provides a degree of epistemic traction against which individual responses to the questions "Who am I?" and "How do I want to be?" can be evaluated as good or bad, or better or worse. This does not mean any kind of consensus will suffice: ideologically motivated consensus and consensus that is a function of false consciousness, for instance, are clearly inadequate. The appropriate form of consensus is between those who are recognized as possessing a certain degree of practical wisdom and moral expertise in matters pertaining to reflective self-inquiry and reflective self-evaluation.

This obviously helps to rescue reflective self-inquiry and self-determination from the brink of existential decisionism, but it leaves a number of questions unanswered. The first question concerns whether a non-question-begging account can be supplied of the vague notion of "understanding something of the matter"—given that there is a wide variety of persons with moral expertise who could fit such a description. If the conditions placed on this notion are too restrictive, then the consensualist conservatism that would result would have the unwanted effect of enforcing only a narrow range of types of intersubjective validation. If the conditions are too broad, however, then it is likely that the interpretive practices of different experts, each with conflicting views of the good life, and each with conflicting epistemic and interpretive norms, would be too diverse to allow for meaningful consensus. Tugendhat's suggestion is that "a person x is more experienced in something than a person y if there is a course of experience from y to x that results in y sharing the value judgments of x, but no course of experience from x to y. Thus, good or better in this sense is what would be acknowledged as such by everyone once they have had the necessary experiences: The consensus is not a consequence of objective criteria, but is itself the sole criterion."[21] But this only pushes the question back one step. The difficulty is to supply the conditions under which the concept of "learning from" is applicable in real-life circumstances. This is particularly acute in pluralist societies with widely divergent ideals of practical wisdom and moral expertise, and conflicting viewpoints on substantive meta-ethical issues: for instance, conflicts about what constitutes the grounds of rationality in matters of reflective self-inquiry, and conflicts about what counts as "objectively preferable" decisions about how to live and how to understand oneself.22

The second problem left unaddressed by Tugendhat's account is that it does not specify clearly what constitutes an adequate consensus. Mere consensus among those with the relevant experience in the matter is not sufficient to underwrite intersubjective objectivity, because it fails to distinguish between the many different forms of consensual agreement. Some forms of consensus, for example, count as meaningful agreement any simple majority among those experienced in the matter; other forms of consensus count as agreement a small but strongly cohesive minority. In addition, Tugendhat does not specify clearly the identity of those persons (with the relevant moral expertise) whose voices constitute a consensus. Besides the fact that they have some experience in the matter, *who* are they? In virtue of what is their role in the validation of reflective self-inquiry effective? Is it their *otherness* with respect to the self, or their *sameness*, which contributes to the validation of the results of reflective self-inquiry?

Neither of these difficulties is fatal. It is enough at this stage to establish that other persons who are experienced in the matter must *somehow* be able to enter into the process of reflective self-inquiry as interlocutors—even if it is not yet clear who they are, how they enter in, and how they reach consensus. I do not work out the questions "Who am I?" and "How should I be?" as an existential Robinson Crusoe. My inquiries must somehow answer to others in ways that are recognizable to them as satisfying certain shared norms of epistemic responsibility. But Tugendhat's emphasis on the *cognitive* character of intersubjective agreement needs to be balanced by an account of the *moral* dimension of the encounter between self and other. It is one thing for the self to be answerable to persons who are experienced in matters of reflective self-inquiry, and whose judgment (in responding to my claims to self-knowledge) shows some degree of practical wisdom; but it is another for the self to pursue reflective self-inquiry because of a sense of *responsibility* for the other persons to whom it must answer. I can be answerable to other persons in the sense of supplying them with plausible reasons that serve to justify the results of my self-inquiries, and that justify to them my choice of a way of life, but I may still be irresponsible, egotistical, and oblivious to the needs of others in the life I have chosen, and in the self-understanding I have endorsed as veridical.

DIALOGIC ENCOUNTER

Mere acknowledgment of the descriptions under which I am identified by others is not sufficient for the acquisition of self-knowledge; nor is mere participation in a community of like-minded others; nor is the mere satisfaction of the conditions of intersubjective cognitive agreement. The further condition that must be satisfied is dialogic encounter: that is, actively engaging another person in a dialogue that is directed to exploring the question "Who am I?" This, as Buber and Levinas argue, is not an activity pursued exclusively by the self and for the self; it is pursued with others and for others, and in a moral context in which the self's responsiveness to others, and its epistemic and moral responsibility for others, reaches an equilibrium with the self's concern for itself. What I learn about myself, and how I integrate it into my conduct, is an acknowledgment of the responsibility that I have to others in my self-investigative practices, because it is others who can be hurt by the inaccurate or self-deceived self-understandings that inform my actions and interpersonal attitudes. One of the primary functions of self-knowledge, in other words, is social and interpersonal, rather than intrapersonal. If the acquisition of self-knowledge is part of a dialogical project, then to be self-knowledgeable is to be an interlocutively and interpersonally responsive agent.

Dialogues, however, come in many different forms, some superficial or motivated by extrinsic considerations (e.g., controlling the other's opinions, or prolonging the conversation for its own sake), and some leading to misunderstanding or alienation. What then are the appropriate conditions for "reflective dialogue"—that is, dialogue that is conducive to reflective self-inquiry and reflective self-evaluation? A reflective dialogue can be characterized as an open-textured process based on the response and address of self and other, through which both interlocutors are united by the desire to achieve mutual and truth-tracking understanding while respecting the moral differences separating them. In raising the question "Who am I?" the self issues a call to the other, and addresses the other as a person who stands in the role of moral witness. The act of addressing and responding to another person in these circumstances is constitutive of the self knowing itself. But how is it constitutive? What is it about the concepts of address and response that secure their central place in self-inquiry?

The philosophy of dialogue begins with the idea that to be a person is to stand in a unique set of relations to other persons. What makes these relations unique is their asymmetry with respect to all other forms of relations, particularly relations to things and events. We do not first establish as objective fact that some creature is a person because it satisfies (for instance) certain determinate conditions of rationality, intentionality, or self-consciousness—and then, at a logically subsequent stage, relate to it in an appropriate way *because* it has satisfied these conditions. Rather, our treating a creature and responding to it in certain ways is somehow *constitutive* of its being a person.[23] Versions of this idea are defended by philosophers across a number of traditions.

According to Buber, Levinas, and others in the tradition of the philosophy of dialogue, one of the central components of "person-constitutive" ways of relating to others is mastery of the unique form of language of personal reference associated with the first-person and second-person perspectives. The language of evocation, and address and response—"addressive language"—is based inter alia on the experience of being the intended target of the second-person nominative pronoun *you*, as uttered by an interlocutor, and the concomitant experience of addressing another with the second-person nominative pronoun *you*.

Levinas adds to this the idea that addressive ways of relating to other persons are essentially ethical in nature: that is, they involve responsiveness, responsibility, desire, and interest. Other forms of relations between selves and others, such as relations that involve the adoption of a stance of knowing, understanding, or explaining, are possible because of these first-order ethical relations. The event at the heart of self-other relations that gives to these relations an ethical dimension is the face-to-face dialogic encounter, which is essentially an evocative relation in which two interlocutors take responsibility for one another in the act of responding to one another. Levinas characterizes the other person's facing the self as something that obligates the self to enter into discourse with it; that is, as an appeal before which the self cannot remain silent. The dialogic encounter that takes place between self and other is not, however, a union, an empathic identification, or a blending of the self with the other into some harmonious synthetic whole: it is a relation between two separated terms, the self and the other.[24] "Discourse is the experience of something absolutely foreign, a pure experience, a traumatism of astonishment."[25] All language, Levinas argues, ultimately refers to this face-to-face dialogic encounter. There is no word for which someone is not ultimately responsible, and which does not ultimately revert to an interlocutor whose facing the self commands the self to respond.[26]

Philosophical accounts of the relation between self and other that under-emphasize the differences between the first- and second-person point of view by modeling the other person to whom the self is related as *another self* are incomplete. A sufficiently rigorous phenomenological description shows that relations between self and other are not relations between two subjects of experience, with each subject encountering the other from its respective first-person point of view *as another subject* occupying a similarly structured first-person point of view. The other to whom the self is related is not a "re-edition of the first person,"[27] which would *per impossibile* be addressed with the first-person locution *I*: the other encountered by the self is the second person, the *You*, which Buber characterizes as the "Thou,"[28] and Levinas characterizes as the "Other."

The idea that self-other relations are essentially relations between two subjectivities is found in fully developed form in Sartre's phenomenology of the look, which describes the dynamics of looking and being looked at that express the existential superiority at stake in the encounter between two conflicting centers of agency.[29] Two selves, both of which are "beings for themselves," are destined to struggle with each other in order to preserve their respective freedom and sense of self, and to fend off objectification at the hands of the other. They oscillate between looking at the other, and thereby retaining the upper hand as the active, superior agent, and being looked at, and thereby being impaled by the other's hostile, freedom-robbing look. Neither one wins in this struggle: there is a ceaseless exchange between one for-itself and the other, first with one freedom subject to violation, and then the other.

As Sartre conceives it, the look that is directed from the for-itself to others is hostile and alienating, because it involves objectifying others and depriving them of the agency that is quintessentially their own. But the look cannot be directed at other persons as they are *for themselves*, that is, as subjects of experience. It is directed at others only insofar as they are quasi-objects, or "freedom-things." Because the encounter with the other threatens the self's freedom, it is the "original fall" of the for-itself.

Sartre's account of the phenomenology of the look follows from conceiving other persons in the self-other relationship as other selves, in all essential respects similar to how the self is *for itself*, with differences being attributable to differences of perspective and mental history. But an essential dimension of the other's reality—viz., the other's otherness—is overlooked when the other person is "duplicated" in the self's own terms. To conceive others in this way is to overlook one of the primary facts of experience: viz., that for each individual person there is only one *I*—namely, oneself. The other person cannot be addressed as *I*, but only as *you*. The force of this "cannot" is both logical and phenomenological.

Thus the otherness that characterizes the other person in the self-other dialogic encounter is not something that can be fully captured by the fact that other persons are different by virtue of different histories or psychological states; or that they are different by virtue of an inobservable inner life. The sense of otherness that Levinas intends is stronger: it is otherness in the sense of transcendence. The other is present to the self in the dialogic encounter in his or her refusal to be contained or comprehended.[30] The other as Other cannot be made explicit as an object. Nothing in this encounter is adequate to any idea by which I might try to measure the other as Other. Levinas's model for the otherness of the other person is not unlike the kind of otherness that would be attributed to God, whose reality is uncontainable, and beyond every idea by which it might be measured.

From this discussion of the philosophy of dialogue, six features of the pragmatics of interlocutive language that is involved in reflective dialogue can be discerned.[31]

First, reflective dialogue is open-textured. The interlocutors who address each other with a view to working out the question "Who am I?" do not know in advance the outcome of the dialogue in which they are engaged; nor do they know how they will be changed by it, and how their original self-understandings will be expanded. Reflective dialogue is therefore to be distinguished from pedagogical dialogue, which follows a program or set of rules and moves toward a determinate end. The direction of pedagogical dialogue is largely predetermined, and the possibility of unanticipated developments is reduced to a minimum.

Second, reflective dialogue requires of both interlocutors a willingness to encounter the other person in such a way that his or her otherness, rather than sameness or like-mindedness, is manifest.[32] There are a number of ways this willingness can be blocked. I can, for instance, systematically interpret the words of my interlocutor into terms that favor my own point of view; or I can hold something back from my interlocutor. But I cannot learn from my interlocutor while covertly remaining committed to the promotion of my own view. If for instance I secretly regard my interlocutor as pathologically motivated, and construe his or her words as symptoms rather than as bona fide reasons, then I cannot learn what he or she thinks about the question I have posed. In a reflective dialogue, I regard the other person as a fully responsible partner in the discussion, and as complying with intersubjectively established norms of responsibility and trustworthiness; but in doing so I am keenly aware that the other person is *other* than me, and not merely a "reedition" of my self.

Third, reflective dialogue has an addressive component: the self addresses the other person with forthrightness, and the other responds in kind. This does not involve the exchange of information or the co-creation of a narrative: it is a spontaneous face-to-face conversation between two interlocutors who are in each other's presence. This aspect of language is easily overlooked because of its pervasiveness and familiarity. Spoken language is often modeled on the enunciation and reception of propositions, or on the exchange of referential statements. But these are abstract models that are removed from the phenomenology of everyday moral discourse. One of the most common events of everyday life is the act of addressing and responding to another person face to face, engaging the other in a way that is frank and unrehearsed in order to establish a commonly understood meaning. Language would be a rootless and impersonal system of signs if it were not anchored in the face-to-face confrontation of interlocutors.

Fourth, reflective dialogue involves an evocative component. My addressing the other person with regard to the question "Who am I?" evokes a range of other-directed emotions and mutually responsive attitudes, to which I respond in kind: for example, care, compassion, sympathy, love, respect, shame, and desire. To engage another person in dialogue is not to acknowledge that the other person's feelings *accompany* his or her carefully considered responses to my question; it is to recognize that these feelings themselves constitute responses to my appeal.

Fifth, reflective dialogue has a nominative component: that is, it involves an exchange based on the utterance by self and other of the pronoun *you*, the pronoun of mutual recognition and response. My sense of myself as interlocutor in the dialogue includes my sense of myself as the referent of the address *you*, spoken by the other person whom I too address as *you*. The pronoun *you* has what might be called elicitative locutionary force. As the pronoun of mutual recognition, it calls forth interlocutors, and situates them in a discursive space where the first-person and third-person pronouns also become appropriate. It is an elicitative speech act.[33]

Finally, reflective dialogue has an existential component: that is, it involves being with other persons and participating in the appropriate kinds of interlocutory, moral, and emotional relations. It does not involve merely thinking about others. It is not possible to address an interlocutor with elicitative locutionary force while maintaining a detached and objective stance. When the other person is addressed with the directness of the nominative second-person pronoun, he or she is not an object of observation; nor is the other person the object of a certain stance (e.g., a stance involving the interpretation of their actions according to a psychodynamic theory). The distinction between the self's theoretical, technical, or aesthetic *stance* to the other person and the self's dialogic *encounter* with the other person is not simply a distinction between perspectives on one and the same self-other relation. That is, it is not merely a matter of seeing the other person first in one way, and then in another way, as the duck-rabbit reversible figure is seen first as a duck, then as a rabbit. The other who is addressed face to face is not part of the same information-yielding dimension that is the object of theoretical, technical, or aesthetic stances. To address the other person is to be called into a conversation that itself brings about an understanding of moral and social identity. It is this original dialogical situation that provides the context for an answer to the question "Who am I?"

The concept of self-knowing is indissolubly tied to the nature of dialogic encounter, and the epistemic and moral responsibility it entails. Outside of the context of a shared form of life, and the linguistic community and the face-to-face interaction that it affords, there is, properly speaking, no self-knowing. Not only does dialogue open the self to itself by opening it to the other person; it is by means of reflective dialogue that persons are "talked into" knowing who they are. Interlocution is a constitutive feature of self-knowing; it is not built up from the contingent interactions of presocial atoms. Knowing who I am is possible only in relation to other persons who constitute a community of interlocutors.

The Stone Angel

Margaret Laurence's novel *The Stone Angel* employs a literary device well-suited to a discussion of the dialogic dimension of self-knowledge: namely, the retrospective survey of a life, at the brink of death, told in the form of a continuous first-person monologue. The novel contains a wealth of allusions to Coleridge's *Rime of the Ancient Mariner;* both works depict aged persons narrating the story of their lives, seeking some final degree of clarity before the end, and discovering (almost haphazardly) that the understanding of the self is contained in the response to a call from the other.

The Stone Angel is rich in metaphors of blindness, insight, and self-deception. It portrays the thoughts of Hagar Shipley, a ninety-year-old woman who is endeavoring to come to terms with the meaning of her life, and the person she has chosen to be. At one level the story traces the external events of the life of Hagar—a fiercely independent and proud woman who grew up under harsh conditions in a small prairie town in Manitoba during the Depression era.[34] At a deeper level it is a story of how Hagar comes to develop a clear awareness of the facts of her life history and moral character, just weeks before her death, after many years of self-blindness and self-deception. The theme of blindness to self is announced early. The stone angel that symbolizes Hagar is a white marble statue standing in memory of her mother, who died giving birth to her: "Above the town, on the hill brow, the stone angel used to stand. . . . Summer and winter she viewed the town with sightless eyes. She was doubly blind, not only stone but unendowed with even a pretense of sight. Whoever carved her had left the eyeballs blank. It seemed strange to me that she should stand above the town, harking us all to heaven without knowing who we were at all." Like the stone angel, Hagar has eyes but no real interpersonal or intrapersonal sight. She is too obdurate to feel much sympathy for others, and to recognize how she stands in relation to their needs and sufferings. At one point, in a moment of defiant lucidity about her blindness, she says, "I could not speak for the salt that filled my throat and for anger—not at anyone, at God, perhaps, for giving us eyes but almost never sight."[35]

The central action of the novel revolves around Hagar's conflict with her son Marvin and his wife Doris, who, after many years of tending to Hagar as she becomes increasingly fragile, have decided to send her to a nursing home. Hagar refuses to leave the house, insisting that she is capable of looking after herself. She is terrified of change. For her, involuntary confinement to a nursing home resembles the situation of the biblical Hagar, banished to the desert. Her attitude is symptomatic of a lifelong pattern of failing to see how she affects others, and how others see her. Her refusal to acknowledge her deteriorating condition closes her off from being aware of the responsibility she has to her son and daughter-in-law, who are repeatedly hurt by the self-protective strategies of self-ignorance and self-deception that inform her actions. At one point, when she has fallen down in her room, she demands to be left alone; but she also knows she cannot stand up on her own. Crying out, she does not recognize the sound of her own voice: "Can this torn voice be mine? A series of yelps, like an injured dog?" Looking in the mirror after the fall, she fails to recognize herself, describing the figure in the glass as "somehow arbitrary and impossible."[36]

In a moment of semi-delusional rebellion against her son's decision, she flees to an isolated part of the British Columbia coast. The journey is doubly symbolic. The "quiet place" she seeks is a place of rejuvenation, a place where she can gain some degree of control over her life; at the same time, the arduous trek down the steep overgrown steps to the shoreline represents a descent into the deepest parts of her self. She camps in an abandoned cannery, with only a handful of foodstuffs, and no warm clothing. During the night a stranger enters the cannery, unaware that it is occupied. He too is burdened with painful memories, and is seeking a quiet refuge for reflection. Hagar is at first terrified, but he shares with her his food and drink, and initiates a conversation that ultimately effects in her a momentous change in how she understands herself.

The conversation begins as an exchange of cautious pleasantries, both speakers maintaining a respectful distance, and both hesitant about where the conversation will take them. The stranger first talks about his family and his work: "He talks and talks. He's a bore, this man, but I find the sound of his voice comforting. The wine warms me. I can't notice the chest pain so much now." As he talks of his marriage, the birth of his son, his loss of faith, and his beliefs about death and the purpose of life, Hagar begins to warm to him: "He's drunk as a lord, but he pours my glass without wasting a drop. He's an experienced hand. But I'm not mocking him, even inwardly. There's a plausibility about this man. I like him now, despite his rabbity face, his nervous gnawing at his mustache. His strangeness interests me and I wonder how I could have thought him a bore."[37]

The rambling narrative to which Hagar had been listening more out of amusement in storytelling than genuine interpersonal openness begins to change direction and take on a more serious tone. She senses the intensity of the stranger's voice, and feels its transformation from monologic narrative to addressive appeal. It becomes clear to her that his words are an injunction to listen and to respond wholeheartedly and exclusively—not necessarily with articulate utterances and insights, but with the careful attention of a moral witness. The scene illustrates how the understanding of the self is contained in the response to a call from the other. The dialogue on which they embark is open-textured, with neither of them knowing where it will lead or how it will change them. It is a dialogue in which they encounter each other as complete strangers, and this serves to foreground for each of them the other's otherness, rather than the other's sameness or like-mindedness. Hagar and the stranger are not close; nor are they like-minded in the strong sense defended by Sandel: they come from different backgrounds and generations. Nor do they consult one another as friends who deliberate together, "offering and assessing by turns competing descriptions of the . . . [persons they are], and of the alternatives [they] . . . face as they bear on . . . [their] identity."[38] But while they are not close, they address and respond to one another face-to-face in a way that is forthright and unrehearsed, with their dialogue turning on the use of the second-person nominative pronoun *you,* the pronoun of mutual recognition and response. Singled out in this way, Hagar's characteristically rigid and proud manner of dealing with others, and her tendency to stereotype others as a defensive reaction to keep them at bay, are temporarily suspended. This gives to their dialogue an evocative character: both Hagar and the stranger evoke from one another certain other-directed emotions and mutually responsive attitudes. The stranger's account of his crisis in religious faith, and his citation of the preacher at his church, is more addressive appeal to Hagar than simple narrative.

> I lean forward, attentive, ease a cramped limb with a hand, and look at this man, whose name I have suddenly forgotten but whose face, now turned to mine, says in plain and urgent silence—Listen. You must listen. He's sitting cross-legged, and he wavers a little and sways as he speaks in a deep loud voice [quoting the preacher at his church].

> "Reveal, oh Lord, to these few faithful ones Thy mysterious purpose, that they may prepare to partake of the heavenly feast in Thy Tabernacle on high and drink the grapes anew in Thine Own Kingdom—"

> He stops. He peers at me to see what I make of it. I look at him and at the shadows streaking now around him. His face recedes, then rushes closer, but only his face, as though the rest of him had ceased to exist. Now I'm afraid, and wish he'd stop, I don't want to hear any more.[39]

Hagar cannot maintain a stance of neutrality to the stranger's appeal; she is implicated and enjoined by the "plain and urgent silence" of his words, which, more like an interlocutive injunction than a moral commandment or imperative, say to her, "Listen. You must listen." The stranger recounts to Hagar how he lost his son in an accident for which he still feels responsible, and which continues to raise in his mind unanswerable questions about the nature of causality and blame. Hagar is astonished by his frankness, and her immediate reaction, a retreat into her habitual defensive posture, is one of condescension: "He thinks he's discovered pain, like a new drug. I could tell him a thing or two. But when I try to think what it is I'd impart, it's gone, it's only been wind that swelled me for an instant with my accumulated wisdom and burst like a belch. I can tell him nothing. I can think of only one thing to say with any meaning. 'I had a son,' I say, 'and lost him.'"[40] The "old" Hagar—proud and emotionally ossified—would have maintained a facade of stoic wisdom, half-heartedly engaging the stranger but remaining inwardly aloof. But in this new setting, aware of his strangeness and of its effect on her own vulnerability, she utters only a simple factual statement that establishes an immediate sense of rapport.

Hagar in turn addresses the stranger and enjoins him to witness her words. In telling him the sequence of events that led to her eldest son's tragic death decades earlier, she opens up a part of her life, and a wealth of feeling, that have for decades been sealed off by complexly integrated behaviors of self-deception, pride, selective forgetting, and class consciousness. She recalls vividly how, in response to the overwhelming guilt she felt upon first hearing the news of her son's death, she made an irrevocable decision to harden herself.

> She [the hospital matron] put a well-meaning arm around me. "Cry. Let yourself. It's the best thing."
>
> But I shoved her arm away. I straightened my spine, and that was the hardest thing I've ever had to do in my entire life, to stand straight then. I wouldn't cry in front of strangers, whatever it cost me.
>
> But when at last I was home, alone in Marvin's old bedroom, and women from the town were sitting in the kitchen below and brewing coffee, I found my tears had been locked too long and wouldn't come now at my bidding. The night my son died I was transformed to stone and never wept at all.[41]

The words she speaks, decades after the fact, and before a stranger whom she cannot see since night has fallen, are cathartic, and they bring her closer to accepting the tragedy and understanding her long-repressed feelings about it. She cries openly, an expression of emotion she never would have allowed herself before: "I'm glad he's here. I'm not sorry I've talked to him, not sorry at all, and that's remarkable."[42] The understanding she achieves in conversation with the stranger could not have been reached in any other way: by exploring the etiology of her feelings and her psychological makeup with a psychodynamic psychotherapist, by experimenting with alternative self-descriptions, or by constructing a narrative life history. Decades of emotional and intellectual habit have closed off these other avenues, and have been incorporated into complex stratagems of denial and selective forgetting. The interlocutive injunction of the stranger is like a provocative force: it calls Hagar into question, and disrupts her conventional self-understanding. It is not merely an instrumental means to insights she would have acquired by other noninterlocutive means; rather, the presence of the stranger as inter-locutor is itself a way in which she comes to know herself. The stranger provokes Hagar to account for herself; he is a witness, neither judging nor interpreting her words according to a prior frame of reference. The conversation between them is thus free of the distortion of stereotyped language and social role play, and therefore free of the objectifying stances that typically characterize more conventional forms of interpersonal behavior. The stranger escapes being pinned down by Hagar's normally shrewd stereotypes by an essential dimension. He "overflows" every idea by means of which she might try to measure him according to her own terms.[43]

Throughout the conversation, perhaps to symbolize his alterity and his refractoriness to Hagar's grasp, the stranger is often in the shadows. The relation between them is not visual; it is not a Sartrean look that enables a "reading" or an objectification of the other person, but a dialogic confrontation based on a nonappropriative respect for the otherness of the person who is expressing himself with unabashed sincerity. The stranger is neither empathetic nor sympathetic; he does not feel toward Hagar a sense of at-oneness.

Later that night Hagar falls asleep, only to awaken in a delusional state in which she believes she is talking to her dead son (although, in fact, it is the stranger to whom she is talking). She expects him to be angry with her, not only for the many years of having to live with the harshly judgmental nature of her love but for the cruel words that were spoken between them just before he bolted out of her house and to his untimely death. Hagar has felt guilty about this fight her whole life, but her imaginary conversation effects a resolution, and allows her to experience for the first time since his death a sense of transfiguring forgiveness. "But when he speaks, his voice is not angry at all. 'It's okay,' he says. 'I knew all the time you never meant it. Everything is all right. You try to sleep. Everything's quite okay.' I sigh, content. He pulls the blanket up around me. I could even beg God's pardon this moment, for thinking ill of Him some time or other. 'I'll sleep now,' I say. 'That's right,' he says. 'You do that.'"[44]

When Hagar awakes the next day, the stranger is gone. But she is changed as a result of the conversation the night before. "He's gone. My memory, unhappily clear as spring water now, bubbles up coldly. It could not have been I, Hagar Shipley, always fastidious if nothing else, who drank with a perfect stranger and sank into sleep huddled beside him. I won't believe it. But it was so. And to be frank, now that I give it a second thought, it doesn't seem so dreadful. Things never look the same from the outside as they do from the inside." With the conversation of the night before rejuvenating her long-repressed ability to experience emotions, she is flooded with feelings of loss for her son John: "Something else occurred last night. Some other words were spoken, words which I've forgotten and cannot for the life of me recall. But why do I feel bereaved, as though I'd lost someone only recently? It weighs so heavily upon me, this unknown loss. The dead's flame is blown out and evermore shall be so. No mercy in heaven."[45]

The stranger has left to notify Marvin and Doris about Hagar, whose physical condition overnight has deteriorated as much as her self-understanding has improved. Hagar is hospitalized, and when the stranger visits her she displays the same haughtiness that the night before she had overcome, angry because he broke his promise not to notify Marvin and Doris. "And so the man goes away, back to his own house and life. I am not sorry to see him go, for I couldn't have borne to speak another word to him, and yet I am left with the feeling that it was a kind of mercy I encountered him, even though this gain is mingled mysteriously with the sense of loss which I felt earlier this morning." While resting, the train of her self-reflections culminates in another moment of insight in which she sees through the web of denial and self-deception she had lived with for so long. The insight lays the ground for a sense of self-acceptance more permanent than she has ever felt before. Hearing a simple verse from a hymn, she soberly takes her measure:

> *All people that on earth do dwell,*
> *Sing to the Lord with joyful voice.*
> *Him serve with mirth, His praise forth tell;*
> *Come ye before Him and rejoice.*

I would have wished it. This knowing comes upon me so forcefully, so shatteringly, and with such a bitterness as I have never felt before. I must always, always, have wanted that—simply to rejoice. How is it I never could? I know, I know. How long have I known? Or have I always known, in some far crevice of my heart, some cave too deeply buried, too concealed? Every good joy I might have held, in my man or any child of mine or even the plain light of morning, of walking the earth, all were forced to a standstill by some brake of proper appearances—oh, proper to whom? When did I ever speak the heart's truth?

Pride was my wilderness, and the demon that led me there was fear. I was alone, never anything else, and never free, for I carried my chains within me, and they spread out from me and shackled all I touched. Oh my two, my dead. Dead by your own hands or by mine? Nothing can take away those years.[46]

This is the culminating moment of Hagar's reflective self-inquiry and reflective self-evaluation. The dialogic encounter with the stranger in the cannery gave her the opportunity to understand herself in the context of addressive experience, in being solicited by the other's call. Wishing to recapture the same dialogic conditions so that she might discuss her impending death, she repeats to the nurse attending her the stranger's imploring words, *"Listen. You must listen."* But the moment is unpropitious; the nurse, who regards her perfunctorily as no more than an elderly patient, is not receptive to her call.

The world is even smaller now. It's shrinking so quickly. The next room will be the smallest of all.

"The next room will be the smallest of the lot."

"What?" the nurse says absent-mindedly, plumping my pillow.

"Just enough space for me."

She looks shocked. "That's no way to talk."

How right she is. An embarrassing subject, better not mentioned. The way we used to feel, when I was a girl, about undergarments or the two-backed beast of love. But I want to take hold of her arm, force her attention. *Listen. You must listen. It's important. It's—quite an event.*

Only to me. Not to her. I don't touch her arm, nor speak. It would only upset her. She wouldn't know what to say.[47]

The same failure to establish the conditions of interlocutive injunction occurs when her teenage grandson visits her in hospital. Hagar reflects with bitter irony on the generational stereotypes that trap both of them, blocking genuine dialogic openness, and the possibility of having a witness to her reflections. "That's what I am to him—a grandmother who gave him money for candy. What does he know of me? Not a blessed thing. I'm choked with it now, the incommunicable years, everything that happened and was spoken or not spoken. I want to tell him. Someone should know. This is what I think. *Someone really ought to know these things.*"[48]

Hagar's addressing the stranger, as a witness in the context of raising the question "Who am I?" is a kind of interlocutive speech act. She is doing more than describing and explaining her character traits and her past, both of which are actions that could be carried out monologically. Her exploration of the question "Who am I?" revolves around the *I* and the *you* of dialogue. She needs a second person to bear witness to her reflective self-inquiries to ensure their meaningfulness. There is no doubt that her illusions, self-ignorance, and self-deceptions have served her well in the challenging environment in which she lived. They have filtered out some of the harsher and more hurtful elements of life, and thereby allowed her to cultivate a range of adaptive self-regarding attitudes and sentiments such as self-esteem and self-contentment. But this has come at a high price. While adaptive from a strictly self-serving point of view, they have functioned as filters or barriers that have prevented her from seeing other persons accurately, and from rejoicing. For most of her life she has been unaware (or only partially aware) of those moral feelings, responses, and actions from others that were directly or indirectly *statements* about how she was affecting them: for example, explicit verbal criticisms, antagonistic or supportive behaviors, or interpersonally directed emotions expressing love, sadness, desire, or sympathy. Unable to perceive these accurately, Hagar conducted herself in a way that was narrowly responsive to the dynamics of her immediate social world, and in keeping with the "proper" social appearances of the community in which she lived. When she finally comes to see with clarity how her selfish decisions and joyless and invulnerable character have adversely affected others around her, and how others have responded with flight or fear, she is placed in a position—at the very end of her long life—to respond more openly and more appropriately, replacing egoistic pride with sympathy, and judgmental distance with acceptance.

Hagar's story shows how the deeper and more pervasive a person's self-opacity or self-deception, the more his or her awareness of other persons is diminished. As fewer aspects of the self are noticeable, and therefore knowable to the person whose self it is, so fewer possibilities for interpersonal conduct and moral responsiveness are presented as viable options. The morally relevant distinctions in interpersonal situations, and in emotional and practical response to others, which would be available to those who are more self-knowledgeable, are not available to those suffering from self-opacity or self-deception. As more aspects of the self, and the self-in-relation, are closed off from view, there comes the risk of a corresponding stunting of emotional and moral growth. The capacity to experience sympathy, regret, desire, and other interpersonally specific emotions and attitudes is directly proportional to the capacity for self-knowledge.

Persons come to know themselves in being known by and responsive to persons other than themselves. By bringing them into contact with an alterity that they cannot contain, nor measure in their own terms, reflective dialogue gives persons a social and interpersonally constituted understanding of the shape of their character, life history, and the values that matter most to them. Understanding of this kind is not acquired for its own sake; it serves the ends of interpersonal responsiveness and responsibility. The response to the question "Who am I?" therefore has a triadic structure: it is for the self, of the self, and before the other. It involves encountering the other person in a face-to-face dialogue that, because it takes the form of injunction, attestation, and avowal,[49] carries the self beyond its narrow first-personal boundaries, and beyond the naive egoism that places it at the center of the world, as the measure of all things.

NOTES

1. INTRODUCTION

1. See H. North, *Sophrosyne: Self-Knowledge and Self-Restraint in Greek and Latin Literature* (Ithaca, N.Y.: Cornell University Press, 1966).

2. Aristotle, *Nichomachean Ethics*, trans. J. A. K. Thomson (Harmondsworth, England: Penguin, 1955), bk. 4, 153–58.

3. F. Nietzsche, *On the Genealogy of Morals*, trans. W. Kaufmann and R. J. Hollingdale (New York: Vintage Books/Random House, 1967), 15.

4. F. Nietzsche, *Daybreak: Thoughts on the Prejudices of Morality*, trans. R. Hollingdale (Cambridge, England: Cambridge University Press, 1982), 115–16, #115.

5. Y. Yovel, *Spinoza and Other Heretics*, vol. 2 (Princeton, N.J.: Princeton University Press, 1989), 136–37.

6. Heidegger's term is *jemeinigkeit*. See M. Heidegger, *Being and Time*, trans. J. Macquarrie and E. Robinson (Oxford: Blackwell, 1962), 68.

7. Not all forms of psychotherapy are insight-oriented. The link between insight and therapeutic change is challenged by the theory of behavioral and strategic psychotherapy, which argues that (1) change is rarely accompanied by insight; (2) insight is often epiphenomenal, or an ex post facto rationalization; and (3) searching for insight can interfere with therapeutic change.

8. See M. Lambert, D. Shapiro, and A. Bergin, "The Effectiveness of Psychotherapy," in *Handbook of Psychotherapy and Behavior Change*, 3d ed., ed. S. Garfield and A. Bergin (New York: John Wiley, 1986); see also J. D. Frank and J. B. Frank, *Persuasion and Healing: A Comparative Study of Psychotherapy*, 3d ed. (Baltimore: Johns Hopkins University Press, 1991).

9. See J. Glass, *Shattered Selves: Multiple Personality in a Postmodern World* (Ithaca, N.Y.: Cornell University Press, 1993); B. S. Held, *Back to Reality: A Critique of Postmodern Theory in Therapy* (New York: W. W. Norton, 1995), chap. 8.

10. W. Somerset Maugham, *The Summing Up* (Harmondsworth, England: Penguin, 1963), 9–10.

11. L. Tolstoy, *The Death of Ivan Ilyich and Other Stories*, trans. R. Edmonds (Harmondsworth, England: Penguin, 1960), 110.

12. Ibid., 137–38.

13. See J. Kekes, *The Examined Life* (University Park, Pa.: Pennsylvania State University Press, 1992), 146.

14. Tolstoy, *Ivan Ilyich*, 152.

15. Ibid., 157.

16. M. Nussbaum, "Finely Aware and Richly Responsible," in *Love's Knowledge* (New York: Oxford University Press, 1989).

17. A. R. Luria, *The Man with a Shattered World*, trans. L. Solotaroff (New York: Basic Books, 1972). See also O. Flanagan, *Consciousness Reconsidered* (Cambridge, Mass.: MIT Press, 1992), for a discussion of the Zasetsky case.

18. Ibid., 42–43.

19. Ibid., 9.

20. E. Erikson, *Identity: Youth and Crisis* (New York: W. W. Norton, 1968), 19.

21. Luria, *The Man with a Shattered World*, 85–86.

22. Ibid., 84.

23. See Flanagan, *Consciousness Reconsidered*, 197.

2. APPROACHES TO THE SELF

1. O. Flanagan, *Varieties of Moral Personality* (Cambridge, Mass.: Harvard University Press, 1991); see also O. Flanagan, *Consciousness Reconsidered* (Cambridge, Mass.: MIT Press, 1992).

2. Flanagan, *Varieties of Moral Personality*, 135.

3. Flanagan, *Consciousness Reconsidered*, 209.

4. See K. V. Wilkes, *Real People: Personal Identity without Thought Experiments* (Oxford, England: Oxford University Press, 1988).

5. Personality prototypicality is not transhistorical. The number of personality prototypes has expanded from four (Galen and Kant) to eight (Jung) to double digits. Gordon Allport inadvertently brought to the fore the problem of the psychometric preservation of the unity of personality by identifying 17,954 personality trait terms in the English language that could be used to distinguish one individual from another. See G. W. Allport and H. Odbert, "Trait-names: A Psycho-Lexical Study," *Psychological Monographs* 47 (1936), vol. 1, no. 211; see also G. W. Allport, *Personality: A Psychological Interpretation* (New York: Holt, 1937).

6. N. D. Sundberg, "The Acceptability of 'Fake' Versus Bona Fide Personality Test Interpretations," *Journal of Abnormal Social Psychology* 50 (1966): 145–47. See also V. M. Dmitruk, R. W. Collins, and D. L. Clinger, "The Barnum Effect and Acceptance of Negative Personal Evaluation," *Journal of Consulting and Clinical Psychology* 41 (1973): 192–94.

7. On "ecological validity," see J. J. Gibson, *The Ecological Approach to Visual Perception* (Boston: Houghton Mifflin, 1979).

8. T. Mischel, *Personality and Assessment* (New York: John Wiley, 1968), 71.

9. D. W. Hamlyn, "Self-Knowledge," in *The Self: Philosophical and Psychological Issues*, ed. T. Mischel (Oxford: Blackwell, 1977), 176.

10. A. O. Rorty, "Adaptivity and Self-Knowledge," in *Mind in Action* (Boston: Beacon Press, 1988), 190.

11. See U. Neisser and D. A. Jopling, eds., *The Conceptual Self in Context: Culture, Experience, Self-Understanding* (New York: Cambridge University Press, 1997).

12. H. Markus, "Self-Schemata and the Processing of Information about the Self," *Journal of Personality and Social Psychology* 35, no. 2 (1977): 64.

13. There are a variety of forms of philosophical narrativism. See D. Dennett, *Consciousness Explained* (Boston: Little, Brown, 1991); D. Carr, *Time, Narrative and History* (Bloomington: Indiana University Press, 1986); D. Spence, *Narrative Truth and Historical Truth: Meaning and Interpretation in Psychoanalysis* (New York: W. W. Norton, 1982); P. Ricoeur, *Time and Narrative*, trans. K. Blamey and D. Pellauer (Chicago: University of Chicago Press, 1988).

14. Flanagan, *Varieties of Moral Personality*, 148–49; see also Carr, *Time, Narrative, and History*, 90.

15. See D. Spence, *Narrative Truth and Historical Truth*.

16. A. O. Rorty, "Adaptivity and Self-Knowledge," 182.

17. Ibid.

18. This is a prominent theme in Sartre's novel *Nausea*. See J. P. Sartre, *Nausea*, trans. L. Alexander (New York: New Directions, 1964), 58.

19. See L. Binswanger's study "The Case of Ellen West," in *Existence: A New Dimension in Psychiatry and Psychology*, ed. R. May, E. Angel, and H. Ellenberger (New York: Simon and Schuster, 1958), 237–364; see also D. Leder, *The Absent Body* (Chicago: University of Chicago Press, 1989); J. H. van den Berg, *A Different Existence: Principles of Phenomenological Psychopathology* (Pittsburgh: Duquesne University Press, 1972); U. Neisser, "Five Kinds of Self-Knowledge," *Philosophical Psychology* 1, no. 1 (1988): 35–59.

20. See D. McKenna Moss, "Distortions in Human Embodiment: A Study of Surgically Treated Obesity," in *Phenomenology: Dialogues and Bridges*, ed. R. Bruzina and B. Wilshire (Albany: State University of New York Press, 1982), 253–68; see also Sartre's

biography of Flaubert, where Sartre identifies as "proto-history" the developmental stage when infants first acquire a primitive somatic sense of self as passive or active, guarded or open, or apathetic or energetic. J. P. Sartre, *The Family Idiot*, trans. C. Cosman (Chicago: University of Chicago Press, 1983), vols. 1 and 2.

3. SELF-DETACHMENT AND SELF-KNOWLEDGE

1. Hampshire's philosophical psychology has evolved significantly from *Thought and Action* (1959) and *Freedom of Mind and Other Essays* (1972) to *Morality and Conflict* (1983) and *Innocence and Experience* (1990). His earlier two works will here be the main center of focus.

2. S. Hampshire, *Thought and Action* (London: Chatto and Windus, 1959).

3. I. Murdoch, *The Sovereignty of Good* (London: Routledge and Kegan Paul, 1970), 7.

4. S. Hampshire, "Disposition and Memory," in *Freedom of Mind and Other Essays* (Oxford: Clarendon, 1972), 176.

5. See D. A. Jopling, "Sub-Phenomenology," *Human Studies* 19 (1996): 153–73.

6. One of the precursors of this view is Spinoza, who describes reflexive cognition as the ability to formulate ideas about ideas: "as soon as anyone knows something, by that very fact he knows that he knows, and at the same time he knows that he knows that he knows, and so on *ad infinitum*." B. Spinoza, *Ethics*, ed. S. Feldman, trans. S. Shirley (Indianapolis: Hackett, 1992), pt. 2, prop. 21, Scholium.

7. F. Brentano, *Psychology from an Empirical Standpoint*, ed. O. Kraus and L. McAlister, trans. A. C. Rancurella, D. Terrell, and L. McAlister (London: Routledge and Kegan Paul, 1973), bk. 1, sec. 2.2, p. 29; see also G. Ryle, "The Systematic Elusiveness of the 'I,'" in *The Concept of Mind* (Harmondsworth, England: Penguin, 1973), 186–89.

8. See J. P. Sartre, *Being and Nothingness*, trans. H. Barnes (London: Methuen, 1969), 43, 160, 199, 335; J. P. Sartre, *Transcendence of the Ego*, trans. F. Williams and R. Kirkpatrick (New York: Noonday Press, 1962).

9. Hampshire, "Sincerity and Single-Mindedness," in *Freedom of Mind*, 236.

10. See D. W. Hamlyn, "Self-Knowledge," in *The Self: Philosophical and Psychological Issues*, ed. T. Mischel (Oxford: Blackwell, 1997).

11. S. Hampshire, *Morality and Conflict* (Cambridge Mass.: Harvard University Press, 1983), 114.

12. Ibid., 55.

13. Hampshire, *Thought and Action*, 214–15.

14. Ibid., 34.

15. Ibid., 244, 20.

16. Ibid., 21.

17. Ibid., 256.

18. See Hampshire, "Sincerity and Single-Mindedness."

19. Hampshire, *Thought and Action*, 175.

20. Hampshire, *Freedom of Mind*, ix; Hampshire, *Thought and Action*, 209–10.

21. Hampshire, *Freedom of Mind*, 14.

22. Spinoza, *Ethics*, pt. 3, prop. 59, n.; pt. 4, prop. 44, Scholium.

23. Hampshire, "Spinoza and the Idea of Freedom," in *Freedom of Mind*.

24. S. Freud, *Dora: An Analysis of a Case of Hysteria* (New York: Collier, 1963), 30.

25. Freud acknowledged the influence of Spinoza's philosophical psychology. See his private correspondence with L. Bickel and S. Hessing, reprinted in S. Hessing, ed., *Speculum Spinozanum, 1677–1977* (London: Routledge and Kegan Paul, 1978); see also W. Bernard, "Psychotherapeutic Principles in Spinoza's *Ethics*," and L. Bickel, "On Relationships between Psychoanalysis and a Dynamic Psychology," in *Speculum Spinozanum*.

26. Freud characterizes psychoanalytic therapy as a kind of self-exploration leading to self-knowledge. See S. Freud, *An Outline of Psycho-Analysis*, trans. J. Strachey (New York: Norton, 1963). Freud describes the therapy as putting the analysand in a position "to extend, by the information we give him, his ego's knowledge of his unconscious" (65). "The method by which we strengthen the patient's weakened ego has as its starting point an increase in the ego's self-knowledge" (70). Again, "we induce the patient's thus enfeebled ego to take part in the purely intellectual work of interpretation, which aims at provisionally filling the gaps in his mental resources" (76).

27. Freud, *Dora*, 32.

28. See A. Grünbaum, *The Foundations of Psychoanalysis: A Philosophical Critique* (Berkeley and Los Angeles: University of California Press, 1984), pt. 1; see also Grünbaum, "Précis of *The Foundations of Psychoanalysis*" and "Author's Response," *Behavioral and Brain Sciences* 9 (1986): 266–81; Grünbaum, *Validation in the Clinical Theory of Psychoanalysis: A Study in the Philosophy of Psychoanalysis* (Madison, Conn.: International Universities Press, 1993), chap.5.

29. See J. D. Frank and J. B. Frank, *Persuasion and Healing: A Comparative Study of Healing*, 3d ed. (Baltimore: Johns Hopkins University Press, 1991).

30. Hampshire, *Thought and Action*, 255.

31. See J. Neu, *Emotion, Thought and Therapy* (London: Routledge and Kegan Paul, 1977).

32. Hampshire's claim, for instance, that the recognition of a causal uniformity "at least is a first step toward finding the means of evading its effects by trying to alter the initial

conditions, or the boundary conditions, upon which the operation depends" (*Thought and Action*, 190) suggests position (3).

33. Hampshire, *Thought and Action*, 132.

34. S. Freud, "The Unconscious," in *The Standard Edition of the Complete Psychological Works of Sigmund Freud*, ed. and trans. J. Strachey (London: Hogarth Press, 1953–74), 14:175; S. Freud, "'Wild' Psycho-Analysis," in *The Standard Edition*, 11:225.

35. Spinoza's philosophical psychology tries to accommodate the complex gradations that exist between knowledge, intention, will, and emotion. Because of the relative weakness of reason, and the failure to which it is susceptible in transforming the passions, knowledge requires compensation in a form other than knowledge in order to be transformative—viz., active non-destructive emotions. An emotion "cannot be restrained nor removed unless by an opposed and stronger emotion" (*Ethics*, pt. 4, prop. 7). Reason requires the energy of the emotions to change the emotions.

36. I. Murdoch, in D. Pears, ed., *Freedom and the Will* (New York: St. Martin's Press, 1963), 101.

37. This is a central point in Sartre and Binswanger's existential psychoanalysis. See L. Binswanger, "The Existential Analysis School of Thought," in *Existence: A New Dimension in Psychiatry and Psychology*, ed. R. May, E. Angel, and H. Ellenberger (New York: Simon and Schuster, 1958), 204; L. Binswanger, *Being in the World: Selected Papers of Ludwig Binswanger*, trans. J. Needleman (New York: Basic Books, 1963).

4. A MYSTERY IN BROAD DAYLIGHT

1. See J. P. Sartre, *Being and Nothingness*, trans. H. Barnes (London: Methuen, 1969), 557–58, for Sartre's criticism of empirical psychology.

2. See E. Tugendhat, *Self-Consciousness and Self-Determination*, trans. P. Stern (Cambridge, Mass.: MIT Press, 1986).

3. See M. Heidegger, *Being and Time*, trans. J. Macquarrie and E. Robinson (Oxford: Blackwell, 1962), 67–68.

4. Sartre, *Being and Nothingness*, 437.

5. J. P. Sartre, "Existentialism Is a Humanism," in *Existentialism and Human Emotions*, trans. B. Frechtman (New York: Citadel, 1957), 42–43.

6. Sartre, *Being and Nothingness*, 39 (emphasis added).

7. M. Merleau-Ponty, *Phenomenology of Perception*, trans. C. Smith (London: Routledge and Kegan Paul, 1962), 406–7.

8. Sartre, *Being and Nothingness*, 457, 480, 479, 176.

9. Ibid., 553–56.

10. Ibid., 468.

11. See J. P. Sartre, *Transcendence of the Ego*, trans. F. Williams and R. Kirkpatrick (New York: Noonday Press, 1962).

12. Sartre, *Being and Nothingness*, 572.

13. Ibid., 328.

14. J. P. Sartre, "Kierkegaard: The Singular Universal," in *Between Existentialism and Marxism*, trans. J. Matthews (London: Verso, 1983), 160.

15. Sartre, *Being and Nothingness*, 479.

16. Ibid., 82, 84.

17. Ibid., 464, 457.

18. Ibid., 461–62.

19. Ibid., 479.

20. Ibid., 570.

21. Similarly, R. M. Hare argues that justification comes to an end when a person is confronted with the decision of whether to accept a way of life; only once it is accepted can justification be based upon the way of life. See R. M. Hare, *The Language of Morals* (New York: Oxford University Press, 1964), 69.

22. Sartre, *Being and Nothingness*, xxviii.

23. Ibid., 571.

24. Ibid., 570.

25. J. P. Sartre, *War Diaries: Notebooks from a Phoney War*, trans. Q. Hoare (London: Verso, 1983), 76.

26. Sartre derives this from Heidegger's claim that "there is some way in which Dasein understands itself in its Being. . . . It is peculiar to this entity that with and through its Being, this Being is disclosed to it" (Heidegger, *Being and Time*, 32; see also 32–35, 67, 317, 414–15).

27. J. P. Sartre, *Sketch for a Theory of the Emotions*, trans. P. Mairet (London: Methuen, 1971), 24.

28. See Sartre, *Being and Nothingness*, 17, 7, 63, 156, 251, 568, 570.

29. Ibid., 563, 569.

30. Ibid., 571; see also 155.

31. Ibid., 303–5, 354–55.

32. Ibid., 463.

33. Ibid., 571; see also 273; see also Sartre, "Kierkegaard," 146.

34. Sartre, *Being and Nothingness*, 463.

35. Ibid., 241; see also 529.

36. Ibid., 286.

37. Sartre, *War Diaries*, 272, 273–74.

38. J. P. Sartre, *The Words*, trans. B. Frechtman (New York: Braziller, 1964).

39. Sartre, *Being and Nothingness*, 574, 568, 570.

40. Sartre, *The Words*, 254.

41. Ibid., 141, 60; Sartre, *Being and Nothingness*, 559.

42. Sartre writes, "When Mme Picard, using the vocabulary that was fashionable at the time, said of my grandfather: 'Charles is an exquisite being,' or 'There's no knowing human beings,' I felt condemned beyond appeal. . . . M. Simonnot, Karlémami, those were human beings. Not I. I had neither their inertia, their depth nor their impenetrability. I was nothing: an ineffaceable transparency. My jealousy knew no bounds the day I learned that M. Simonnot, that statue, that monolithic block, was, in addition, indispensable to the universe" (*The Words*, 90).

43. See *Being and Nothingness*, pt. 1, chap. 2.

44. Sartre, *The Words*, 153, 193, 197, 199.

45. Ibid., 198; see also 252.

46. Ibid., 254, 255. The translation of *qui perd gagne* has been altered from "winner loses" to the more accurate "loser wins."

47. See J. Fell, "Sartre's *Words*: An Existential Self-Analysis," *Psychoanalytic Review* 55, no. 3 (1968).

48. Sartre, *The Words*, 117, 252–53, 255. Upon reading his description of his childhood, and particularly his statement "I loathe my childhood and whatever has survived of it" (*The Words*, 164), Sartre's mother declared that her son had obviously not understood his childhood.

49. Sartre, *Being and Nothingness*, 155.

50. Sartre's account of the precise relation between the lived and the known is unclear, because it fails to distinguish between the following three claims: (a) that knowledge is a secondary structure resting upon the primary tier of prereflective experience; (b) that knowledge is existentially incompatible with prereflective experience; and (c) that knowledge falsifies prereflective experience. All three claims are made at different stages of the argument, but failure to distinguish between them leads to a number of confusions. Claim (a), for example, fails to distinguish between logical primacy, epistemic primacy, and psychological primacy.

51. See Sartre, *Being and Nothingness*, 155–63, 335. Sartre later took up some of these themes in *Notebooks for an Ethics*, trans. D. Pellauer (Chicago: University of Chicago Press, 1992).

52. Sartre, *Being and Nothingness*, 476.

53. I. Murdoch, *The Sovereignty of Good*, 37; Sartre, *The Words*, 238.

54. This is also Merleau-Ponty's criticism. To identify persons with their fundamental projects amounts to saying that their lives are already made, and that the development of lives is nothing but a repetition of primordial choices. It is impossible "to name a single gesture which is absolutely new in regard to that way of being in the world which, from the very beginning, is myself. There is no difference between saying that our life is completely constructed and that it is completely given." M. Merleau-Ponty, *Sense and Nonsense*, trans. H. Dreyfus and P. Dreyfus (Evanston, Ill.: Northwestern University Press, 1964), 21.

5. "THE MAN WITHOUT QUALITIES": IRONY, CONTINGENCY, AND THE LIGHTNESS OF BEING

1. R. Rorty, "Freud and Moral Reflection," in *Pragmatism's Freud: The Moral Disposition of Psychoanalysis*, ed. J.H. Smith and W. Kerrigan (Baltimore: Johns Hopkins University Press, 1986), 11–12.

2. R. Rorty, *Contingency, Irony and Solidarity* (New York: Cambridge University Press, 1989), 19.

3. R. Rorty, "The World Well Lost," in *Consequences of Pragmatism* (Brighton, England: Harvester Press, 1982), 13.

4. R. Rorty, "Nineteenth-Century Idealism and Twentieth-Century Textualism," in *Consequences of Pragmatism*, 140.

5. R. Rorty, "Epistemological Behaviorism and the De-Transcendentalization of Analytic Philosophy," in *Hermeneutics and Praxis*, ed. R. Hollinger (Notre Dame, Ind.: Notre Dame University Press, 1985), 104; R. Rorty, "Postmodernist Bourgeois Liberalism," *Journal of Philosophy* 80, no. 10 (1983): 585.

6. Ibid.

7. Rorty, "Freud and Moral Reflection," 12; Rorty, *Contingency, Irony, and Solidarity*, 73.

8. F. Nietzsche, *Beyond Good and Evil*, trans. W. Kaufmann (New York: Vintage Press, 1966), 94.

9. Ibid., 57.

10. Nietzsche writes; "Be your self! All you are now doing, thinking, desiring, is not you yourself!" F. Nietzsche, *Untimely Meditations*, trans. R. J. Hollingdale (Cambridge, England: Cambridge University Press, 1983), 3:1, 127.

11. See C. Guignon and D. Hiley, "Biting the Bullet: Rorty on Private and Public Morality," in *Reading Rorty*, ed. A. Malachowski (Oxford: Blackwell, 1990), 356–57.

12. F. Nietzsche, *On the Advantage and Disadvantage of History for Life*, trans. P. Preuss (Indianapolis: Hackett, 1980), 28.

13. Rorty, "Freud and Moral Reflection," 8, 11. This resembles Rorty's deflationary account of Taylor's view that humans are unique because they are self-interpreting animals. See R. Rorty, *Philosophy and the Mirror of Nature* (Oxford: Blackwell, 1980), 350–52.

14. Ibid.

15. R. Rorty, "The Contingency of Selfhood," *London Review of Books*, May 8, 1986, 14–15.

16. P. Rieff, *Freud: The Mind of the Moralist*, 3d ed. (Chicago: University of Chicago Press, 1979), 70.

17. S. Freud, "Fixation to Traumas—The Unconscious," in *The Standard Edition of the Complete Psychological Works of Sigmund Freud*, ed. and trans. J. Strachey (London: Hogarth Press, 1953–74), 16: 284–85.

18. S. Freud, "A Difficulty in the Path of Psychoanalysis," in *The Standard Edition of the Complete Psychological Works of Sigmund Freud*, 17:143.

19. D. Davidson, "Paradoxes of Irrationality," in *Philosophical Essays on Freud*, ed. R. Wollheim and J. Hopkins (Cambridge, England: Cambridge University Press, 1982).

20. Rorty, "Freud and Moral Reflection," 5, 7.

21. Ibid., 8.

22. Rorty's interpretation of the goals of psychoanalysis stands in sharp contrast to Freud's understanding. Freud identified himself as an advocate of the rationalist tradition of Spinoza, and defended the claim of reason for its own sake. In 1931 Freud wrote, "I readily admit my dependence on Spinoza's doctrine. . . . I conceived my hypotheses from the atmosphere created by him." S. Freud, letter to Dr. L. Bickel, 23 June, 1931; quoted in W. Bernard, "Psychotherapeutic Principles in Spinoza's *Ethics*," in *Speculum Spinozanum, 1677–1977*, ed. S. Hessing (London: Routledge and Kegan Paul, 1978), 63. Freud considered analytic intervention as a powerful tool that aids the conscious self in its conquest of the unconscious through the exploration and interpretation of the psyche: "We must not forget that the analytic relationship is based on a love of truth; that is, on a recognition of reality, and that it precludes any other kind of shame or deceit." S. Freud, "Analysis Terminable and Interminable," in *The Standard Edition*, 18:209–54 (emphasis added).

23. Rorty, "Freud and Moral Reflection," 9.

24. See A. E. Bergin, "The Evaluation of Therapeutic Outcomes," in *Handbook of Psychotherapy and Behavior Change*, ed. A. E. Bergin and S. Garfield (New York: John Wiley, 1971), 217–70. See also B. S. Held, *Back to Reality: A Critique of Postmodern Theory in Therapy* (New York: W. W. Norton, 1995).

25. R. Musil, *The Man without Qualities,* trans. E. Wilkins and E. Kaiser (London: Picador/Pan, 1979), 1:7.

26. *Urlaub vom Leben,* or "leave from life," is a term the character Ulrich uses to characterize his experimental withdrawal from life. The phrase "master of the hovering life" is from the title of F. G. Peters's *Robert Musil, Master of the Hovering Life: A Study of the Major Fiction* (New York: Columbia University Press, 1978).

27. As a student, Musil worked with the psychologist Carl Stumpf and wrote a doctoral dissertation on the physicist-philosopher Ernst Mach. During this time Musil developed an affinity for analytic positivism and nominalism, as well as a lasting skepticism toward psychoanalysis and phenomenology.

28. Musil, *The Man without Qualities,* 174–75.

29. Ibid., 2:210.

30. Even as a child Ulrich had ruminated about the arbitrary manner in which the world had come into being, writing in one of his essays that when God looked upon His creation, He said to Himself, "It could just as easily be some other way." Ibid., 1:15.

31. Ibid., 1:176, 186. The phrase "presence in the world" can also be translated as "Being-in-the-world."

32. G. Ryle, "The Systematic Elusiveness of the 'I,'" in *The Concept of Mind* (Harmondsworth, England: Penguin, 1973), 186–89.

33. O. Sacks, *The Man Who Mistook His Wife for a Hat and Other Clinical Tales* (New York: Harper and Row, 1970), 43–54.

34. See U. Neisser, ed., *The Perceived Self: Ecological and Interpersonal Sources of Self-Knowledge* (New York: Cambridge University Press, 1993); J. L. Bermúdez, A. Marcel, and N. Eilan, eds., *The Body and the Self* (Cambridge, Mass.: MIT Press, 1995).

35. James evokes the sense of personal identity through contrastive means, by calling attention to pathologies in which identity-constitutive feelings and moods are eroded, and a prevailing sense of uncanny passivity emerges. See W. James, *The Principles of Psychology* (Cambridge, Mass.: Harvard University Press, 1899), chap. 10, "The Consciousness of Self," especially 356–57.

36. Musil, *The Man without Qualities,* 1:343–44.

37. See P. Ricoeur, *Time and Narrative,* trans. K. Blamey and D. Pellauer (Chicago: University of Chicago Press, 1988), vol. 3. Ricoeur calls this the aporia of the inscrutability of time, that which in time eludes all representation and remains inaccessible to conceptualization.

38. M. Merleau-Ponty, *Phenomenology of Perception,* trans. C. Smith (London: Routledge and Kegan Paul, 1962), 393. To this Merleau-Ponty adds: "[An] act confers a certain quality upon us for ever, even though we may afterwards repudiate it and change our beliefs. . . . What we have experienced is, and remains, permanently ours; and in old age

a man is still in contact with his youth. Every present as it arises is driven into time like a wedge and stakes its claim to eternity. Eternity is not another order of time, but the atmosphere of time." See also Sartre's description of "pure events" in "Writing for One's Age," appendix to *What is Literature?* trans. B. Frechtman (London: Methuen, 1967), 233–34.

39. Sartre's account of radical choice cannot be divested from his account of the fundamental project, and the distinction between self-deceptive and authentic ways of being. From a Sartrean point of view, Rorty's ironist is in bad faith.

40. See C. Guignon, "Pragmatism or Hermeneutics? Epistemology after Foundationalism," in *The Interpretive Turn*, ed. D. Hiley, J. Bohman, and R. Shusterman (Ithaca, N.Y.: Cornell University Press, 1991), 94; see also C. Taylor, "Overcoming Epistemology," in *After Philosophy: End or Transformation?* ed. K. Baynes, J. Bohman, and T. McCarthy (Cambridge, Mass.: MIT Press, 1987), 482.

6. DIALOGIC SELF-KNOWING

1. See O. Flanagan, *Varieties of Moral Personality* (Cambridge, Mass.: Harvard University Press, 1991), 147.

2. M. Sandel, *Liberalism and the Limits of Justice* (New York: Cambridge University Press, 1982), 173.

3. Ibid., 143.

4. O. Flanagan, "Identity and Strong and Weak Evaluation," in *Identity, Character and Morality*, ed. O. Flanagan and A. O. Rorty (Cambridge, Mass.: MIT Press, 1990), 57; see also O. Flanagan, *Self-Expressions: Mind, Morals and the Meaning of Life* (Oxford: Oxford University Press, 1996), chap. 9.

5. Flanagan, *Varieties of Moral Personality*, 145.

6. Sandel, *Liberalism and the Limits of Justice*, 17; see also Flanagan, *Varieties of Moral Personality*, 156.

7. Flanagan, *Varieties of Moral Personality*, 156.

8. Sandel, *Liberalism and the Limits of Justice*, 181.

9. Levinas describes this face-to-face confrontation with the other as a "moral summons that makes the self aware of its arbitrary freedom." *Totality and Infinity*, trans. A. Lingis (Pittsburgh: Duquesne University Press, 1969), 196, 51.

10. E. Tugendhat, *Self-Consciousness and Self-Determination*, trans. P. Stern (Cambridge, Mass.: MIT Press, 1986), 249.

11. C. Taylor, "Responsibility for Self," in *The Identities of Persons*, ed. A. O. Rorty (Berkeley and Los Angeles: University of California Press, 1976), 296; see also C. Taylor, *Sources of the Self* (Cambridge, Mass.: Harvard University Press, 1989), C. Taylor, "What Is Human

Agency?" in *The Self: Psychological and Philosophical Issues,* ed. T. Mischel (Oxford: Blackwell, 1977), 103–35.

12. Taylor, "What Is Human Agency?" 130.

13. Taylor, "Responsibility for Self," 297. This parallels Gadamer's claim that all understanding involves learning how to be responsive: that is, learning how to participate, listen, and be open to what the text is saying. Gadamer describes this as the pathos of being open to the text, and of allowing it to speak. Openness makes it possible to become aware of the self's prejudices and attachments that conceal the meaning of the text. See H. G. Gadamer, *Truth and Method,* 2d ed., trans. rev. by J. Weinsheimer and D. G. Marshall (New York: Continuum, 1993).

14. Ibid., 298.

15. Ibid.

16. Tugendhat, *Self-Consciousness and Self-Determination,* 217.

17. Ibid., 265.

18. Ibid., 175, 265, 213.

19. Ibid., 217.

20. Ibid., 249. See also 253, 220.

21. Ibid., 247.

22. Tugendhat's reliance upon consensus also makes the intersubjective validation of personal discoveries and decisions circumstance-dependent, and therefore a matter of moral luck: for without access to interlocutors with the requisite experience, there may be no hope of being exposed to adequate feedback.

23. D. Dennett, "Conditions of Personhood," in *Brainstorms: Philosophical Essays on Mind and Psychology* (Cambridge, Mass.: MIT Press, 1978), 270.

24. Levinas, *Totality and Infinity,* 195.

25. Ibid., 73.

26. Ibid., 202.

27. M. Theunissen, *The Other: Studies in the Social Ontology of Husserl, Heidegger, Sartre, and Buber,* trans. C. MacAnn (Cambridge, Mass.: MIT Press, 1984), pt. 3.

28. M. Buber, *I and Thou,* trans. R. G. Smith (New York: Scribners, 1958).

29. Sartre, *Being and Nothingness,* trans. H. Barnes (London: Methuen, 1967), 252–302.

30. Levinas, *Totality and Infinity,* 194.

31. These six central features (among others) are also found operating in dialogic psychotherapy. See M. Friedman, *The Healing Dialogue in Psychotherapy* (New York: Jason Aronson,

1985); M. Friedman, *Dialogue and the Human Image: Beyond Humanistic Psychology* (Newbury Park, Calif: Sage, 1992); and R. Anderson and K. N. Cissna, eds., *The Martin Buber–Carl Rogers Dialogue: A New Transcript with Commentary* (Albany: State University of New York Press, 1997).

32. See Levinas, *Totality and Infinity*, sec. 1.

33. See D. A. Jopling, "Cognitive Science, Other Minds, and the Philosophy of Dialogue," in *The Perceived Self: Ecological and Interpersonal Sources of Self-Knowledge*, ed. U. Neisser, (New York: Cambridge University Press, 1993), 290–309; see also A. Baier, "Cartesian Persons," in *Postures of the Mind: Essays on Mind and Morals* (Minneapolis: University of Minnesota Press, 1985).

34. Laurence describes Hagar as a hardened pioneer, "one hell of an old lady, a real tartar. She's crabby, snobbish, difficult, proud as lucifer for no reason, a trial to her family…. [P]ioneers are pig-headed old egotists who can't relinquish the reins." A. Wiseman, afterword to *The Stone Angel*, by M. Laurence (Toronto: McClelland and Stewart, 1968), 312–13.

35. Laurence, *The Stone Angel*, 3, 173.

36. Ibid., 31, 38.

37. Ibid., 224, 230.

38. Sandel, *Liberalism and the Limits of Justice*, 181.

39. Laurence, *The Stone Angel*, 232.

40. Ibid., 233–34.

41. Ibid., 242–43.

42. Ibid., 245.

43. See Levinas, *Totality and Infinity*, sec. 1, pt. A.

44. Laurence, *The Stone Angel*, 247–48.

45. Ibid., 249–50.

46. Ibid., 253, 292.

47. Ibid., 232, 282.

48. Ibid., 296.

49. P. Ricoeur, *Oneself as Another*, trans. K. Blamey (Chicago: University of Chicago Press, 1992), 10th study.

BIBLIOGRAPHY

Allport, G. W. *Personality: A Psychological Interpretation.* New York: Holt, 1937.

Allport, G. W., and H. Odbert. "Trait-names: A Psycho-Lexical Study." *Psychological Monographs,* vol. 47, no. 1 (1936): 1–171.

Anderson R., and K. N. Cissna, eds. *The Martin Buber–Carl Rogers Dialogue: A New Transcript with Commentary.* Albany: State University of New York Press, 1997.

Aristotle. *Nichomachean Ethics.* Translated by J. A. K. Thomson. Harmondsworth, England: Penguin, 1955.

Baier, A. *Postures of Mind: Essays on Mind and Morals.* Minneapolis: University of Minnesota Press, 1985.

Bergin, A. E. "The Evaluation of Therapeutic Outcomes." In *Handbook of Psychotherapy and Behavior Change,* edited by A. E. Bergin and S. Garfield, 217–70. New York: John Wiley, 1971.

Bermúdez, J. L., A. Marcel, and N. Eilan, eds. *The Body and the Self.* Cambridge, Mass.: MIT Press, 1995.

Bernard, W. "Freud and Spinoza." *Psychiatry* 9, no. 2 (May 1946): 99–108.

———. "Psychotherapeutic Principles in Spinoza's *Ethics.*" In *Speculum Spinozanum: 1677–1977,* edited by S. Hessing, 63–80. London: Routledge and Kegan Paul, 1978.

Binswanger, L. "The Existential Analysis School of Thought." In *Existence: A New Dimension in Psychiatry and Psychology,* edited by R. May, E. Angel, and H. Ellenberger, 191–213. New York: Simon and Schuster, 1958.

———. *Being in the World: Selected Papers of Ludwig Binswanger.* Translated by J. Needleman. New York: Basic Books, 1963.

Brentano, F. *Psychology from an Empirical Standpoint.* Edited by O. Kraus and L. McAlister; translated by A. C. Rancurella, D. Terrell, and L. McAlister. London: Routledge and Kegan Paul, 1973.

Buber, M. *I and Thou.* Translated by R. G. Smith. New York: Scribners, 1958.

Carr, D. *Time, Narrative and History.* Bloomington: Indiana University Press, 1986.

Davidson, D. "Paradoxes of Irrationality." In *Philosophical Essays on Freud,* edited by

R. Wollheim and J. Hopkins, 289–305. Cambridge, England: Cambridge University Press, 1982.

Dennett, D. "Conditions of Personhood." In *Brainstorms: Philosophical Essays on Mind and Psychology*. Cambridge, Mass.: MIT Press, 1978.

———. "The Origins of Selves." *Cogito* 1 (1989): 163–73.

———. *Consciousness Explained*. Boston: Little, Brown, 1991.

Dmitruk, V. M., R. W. Collins, and D. L. Clinger. "The Barnum Effect and Acceptance of Negative Personal Evaluation." *Journal of Consulting and Clinical Psychology* 41 (1973): 192–94.

Elster, J., ed. *The Multiple Self*. New York: Cambridge University Press, 1985.

Erikson, E. *Identity: Youth and Crisis*. New York: W. W. Norton, 1968.

Fell, J. "Sartre's *Words*: An Existential Self-Analysis." *The Psychoanalytic Review* 55, no. 3 (1968): 426–41.

Fingarette, H. *Self-Deception*. London: Routledge and Kegan Paul, 1969.

Flanagan, O. *Consciousness Reconsidered*. Cambridge, Mass.: MIT Press, 1992.

———. "Identity and Strong and Weak Evaluation." In *Identity, Character and Morality*, edited by O. Flanagan and A. O. Rorty, 37–65. Cambridge, Mass.: MIT Press, 1990.

———. *Self-Expressions: Mind, Morals, and the Meaning of Life*. New York: Oxford University Press, 1996.

———. *Varieties of Moral Personality*. Cambridge, Mass.: Harvard University Press, 1991.

Frank J. D., and J. B. Frank. *Persuasion and Healing: A Comparative Study of Psychotherapy*. 3d. ed. Baltimore: Johns Hopkins University Press, 1991.

Freud, S. "Analysis Terminable and Interminable." In *The Standard Edition of the Complete Psychological Works of Sigmund Freud*, edited and translated by J. Strachey, vol. 23, 209–71. London: Hogarth Press, 1953–74.

———. "A Difficulty in the Path of Psychoanalysis." In *The Standard Edition of the Complete Psychological Works of Sigmund Freud*, vol. 17, 135–44.

———. *Dora: An Analysis of a Case of Hysteria*. New York: Collier, 1963.

———. "Fixation to Traumas—The Unconscious." In *The Standard Edition of the Complete Psychological Works of Sigmund Freud*, vol. 16, 273–85.

———. *An Outline of Psycho-Analysis*. Translated by J. Strachey. New York: Norton, 1963.

———. "The Unconscious." In *The Standard Edition of the Complete Psychological Works of Sigmund Freud*, vol. 14, 159–215.

———. " 'Wild' Psycho-Analysis." In *The Standard Edition of the Complete Psychological Works of Sigmund Freud*, vol. 11, 219–27.

Friedman, M. *Dialogue and the Human Image: Beyond Humanistic Psychology.* Newbury Park, Calif.: Sage, 1992.

——. *The Healing Dialogue in Psychotherapy.* New York: Jason Aronson, 1985.

Gadamer, H. G. *Truth and Method.* 2d ed. Translated and revised by J. Weinsheimer and D. G. Marshall. New York: Continuum, 1993.

Gibson, J. J. *The Ecological Approach to Visual Perception.* New Jersey: Erlbaum, 1986.

Glass, J. *Shattered Selves: Multiple Personality in a Postmodern World.* Ithaca, N.Y.: Cornell University Press, 1993.

Grünbaum, A. *The Foundations of Psychoanalysis: A Philosophical Critique.* Berkeley and Los Angeles: University of California Press, 1984.

——. "Précis of *The Foundations of Psychoanalysis*" and "Author's Response." *Behavioral and Brain Sciences* 9 (1986): 266–81.

——. *Validation in the Clinical Theory of Psychoanalysis: A Study in the Philosophy of Psychoanalysis.* Madison, Conn.: International Universities Press, 1993.

Guignon, C. "Pragmatism or Hermeneutics? Epistemology after Foundationalism." In *The Interpretive Turn,* edited by D. Hiley, J. Bohman, and R. Shusterman, 81–101. Ithaca, N.Y.: Cornell University Press, 1991.

Guignon, C., and D. Hiley. "Biting the Bullet: Rorty on Private and Public Morality." In *Reading Rorty,* edited by A. Malachowski, 339–69. Oxford: Blackwell, 1990.

Hamlyn, D. W. "Self-Knowledge." In *The Self: Philosophical and Psychological Issues,* edited by T. Mischel, 170–202. Oxford: Blackwell, 1977.

Hampshire, S. *Freedom of Mind and Other Essays.* Oxford: Clarendon, 1972.

——. *Freedom of the Individual.* London: Chatto and Windus, 1975.

——. *Innocence and Experience.* Cambridge, Mass.: Harvard University Press, 1989.

——. *Morality and Conflict.* Cambridge, Mass.: Harvard University Press, 1983.

——. *Spinoza.* Harmondsworth, England: Penguin, 1951.

——. *Thought and Action.* London: Chatto and Windus, 1959.

Hare, R. M. *The Language of Morals.* New York: Oxford University Press, 1964.

Harré, R. *Personal Being: A Theory for Individual Psychology.* Cambridge, Mass.: Harvard University Press, 1984.

Heidegger, M. *Being and Time.* Translated by J. Macquarrie and E. Robinson. Oxford: Blackwell, 1962.

Held, B. S. *Back to Reality: A Critique of Postmodern Theory in Therapy.* New York: W. W. Norton, 1995.

Hessing, S., ed. *Speculum Spinozanum, 1677–1977.* London: Routledge and Kegan Paul, 1978.

James, W. *The Principles of Psychology.* Cambridge, Mass.: Harvard University Press, 1899.

Jopling, D. A. "Cognitive Science, Other Minds, and the Philosophy of Dialogue." In *The Perceived Self: Ecological and Interpersonal Sources of Self-Knowledge,* edited by U. Neisser, 290–309. New York: Cambridge University Press, 1993.

———. "Sartre's Moral Psychology." In *The Cambridge Companion to Sartre,* edited by C. Howells, 103–39. New York: Cambridge University Press, 1992.

———. "A Self of Selves?" In *The Conceptual Self in Context: Culture, Experience, Self-Understanding,* edited by U. Neisser and D. A. Jopling, 249–67. New York: Cambridge University Press, 1997.

———. "Sub-Phenomenology." *Human Studies* 19 (1996): 153–73.

———. "'Take away the Life-lie . . .': Positive Illusions and Creative Self-Deception." *Philosophical Psychology* 9, no. 4 (1996): 525–44.

Kekes, J. *The Examined Life.* University Park: Pennsylvania State University Press, 1988.

Laing, R. D. *The Divided Self.* Harmondsworth, England: Penguin, 1973.

Lambert, M., D. Shapiro, and A. Bergin. "The Effectiveness of Psychotherapy." In *Handbook of Psychotherapy and Behavior Change,* edited by S. Garfield and A. Bergin. 3d ed. New York: John Wiley, 1986.

Laurence, M. *The Stone Angel.* Toronto: McClelland and Stewart, 1968.

Leder, D. *The Absent Body.* Chicago: University of Chicago Press, 1989.

Levinas, E. *Totality and Infinity.* Translated by A. Lingis. Pittsburgh: Duquesne University Press, 1969.

Lloyd, G. *Being in Time: Selves and Narrators in Philosophy and Literature.* New York: Routledge, 1993.

———. *Part of Nature: Self-Knowledge in Spinoza's Ethics.* Ithaca, N.Y.: Cornell University Press, 1994.

Luria, A. R. *The Man with a Shattered World.* Translated by L. Solotaroff. New York: Basic Books, 1972.

MacIntyre, A. *After Virtue.* 2d ed. Notre Dame, Ind.: University of Notre Dame Press, 1984.

Markus, H. "Self-Schemata and the Processing of Information About the Self." *Journal of Personality and Social Psychology* 35, no. 2 (1977): 63–78.

Martin M., ed. *Self-Deception and Self-Understanding: New Essays in Philosophy and Psychology.* Lawrence: University Press of Kansas, 1985.

McKenna Moss, D. "Distortions in Human Embodiment: A Study of Surgically Treated Obesity." In *Phenomenology: Dialogues and Bridges,* edited by R. Bruzina and

B. Wilshire, 253–68. Albany: State University of New York Press, 1982.

Mclaughlin, B. P., and A. O. Rorty, eds. *Perspectives on Self-Deception*. Berkeley and Los Angeles: University of California Press, 1988.

Mead, G. H. *Mind, Self and Society*. Edited by C. W. Morris. Chicago: University of Chicago Press, 1934.

Merleau-Ponty, M. *Phenomenology of Perception*. Translated by C. Smith. London: Routledge and Kegan Paul, 1962.

———. *Sense and Nonsense*. Translated by H. Dreyfus and P. Dreyfus. Evanston, Ill.: Northwestern University Press, 1964.

Mischel, T. *Personality and Assessment*. New York: John Wiley, 1968.

Mischel, T., ed. *The Self: Philosophical and Psychological Issues*. Oxford: Blackwell, 1977.

Murdoch, I. *The Sovereignty of Good*. London: Routledge and Kegan Paul, 1970.

Musil, R. *The Man without Qualities*. Translated by E. Wilkins and E. Kaiser. London: Picador/Pan, 1979.

Nagel, T. *Mortal Questions*. New York: Cambridge University Press, 1979.

Nehamas, A. *Nietzsche: Life as Literature*. Cambridge, Mass.: Harvard University Press, 1985.

Neisser, U. "Five Kinds of Self-Knowledge." *Philosophical Psychology* 1, no. 1 (1988): 35–59.

Neisser, U., ed. *The Perceived Self: Ecological and Interpersonal Sources of Self-Knowledge*. New York: Cambridge University Press, 1993.

Neisser, U., and R. Fivush, eds. *The Remembering Self: Construction and Accuracy in the Self-Narrative*. New York: Cambridge University Press, 1994.

Neisser, U., and D. A. Jopling, eds. *The Conceptual Self in Context: Culture, Experience, Self-Understanding*. New York: Cambridge University Press, 1997.

Neu, J. *Emotion, Thought and Therapy*. London: Routledge and Kegan Paul, 1977.

Nietzsche, F. *Beyond Good and Evil*. Translated by W. Kaufmann. New York: Vintage Press, 1966.

———. *Daybreak: Thoughts on the Prejudices of Morality*. Translated by R. Hollingdale. Cambridge, England: Cambridge University Press, 1982.

———. *On the Advantage and Disadvantage of History for Life*. Translated by P. Preuss. Indianapolis: Hackett, 1980.

———. *On the Genealogy of Morals*. Translated by W. Kaufmann and R. J. Hollingdale. New York: Vintage Books/Random House, 1967.

———. *Untimely Meditations*. Translated by R. J. Hollingdale. Cambridge, England: Cambridge University Press, 1983.

North, H. *Sophrosyne: Self-Knowledge and Self-Restraint in Greek and Latin Literature*. Ithaca, N.Y.: Cornell University Press, 1966.

Nussbaum, M. *Love's Knowledge*. New York: Oxford University Press, 1989.

Pears, D., ed. *Freedom and the Will*. New York: St. Martin's Press, 1963.

Peters, F. G. *Robert Musil, Master of the Hovering Life: A Study of the Major Fiction*. New York: Columbia University Press, 1978.

Ricoeur, P. *Oneself as Another*. Translated by K. Blamey. Chicago: University of Chicago Press, 1992.

———. *Time and Narrative*. Translated by K. Blamey and D. Pellauer. Chicago: University of Chicago Press, 1988.

Rieff, P. *Freud: The Mind of the Moralist*. 3d ed. Chicago: University of Chicago Press, 1979.

Rorty, A. O. "Adaptivity and Self-Knowledge." *Inquiry* 18 (1975): 1–22.

———. *Mind in Action*. Boston: Beacon Press, 1988.

Rorty, A. O., ed. *The Identities of Persons*. Berkeley and Los Angeles: University of California Press, 1976.

Rorty, R. *Consequences of Pragmatism*. Brighton, England: Harvester Press, 1982.

———. *Contingency, Irony and Solidarity*. New York: Cambridge University Press, 1989.

———. "The Contingency of Selfhood." *London Review of Books* (May 8, 1986): 11–15.

———. "Epistemological Behaviorism and the De-Transcendentalization of Analytic Philosophy." In *Hermeneutics and Praxis*, edited by R. Hollinger, 89–121. Notre Dame, Ind.: Notre Dame University Press, 1985.

———. "Freud and Moral Reflection." In *Pragmatism's Freud: The Moral Disposition of Psychoanalysis*, edited by J. H. Smith and W. Kerrigan, 1–27. Baltimore: Johns Hopkins University Press, 1986.

———. *Philosophy and the Mirror of Nature*. Oxford: Blackwell, 1980.

———. "Postmodernist Bourgeois Liberalism." In *Objectivity, Relativism and Truth: Philosophical Papers*, 1:197–202. New York: Cambridge University Press, 1991.

Ryle, G. *The Concept of Mind*. Harmondsworth, England: Penguin, 1973.

Sacks, O. *The Man Who Mistook His Wife for a Hat and Other Clinical Tales*. New York: Harper and Row, 1970.

Sandel, M. *Liberalism and the Limits of Justice*. New York: Cambridge University Press, 1982.

Sartre, J. P. *Being and Nothingness*. Translated by H. Barnes. London: Methuen, 1969.

———. "Consciousness of Self and Knowledge of Self." Translated by M. Lawrence and

N. Lawrence. In *Readings in Existential Phenomenology*, edited by N. Lawrence and D. J. O'Connor, 113–42. Englewood Cliffs, N.J.: Prentice Hall, 1967.

———. *Existentialism and Human Emotions*. Translated by B. Frechtman. New York: Citadel, 1957.

———. *The Family Idiot*. Translated by C. Cosman. Vols. 1 and 2. Chicago: University of Chicago Press, 1983.

———. "Kierkegaard: The Singular Universal." In *Between Existentialism and Marxism*, translated by J. Matthews, 141–69. London: Verso, 1983.

———. *Nausea*. Translated by L. Alexander. New York: New Directions, 1964.

———. *Notebooks for an Ethics*. Translated by D. Pellauer. Chicago: University of Chicago Press, 1992.

———. *Sketch for a Theory of the Emotions*. Translated by P. Mairet. London: Methuen, 1971.

———. *Transcendence of the Ego*. Translated by F. Williams and R. Kirkpatrick. New York: Noonday Press, 1962.

———. *War Diaries: Notebooks from a Phoney War*. Translated by Q. Hoare. London: Verso, 1983.

———. *What is Literature?* Translated by B. Frechtman. London: Methuen, 1967.

———. *The Words*. Translated by B. Frechtman. New York: Braziller, 1964.

Shoemaker, S. *Self-Knowledge and Self-Identity*. Ithaca, N.Y.: Cornell University Press, 1963.

Somerset Maugham, W. *The Summing Up*. Harmondsworth, England: Penguin, 1963.

Spence, D. *Narrative Truth and Historical Truth: Meaning and Interpretation in Psychoanalysis*. New York: W. W. Norton, 1982.

Spinoza, B. *Ethics*. Edited by S. Feldman, translated by S. Shirley. Indianapolis: Hackett, 1992.

Strawson, P. F. *Freedom and Resentment and Other Essays*. London: Methuen, 1974.

Sundberg, N. D. "The Acceptability of 'Fake' versus Bona Fide Personality Test Interpretations." *Journal of Abnormal Social Psychology* 50 (1966): 145–47.

Taylor, C. "Overcoming Epistemology." In *After Philosophy: End or Transformation?* edited by K. Baynes, J. Bohman, and T. McCarthy, 464–88. Cambridge, Mass.: MIT Press, 1987.

———. "Responsibility for Self." In *The Identities of Persons*, edited by A. O. Rorty, 281–99. Berkeley: University of California Press, 1976.

———. *Sources of the Self*. Cambridge, Mass.: Harvard University Press, 1989.

———. "What is Human Agency?" In *The Self: Psychological and Philosophical Issues*, edited by T. Mischel, 103–35. Oxford: Blackwell, 1977.

Theunissen, M. *The Other: Studies in the Social Ontology of Husserl, Heidegger, Sartre, and Buber.* Translated by C. MacAnn. Cambridge, Mass.: MIT Press, 1984.

Tolstoy, L. *The Death of Ivan Ilyich and Other Stories.* Translated by R. Edmonds. Harmondsworth, England: Penguin, 1960.

Toulmin, S. "Self-Knowledge and Knowledge of Self." In *The Self: Psychological and Philosophical Issues,* edited by T. Mischel, 291–317. Oxford: Blackwell, 1977.

Tugendhat, E. *Self-Consciousness and Self-Determination.* Translated by P. Stern. Cambridge, Mass.: MIT Press, 1986.

Van den Berg, J. H. *A Different Existence: Principles of Phenomenological Psychopathology.* Pittsburgh: Duquesne University Press, 1972.

Wilkes, K. V. *Real People: Personal Identity without Thought Experiments.* Oxford, England: Oxford University Press, 1988.

Yovel, Y. *Spinoza and Other Heretics.* 2 vols. Princeton, N.J.: Princeton University Press, 1989.

INDEX

DUE